THE REAL
DUKE ELLINGTON

THE REAL
DUKE
ELLINGTON

DON
GEORGE

Robson Books

The author gratefully acknowledges permission from the following to reprint material in this book:

Chappell & Co., Inc., for lyrics from "I'm Beginning to See the Light," by Don George, Harry James, Duke Ellington and Johnny Hodges, copyright © 1944 by Alamo Music, Inc. Copyright renewed, controlled by Chappell & Co., Inc. (Intersong Music, Publisher). International Copyright Secured. All rights reserved.

Columbia Records, for use of liner notes by George Avakian from the Columbia Records album, *Ellington in Newport*.

Melody Maker Magazine, for "Amazing Ellington" feature, published in *Rhythm Magazine* in 1933.

Ricki Music, Inc., for lyrics from "Sweet Man," by Don George, copyright © 1981 by Ricki Music, Inc.

Tempo Music, Inc., for lyrics from the following songs: "Time's A-Wastin'," by Don George, Duke Ellington and Mercer Ellington, copyright © 1945 by Tempo Music, Inc.; "To Know You Is to Love You," by Don George and Duke Ellington, copyright © 1958 by Tempo Music, Inc.; "The Lonely Ones," by Don George and Duke Ellington, copyright © 1959 by Tempo Music, Inc.; "Baby, You're Too Much," by Don George and Duke Ellington, copyright © 1967 by Tempo Music, Inc.

Tempo Music, Inc., and Ricki Music, Inc., for lyrics from the following songs: "I Ain't Got Nothin' but the Blues," by Don George and Duke Ellington, copyright © 1944 by Edwin H. Morris & Co., Inc. Copyright renewed 1972 by Tempo Music Inc., and Ricki Music, Inc.; "Every Hour on the Hour," by Don George and Duke Ellington, copyright © 1945 by Melrose Music Corp. Copyright renewed 1973 by Tempo Music, Inc., and Ricki Music, Inc.; "I'm Afraid," by Don George and Duke Ellington, copyright © 1948 by Consolidated Music Pub., Inc. Copyright renewed 1976 by Tempo Music, Inc., and Ricki Music, Inc.

Z A Music, Inc., for lyrics from "What Is It Like Where She Has Gone?" by Allison Assante, copyright Z A Music, Inc.

FIRST PUBLISHED IN GREAT BRITAIN IN 1982 BY ROBSON BOOKS LTD., BOLSOVER HOUSE, 5–6 CLIPSTONE STREET, LONDON W1P 7EB COPYRIGHT © 1981 DON GEORGE

British Library Cataloguing in Publication Data

George, Don
  The real Duke Ellington.
  1. Ellington, Duke 2. Jazz musicians—Biography
  I. Title.
785.42′092′4   ML410.E44

ISBN 0-86051-166-9

Printed and bound in Great Britain by Mackays of Chatham Ltd

For my friend Lady Allison Assante, and my daughter Ricki, Duke's favorite niece.

Acknowledgements

I am extremely grateful to the following people who shared their memories with me—

Phoebe Jacobs, the great PR lady

Brooks Kerr, Duke's protégé

Glen Kittler, good friend

Marian Logan, Dr. Arthur Logan's widow

Toney Watkins, singer, dancer, Duke's confidante

Sonny Greer, who originally brought Duke to New York

Pastor John Garcia Gensel, "Shepherd of the Night Flock"

—and certainly to Elisabeth Jakab, senior editor at Putnam's, who is stimulating, inspirational and wonderful to work with. And a great big Hallelujah to Howard Beldock, a friend and attorney, who put me together with Elisabeth Jakab to make this book a reality.

Many, many thanks for their gracious cooperation to: Alvin Ailey, Lady Allison Assante, George Avakian, Louis Bellson, Tony Bennett, Richard Burton, Fred Cohen, Stanley Dance, Dr. Judianne Densen-Gerber, Ms. Edith Exton, José Ferrer, Luther Henderson, Jon Hendricks, Al Hibbler, Geoffrey Holder, Quincy Jones, Peggy Lee, Lyle Leverich, Anita Porter, Otto Preminger, Sam Shaw, Billy Taylor, Sam Vaughan, George Wein, Bernice Wiggins and Shela Xoregos.

Contents

Words & Music by Don George
A.S.C.A.P., A.G.A.C.

Sweet Man

VERSE : WISTFULLY (AD LIB)

1. Once there was a sweet man, a warm and lov-ing sweet man, who
2. He was bold and dar-ing, and he was kind and car-ing, as

walked be-side me on-ly yes-ter day_____ . But the
he made life a song a-long the way_____ . No one

blues came af-ter the mu-sic and the laugh-ter,
e-vil eyed me when he was here be-side me,

how I wish he had-n't gone a-way_____ : } He was
how I wish that he was here to-day_____

Sweet Man – D. George

CHORUS: WALKING BLUES (MED. SLOW)

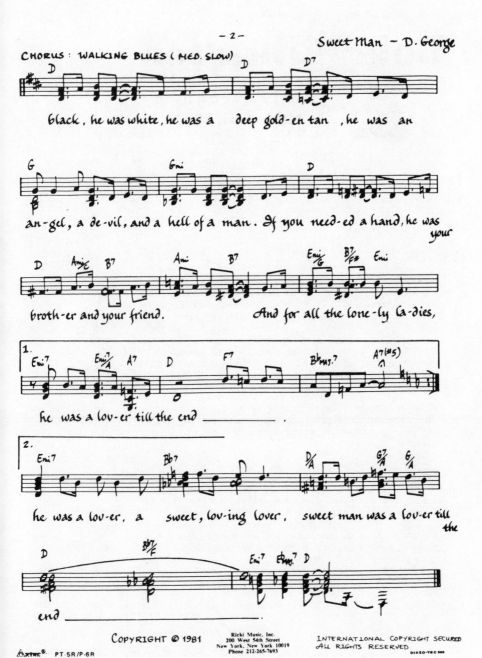

black, he was white, he was a   deep gold-en tan , he was an

an-gel, a de-vil, and a hell of a man. If you need-ed a hand, he was your

broth-er and your friend.   And for all the lone-ly la-dies,

1.
he was a lov-er till the end _____ .

2.
he was a lov-er, a   sweet, lov-ing lover,   sweet man was a lov-er till the

end _____ .

Axtec® PT-5R/P-6R   DIAZO-TEC 900

Duke Ellington
inc.
1619 Broadway
New York 19, N. Y.

August 9, 1961

Don George, one of my songwriting partners, is having
a one-man showing of his paintings at the Southampton
Art Gallery East, 11 South Main Street, Southampton,
Long Island, beginning August 25 thru September 7,
1961.

In addition to his painting, Don is also one of our
foremost songwriters. Among the songs Don and I have
written together are, "I'm Beginning To See The Light",
"I Ain't Got Nothin But The Blues", "Every Hour On The
Hour" and many others. Don Also wrote songs for such
films as "Giant", "With A Song In My Heart", "Roadhouse",
"The Fabulous Dorseys", and many, many others, and is
the sole perpetrator of the song, "The Yellow Rose Of
Texas".

I find Don's paintings unusual and exciting and I am
delighted that he is receiving recognition as an important artist. I know that if you visit the gallery
during Don's one-man show you will be as thrilled as
I am with his work.

I particularly suggest that you attend the champagne
preview at the gallery on Friday evening, August 25th,
from 9:00 to 12:00 P.M.

Sincerely,

"Mama, Mama," the boy cried, "when I grow up I'm going to be rich and famous and everybody is going to call me Duke; and Mama, I'm going to make a lot of money and buy you clothes and anything you want."

PART ONE

The Capitol Theatre, October 1943

I WALKED PAST THE CAPITOL THEATRE ENTRANCE, WHERE THE BIG SIGN READ:

DUKE ELLINGTON

LENA HORNE

First Show   1:15 P.M.
Tickets .75 including war tax, till One P.M.

PLUS Feature Film

L
I
V
E

O
N

S
T
A
G
E

Past the Rismont Tea Room, where one of our more famous actors had romanced the owner's daughter in order to keep his belly full while he was struggling to make it; past the Nat Lewis Haberdashery shop, where the chorus girls brought their Johns to spring for goodies the girls returned the next day for half the money back; where Rosemary Clooney ordered an initialed sweater for husband José Ferrer, and the monogram was printed with an *H* for José. I headed south on Broadway to the corner of Fiftieth Street and turned west to the Capitol Theatre stage door.

When I walked in, the rheumy-eyed stage doorman asked, "Who do you want to see?"

"Duke Ellington," I replied.

"He's onstage."

"I'll wait."

"Who are you?"

I took a shot. What the hell, I had nothing to lose.

"I'm his brother."

The doorman looked skeptically at my blond hair and white skin but didn't challenge me. He gestured wearily over his shoulder. "First room at the top of the stairs."

The room was painted battleship gray. There was no closet; just an open pipe rack with fifteen or twenty suits hanging from it; perhaps a dozen pairs of shoes lined up on the floor; a dressing table built into the wall, with naked light bulbs sitting disconsolately around a mirror that needed resilvering; a sink in the corner that seemed to be handier for urinary purposes than any more formal ablutions; a cot and a chair. The john was in the hall.

I sat down to wait for Duke.

Soon there were footsteps on the stairs, noises in the hall. The first show was over. The door opened and Duke walked in, followed by his valet, short, dark-black Jonesie. Neither of them looked at me. Duke stripped down, and Jonesie hung up his clothes and left. Duke toweled himself, put on an old cotton robe, settled a silk-stocking cap on his head to help caucasian his hairdo, lay down on the cot and fell fast asleep.

He looked regal even in repose. Lying there on his back, snoring slightly, he possessed more majesty than most vertical dignitaries with all their borrowed pomp and circumstance. The pouches under his eyes gave him the vaunted bedroom look that attracted women to him by the droves. His skin was neither black nor brown nor beige but, as Lady Allison Assante later described him, he was the golden man, the twentieth century Genghis Khan.

There was a knock on the door, and a voice came over the tiny loudspeaker on the wall: "Half-hour." Duke's breathing didn't miss a beat. Another knock, and the loudspeaker hoarsely declared, "Fifteen minutes." Duke still didn't budge. When the count reached "Five minutes," Jonesie entered and started laying out Duke's clothes. Duke got up, scratched himself, sauntered over to the mirror, looked at his teeth, took off the stocking cap, squirted some drops into his eyes, reached for a huge marshmallow of a powder puff, dipped it into the

18

Johnson's baby talc and proceeded to apply it vigorously to his upper and lower décolleté. Then with the aid of Jonesie, he permitted himself to be dressed and left for the next show.

Feeling adventurous, I opened the door of the dressing room and stepped into the hall. Just then, down the stairs from the second landing came the stuff of dreams. Breathtakingly gowned, with her upturned nose and breasts aiming at the stars, Lena Horne smiled at me on her way to the stage, and I practically levitated all the way back into the dressing room.

After the second show Duke walked in, followed by Jonesie. Again neither of them looked at me. Duke stripped. Jonesie hung up Duke's clothes and left. Duke toweled himself, put on the old cotton robe and the the stocking cap, lay down on the cot and went to sleep.

Me, I just sat.

At the half-hour after the third show, Jonesie came in with a tray for Duke. Steak, chopped liver, lettuce and tomatoes, orange juice, apple pie and ice cream. Duke ate the apple pie and ice cream first, then finished the rest of the tray. He got up, went through the teeth, stocking cap, eyedrops, powder-puff bit, got dressed with the help of Jonesie and left for the stage. I hadn't eaten all day.

After the fourth and last show, Duke, still ignoring me, changed into his street clothes. Sonny Greer, Duke's drummer, came in and asked him for some money. Duke said, "I just lead the band. I'm a musician like you." He put Sonny on for a while, then gave him the money. They walked out, through for the night, leaving me there with the light on.

Vaudeville was alive and well. Every theater in the Broadway area was jumping with great talent. And on the second day of my vigil, the cream poured in to pay their respects to Duke.

Cab Calloway, the Hi-De-Ho Man, who was high decibeling "Minnie the Moocher" at the Strand Theatre, stopped by to give Duke a couple of winners at the track, which Duke wisely refrained from playing. Sophie Tucker, the Last of the Red-Hot Mamas, restlessly maneuvered her glorious bulk from starring in the two-a-day at the Palace, while Orson Welles dropped in

19

to decorate the scene and to discuss collaborating on a musical version of *Aesop's Fables* with Duke.

All sixty-one inches of Billy Strayhorn, Duke's co-arranger, co-composer, etc. (fondly called Sweetpea by everyone), smilingly entertained the callers when it was necessary for Duke to go onstage.

While all this was going on, I was occasionally included in the conversation by the visitors, who obviously imagined that I was part of Duke's entourage, but Duke, with the greatest of dexterity, continued to ignore me, looking over, under, around and through me.

On the third day, after the first show, Duke turned to me and asked, "Who are you?"

"Don George."

"What do you do?"

"I write lyrics."

"What do you want?"

"I want to write with you."

He turned away and completely ignored me for the rest of the day.

The next day when I came in there was a small white piano sitting in the corner of the dressing room, smiling at me. I was about to go over and shake hands with it when Duke walked in.

"I thought you might like it," he remarked casually.

Me (trying to be cool): "I sure do."

He sat down at the piano. "You got any songs going now?"

" 'I Never Mention Your Name.' It's on the Hit Parade."

"Good song. Got any titles?"

One of the first songs we wrote was "I'm Beginning to See the Light."

It was the start of a collaboration that lasted over thirty years, not only as songwriters but as buddies. We wrote together, we traveled together, we shared hotel suites, we shared women and most of all we shared an indestructible affection and understanding.

There are writers who fight tooth and nail when they work together; writers who don't talk to each other; I even remem-

20

ber a writer who told me that he did his best work after he masturbated. But as far as we were concerned, there was no tryout period, no acclimatization. The songs just seemed to write themselves.

"Don."

"Yes, Duke."

"You're my friend, aren't you?"

"Of course, Duke."

"I hope you'll do me a favor."

"You know I will."

"Well, Don, when we're working in New York, Evie comes around an awful lot.* I never know when to expect her."

"Yes, Duke."

"I like to go up to Lena's dressing room and visit with her every now and then. We're such old friends. But I wouldn't want Evie to find me there because she's so jealous. It's a real problem."

"What do you want me to do?"

"When I go up to Lena's, just sit at the top of the stairs and keep an eye on the stage door. When Evie comes in, bang your keys against the railing. I'll hear you."

"Okay, buddy."

It became a game that Duke never lost. Evie would open the stage door, I'd bang the keys on the railing, and in a flash Duke would be descending the stairs.

I took to roaming the streets around the Capitol Theatre while Duke was onstage. I had been brought up in the neighborhood, and the streets were really memory lanes to me.

Around the corner, on Fifty-first Street, I remembered the place where an Italian restaurant, the Vesuvius, used to be. It had been torn down when they built the Capitol. I could still picture Mama and Papa Lettieri, Mama at the cash register and Papa doing the cooking and the three kids I had shared part of my childhood with. Renato, a beautiful boy who slowly died of multiple sclerosis; Albina and Americus, whom we called Rickey. It never occurred to me that it was anything but natural and normal to see Rudolph Valentino, Enrico Caruso and Gabriele

*Evie was Duke's common-law wife.

D'Annunzio's grandson having dinner together there with the tablecloth turned so that a corner was facing each of them, with the corners, like spaghettied ski slopes, tucked into their shirt collars for napkins.

"Don, what do your girl friends do with their old silk stockings?"
"Throw them away, I guess."
"Do you think it might make them happy to know their stockings were gracing the brow of Edward Kennedy Ellington?"
"I'm sure they'd be thrilled," I answered, tongue in cheek.
"Don't forget to get me some, now."
"I won't."

It was closing night for Duke and the band at the Capitol. Jonesie was busy packing Duke's wardrobe for the trip to the next stop, Toronto. Sweetpea was checking some music with Tom Whaley, the copyist, in the corner.
"Jonesie, did we take care of everybody—the stagehands and the doorman?"
"Yes, Duke."
"You're sure, now."
"I'm sure, man. We're straight with everybody."
"Good. We always want people to be glad to see us again. And Jonesie, be careful with the master's attire."
The fellows in the band kept dropping in to check on the time the bus left for Toronto, but although I did everything but climb in his pocket, Duke said nothing about my going along.

The next day I took the train to Toronto and arrived at Duke's hotel late in the afternoon. I registered and called Duke from the lobby.
"How ya doing, buddy?"
"Don! How are things in New York?"
"I really wouldn't know."
"Is something wrong, man?"
"No, everything's fine. I just checked into the hotel."
"You mean you're here?"
"I figured we could get some work done."

Pause—pause—pause.

"Did you bring the stockings?"

Duke had me moved into his suite. There were two bedrooms with a large living room in between, and an upright
piano spread-eagled against the wall.

"Have you eaten?" Duke asked.

"Not yet," I replied.

It was then that I got my first real lesson in people-stroking
diplomacy from the master (or How to Make People Love You
Madly on First Contact).

Duke picked up the telephone. "Room service, please
. . . This is Duke Ellington in 805. I would like to speak to the
chef."

Pause.

"Hello, Monsieur Chef? This is Duke Ellington."

Pause.

"Yes, from the States."

"No, the band is at another hotel. I checked into this hotel
because you're here. Everyone agrees you're the greatest chef
in Canada."

Pause.

"Please, there's no need to thank me; I'm just repeating what
everyone says."

Pause.

"One order of double lamb chops, some chopped liver, lettuce and tomatoes, apple pie with ice cream: yes, broccoli will
be fine; and a glass of hot water and lemon."

Duke looked at me inquiringly.

I nodded my head.

"Better make that two of everything."

He hung up the phone.

I asked Duke, "How long have you known this fellow?"

Duke (over his shoulder on his way to the bathroom), "I never even heard of him before."

When the bellman wheeled in the wagon with the food,
Duke had just taken a shower and was standing in the middle
of the room with nothing on but a towel tucked around his
middle and a silk stocking on his head.

The bellman took one look at Duke and exclaimed excitedly,

23

"I know you. Everybody knows you. You're that great wrestler from the States."

I have never seen anyone expand his chest as fast and as far as Duke did. It must have gone out at least six inches. The bellman took some time to set up the table and serve the food. As long as he was still there, Duke didn't want to exhale and ruin his image.

The bellman walked to the door and paused, one hand on the knob. "I used to be in the theater."

I answered perfunctorily, one eye on the food and one eye on Duke, who had both eyes on the food. "Yes?"

The bellman wouldn't quit. "I used to be in vaudeville. I had a balancing act. I could balance a Coca-Cola bottle on my nose with a cigarette paper standing up on the end of it."

Duke was still holding his breath. I was hungry but had to see this.

"That's not easy to believe. The Coke bottle maybe, but the cigarette paper?"

"No, really. I could do it. I can *still* do it."

"You can? Will you show us?"

"Sure."

He dug down in the wagon and came up with a Coke bottle and a cigarette paper, excited about doing his act for the great wrestler from the States.

Sure enough, he did the trick, and we acted very impressed. When he finally left, Duke let all the air out, collapsed in a chair, muttered something about the bellman's ancestry and we both broke up.

As a prelude to the meal, Duke squeezed the lemon into the hot water and drank it.

He ate the pie and ice cream first, explaining that the greatest thing the Orientals ever invented in their culture and civilization was the sublime enchantment of starting a meal with a sweet.

He followed his breakfast with eleven vitamin pills, which he had lined up beside his plate. (The black one puzzled me.)

Duke didn't finish his lamb chops but wrapped part of one

24

in a napkin and abandoned it, a subconscious memorial, I later learned, to his leaner days.

Duke was working at the Queensway, one of the better clubs in Toronto, and was really cock o' the walk. He was invited into the finest homes and officers' clubs and always took me with him. It was a ball. They couldn't do enough for us. They drove us anyplace we wanted to go and occasionally to places we didn't!

One night we were being driven to the officers' mess at one of the swankier clubs, where Duke was to be guest of honor. The conversation, as often happened in those days, veered to the subject of the situation in Europe. A couple of the high-ranking officers in the car allowed as how Hitler wasn't so bad. After all, he was getting rid of some of "those people." I thought of Duke, a black man. If he hadn't been a universally recognized genius, these people probably wouldn't even speak to him, much less honor him at their club. Almost all the Torontonians we had met were warm, loving people, and these bastards were certainly not representative of anyone other than themselves.

Very loudly and distinctly, I said, "Duke, I wonder if our friends realize there's a non-Aryan sitting in the backseat."

The rest of the evening proceeded with a dull thud until after the dinner and the speeches, when one of the politicians' wives, a lovely lady who was standing in for her husband, corralled Duke and myself and took us with a lady friend back to her stately home for a late meal.

Her husband was away on government business, and there we all were in the kitchen, having a grand time. It was about three in the morning, and Duke and I were scrambling eggs when down came a voice from above the great winding staircase.

"Julia, Julia, what are you doing down there?"

We hadn't realized her mother was up there all the time.

The mayor was a great guy. He named one day Duke Ellington Day, and the people really turned it on—flags, music, food, girls, dancing; joy, joy, joy.

25

We wrote a song or a piece of a song every day.

It was easy to see why the Duke loved Toronto. The city was clean and green and soft and warm and wonderful. And the people were the same. The streets were immaculate, open and friendly, and the chef at the hotel could make even burned toast taste great.

On the other side of the world, there was a war going on, but here the pubs opened at 4 P.M. and a fellow, if he was lucky, could indulge himself in a pint of warm ale. And if he was luckier still, he might have met the two beautiful charmers I ran into at one of the pubs, who invited me to a party later that evening. Duke joined us at the party after he got through work, and after a few "God Save the Kings," the four of us hightailed it back to the hotel.

The girls had been there all night and all day, and now it was time for them to get dressed and leave. Duke and I, was usual, were working on a song. One of the girls, kind of high on Lincoln Inn rye whiskey, a native product, was sitting on top of the upright piano, her bare feet hanging over the keys, her toes chasing Duke's fingers as he reached for the chords, between and around her legs. She finally stood up on top of the piano and spread her arms, screaming, "Whee, I'm a B-25," and dove through the air. I broke her fall just before she hit the ground and turned to her friend for help.

"She's been listening to the radio too much about the war," her friend said. We got her dressed, and in the process she spied Duke's huge powder-puff and talc ensemble and proceeded to powder her face with it. A grinning bellhop finally came and helped the girls to a cab, and Duke started to get ready to go to work.

It was after 3 A.M. Duke and the band had finished their week at the Queensway and were getting ready to jump off on a series of one-nighters. We were sitting around swapping stories while we waited for the instruments to be loaded on the bus. Duke had finished his first quart of ice cream and was working on the second, looking at me out of the corner of his eye as though he was afraid I might want some.

We were clowning around about the old days, before we had

met. Duke and Sweetpea and I were comparing notes as to who had been the best soda jerk, which we all had started out as, at different times, in different places.

Sonny spoke up. "Hey, Duke. How come you never tell about when you were a dishwasher at the Plaza Hotel in Asbury Park?"

Duke, grinning, "A man's got to have some secrets."

Just then Jonesie walked in, a worried look on his face. "Anybody seen the road manager? I can't find him anyplace."

Sonny turned to Duke. "I saw him last night at the club when he picked up our money. Didn't he bring it to you?"

Duke shook his head. "I haven't seen him. Why don't we check the desk."

All eyes were on Sonny as he picked up the room phone, got the switchboard, asked for the front desk, listened quietly, then hung up. "He checked out last night."

His face clouded and his voice rose.

"Man, ain't that a pisser? Here's a guy we've been working with for a long time. We trusted him, and he pulls this on us. Who the hell does he think he is? I'm going to call some of the boys in New York. They'll know how to get the money back."

Sweetpea took the floor. "We wouldn't want to do that, Sonny. Those boys play awful rough. Why don't we just call the police up here and let them handle it?"

Sonny and Sweetpea went back and forth and round and round, Sonny pitching for the boys and Sweetpea for the law.

Finally Duke, wearing an expression of infinite calm, held up his hand for silence.

"We'll do nothing," he said. "Let him have the money. Apparently he needs it more than I do."

Edna

"SAY, DON."

"I'm right here behind you, Duke."

"Look, man. Anytime you've been with a lady that you

shouldn't have been with, make sure you take a shower before you go home."

"What's on your mind, buddy?"

"I was just thinking about when I was married to Edna, and I'd been with this other lady who was wearing a lot of cologne, and I came home and got in bed and a big whiff of cologne came up when I pulled the sheet down over me. I thought Edna was asleep, but she rolled over and turned on the light and got the gun she kept in her night table. Man, she just laid it up against my head and she said, 'You son-of-a-bitch, I'm going to kill you. You've been with another woman.' "

"What the devil did you do, Duke?"

"I thought real fast. I said, 'No, no, you just listen to *me*. What happened was that I was at the turkish bath with the fellows and that's the kind of soap they use.' "

"Did she buy it?"

"She bought it." He got up, stretching. "Don, we can't permit anything to interfere with man's inalienable right to have a little pussy on the side."

The Brill Building

THE BRILL BUILDING STANDS ON THE NORTHWEST CORNER OF FORTY-NINTH Street and Broadway. It is a fourteen-story white brick building with a terrace that surrounds the entire penthouse floor.

The second floor of the building has been occupied in the glamorous past by such internationally known nightclubs as the Hurricane and the Zanzibar, which were entered by a separate mirrored stairway leading from the street.

The greatest popular songs, the greatest theatrical songs and the greatest film songs have been written and published in the Brill Building, which has been known throughout the decades as Tin Pan Alley.

It has given birth and sustenance to the greatest songwriters in the world. Duke Ellington, Harold Arlen, Hoagy Carmichael, Johnny Mercer, George and Ira Gershwin and so many of the other greats were spawned there.

I know the building well. My first song was published there, and my first hit.

One day, I guess it was either 1938 or 1939, I was standing in the lobby of the Brill Building looking across Broadway at the Rivoli Theatre, which is directly opposite. A little, thin fellow was standing to my right. There was a Gary Cooper picture playing at the Rivoli, and a huge photo of Cooper—at least one story tall—was above the marquee of the theater. Thinking aloud, I said, "Wow, look at the size of Cooper's picture."

The little fellow's voice rang out loud and clear. "Kid, when my film plays the Rivoli, my picture will be clear up to the top of the flagpole."

(To myself.) "Who does this character think he is?"

Later on, of course, he turned out to be Frank Sinatra.

It was at the Brill Building that Duke and I first met Tony Bennett whose contract with Columbia Records was about to be dropped after one final recording date. Tony recorded "Because of You" on that date and became a fantastic star, an evergreen, and a lifelong buddy of ours.

Duke's office was on the sixth floor, and we hung out there sometimes in the late afternoons when Duke's band was playing at the Hurricane downstairs in the building.

Duke never went directly home after work. He'd sit around and talk with whichever friends dropped in to hear him play. Peggy Lee, Ed Sullivan, Charlie Barnet, Tommy Dorsey (whose office was in the penthouse) and all his other buddies, as a mark of respect, courtesy and love, were constant stay-up-lates with Duke.

Finally we would go to the Stage Delicatessen to pick up corned beef sandwiches, roast beef sandwiches with cole slaw and russian dressing, and go back to Duke's apartment to write.

Duke had a strange way of composing. Most tune writers wrote the melody first, then worked out the chord structure behind it, but Duke wrote the chords and that was that. I needed a melody to hang onto. At first I felt as though I were feeling my way through a labyrinth and had forgotten to unwind the string behind me that would return me to the entrance; but gradually, through some form of musical osmosis, the words fell in the right places and lo! . . . we had a song.

Duke wrote something every single night. Before the chicks, during the chicks and after the chicks, he just wrote. He was afraid to go to sleep while it was dark. Perhaps because of his fear of death, he didn't sleep nights. Whatever his gig was— vaudeville, concerts, one-nighters, nightclubs—Duke saw to it that a piano was available at the end of the gig, and alternating among the conversations and the songwriting and the ladies, he would remain occupied all night.

Sometimes we'd walk out of places when the streets were alive with people going to work, while he was on his way home to sleep. He'd look around and say, "Goddamn! Have all these people been up all night?"

Lena's Hat

IN THE DRESSING ROOM AT THE APOLLO THEATRE ON 125TH STREET IN NEW York City, Duke is sitting chatting with Ella Fitzgerald, his co-star in the show. Lena Horne drops in unexpectedly to visit, wearing an attractive hat. Duke rises to the occasion.

"You sure make that hat look pretty."

Ella waves a disdainful hand. "Don't pay any attention to him, honey. He talks like that to everybody."

Bernice Wiggins

ONE AFTERNOON WHILE DUKE WAS OUT OF TOWN, I VISITED WITH BERNICE Wiggins, a cousin of Duke's, a wonderfully warm, friendly woman nearly the same age as Duke, who had been brought up with him in Washington, D.C.

BERNICE [smiling]: Come on in and rest your coat, Don.

ME [kissing her on both cheeks]:   Thank you.

BERNICE: Is everything all right? There's nothing wrong with Duke, is there?

ME: No, he's fine. I was just thinking how I hadn't seen you in a while, and I thought I'd stop by.

BERNICE: Would you like some tea? I was just about to have some.

[After the tea and Fig Newtons, the conversation as usual veered to Duke.]

BERNICE [reminiscing]: He used to come in from school . . . he used to come in to get his dinner and he would

30

say, "You know, Mother, I'm going to be one of the greatest men in the world." And she used to say, "Oh, boy, hush your mouth." He'd say, "Yes, I am, Mother." Then he would kiss her—just kiss her and kiss her when she would be scolding him. And he would say, "I'm going to have everybody in the world calling me Duke." And then he used to make me turn around. I was his audience. And I used to get so mad at him because I had to pay strict attention to what he was saying. Then he would bow forward, he would bow to the left, he would bow to the right. Then he would say, "Now I'm going to tell you. Everybody in the world is going to call me Duke Ellington. I'm ze Duke, ze great, ze grand, and ze glorious Duke." And we used to laugh. It was so funny.

ME: How old was he then?

BERNICE: Well, he was seventeen, going onto eighteen. Going to school. And he predicted his future. This has never been mentioned. But this is God's . . . heaven's truth, I'm sittin' here tellin' it. He predicted his future. And everybody in the whole world called him Duke. And then he said, too, "I'm going to bow before kings and queens." And he did. So that was his life.

ME: Kings, queens, presidents . . .

BERNICE: Even presidents. Everybody. He has . . . and I was surprised. I had a picture I had taken out of the paper, because we didn't hear too much of it, but he even played piano with President Truman in the White House. That's going way back. A duet together. They both sat at the same piano.

[Her face became animated. She was speaking more proudly now.]

BERNICE: One of my greatest moments was when he was invited to the Waldorf-Astoria Hotel, and that was around 1936 or '5. And in his honor, and with Paderewski and Stravinsky, he was one of the first Negroes that had ever been so highly honored, and his music was recognized then by these great musicians.

ME: You mean Paderewski and Stravinsky were really there? There at the Waldorf?

[Her big eyes glowed even brighter.]

BERNICE: They were present in honor of him. In 1936. No, it had to be . . . Aunt Daisy died in '35.* It could have been in the latter part of '35, or '36. It was during that time, yes. And that was my proudest moment. To think that Paderewski and Stravinsky were sitting in honor of him, why, it was marvelous.

ME: I would certainly think so.

BERNICE: Yes, indeed. One of my greatest moments. I tell you, we've had many in honor of him. But that was one of the first because it hadn't happened to any of the other Negro musicians, you know, and he's been hailed the highest and best. And he has proven himself. He has proven himself. And then it opened many doors to other musicians. And what makes it so nice, you know *they* give him the honors of some of their successes. Isn't that beautiful? They give him the honors. It's really beautiful. I think I could go on and on and on but there's no end to this story . . .

[She rocked back and forth in remembrance.]

BERNICE: In our young childhood . . . he was young himself, because he wasn't much older than I was . . . anyway, he would come around and check on us. Sometimes we would be playing and we would love to see him because he played on this jew's harp, "Casey Jones." And, oh boy, this . . . I don't know what you called that dance then—buck and wing or something—and we thought he was the greatest thing that ever lived. And he was in short pants.

ME: [I've never seen Duke even do a ballroom dance.] This is the first I've heard of Duke as a dancer. Tell me about his dancing.

BERNICE: That's right. It was kind of like tap dancing—buck and wing. He could do that, dear. He could play that jew's harp, anything he wanted, during those days, years, that music was famous, as a young boy, he could play it. I never seen nothin' like it. And when he come around he was entertaining us because we were five, six and seven years old and we were so happy to see him, so we thought he was the grandest thing in the world. I'm glad we lived long enough to even really believe, realize and see that he was the greatest thing in the world.

*Aunt Daisy was Duke's mother.

32

ME [hugging Bernice in wholehearted agreement]: Not only to you, Bernice. Not just to you alone.

BERNICE: There was not a day that he didn't want to know something about some of his people. Isn't that something? All the history that he made, all the music and everything, it was always "Where's so-and-so? How's so-and-so?" Or if they're sick he would take care of their hospital bills. If they die, he wanted to know where they're going to be buried. The money's there. Oh, he was just a wonderful man. And not only his relatives. His friends. People that he didn't know of. And if someone would come to him and tell him the plight of somebody, he would want to know, "Where are they? . . . Who are they?" and then he would see that you go take care of them or you'll go pay their rent.

He was a man that loved and wanted love and knew nothing but love. It came out of his life as a child. Love. His mother, his father, and his sister. It was love. And that word was so easy put together. God-love. God-love. And still, after all

L

GOD

V

E

his popularity in music and the tapes of music, he was always with God. He was religious. Religious man. It was in the family. Came from his grandmother, his grandfather. And we also have a minister in our family, and years back we were raised the old-fashioned way. Christian way. [Smiling fondly.]

And he always had advice for us young girls. He was supposed to be like our father to us, you know, young as he was. And I first come to New York and I was married and had a girl about six years old, and he give me lectures now. "Now you're comin' to New York and there's gonna be nice times up here. I don't want you to come up here and get all excited over these men and everything because you've gotta look out for yourself and I don't want no trouble." Now this was the way he saw us. He seen to it, too. He seen that we wouldn't get near the men to even have anything to say to them. If you were his cousin, he wanted you to be a lady, stay a lady. And that's the way we had to be. Checked on us going and coming.

ME [whimsically]:   He was just protecting you from people like himself.

BERNICE: Well, he was a good man. We loved him. If he didn't dedicate himself solely to one woman, it was because all women were beautiful to him. He loved them all and they all loved him. So you see . . .

The Hurricane

IN DUKE'S DRESSING ROOM AT THE HURRICANE, BILLY STRAYHORN BROUGHT me a lead sheet of one of Duke's tunes that I was writing a lyric for. I was sitting at the dressing table penciling in the lyric on the lead sheet when Duke's doctor, Arthur Logan, walked in. The dressing room was about ten or twelve feet away from the stand where the band was playing. They were really blasting away. It was tremendously loud. Logan said to me, "Don, how in the world can you write a lyric here; how can you concentrate with all that noise going on?" I looked up and said, "What noise?" I was concentrating so, I hadn't heard the band.

The song I was working on was called "I'm Afraid." Actually it turned out eventually to be the song that Duke used on his ladies when he was attempting to pamper his libido and all else failed. When they didn't respond to the halo-on-the-ceiling bit, or his birthday gambit—"Every day I meet a pretty girl it's my birthday" or "I knew you walked into the room because the whole room got lighter" or "I can just picture you sitting on a crescent moon"—when the lady responded to none of these, Duke would get her to a piano and with a little-lost-boy-take-pity-on-me look on his face would sing this song. Duke was not much of a singer but he was one hell of an actor. He told me it never failed, never missed.

I'M AFRAID

I'M AFRAID of wanting you too much
So AFRAID of trembling at your touch
This is no time to start
Flashing your eyes at me
I have to watch my heart

34

It bruises so easily
Don't insist, there's much too much concerned
If we kissed, my mem'ries might get burned
And if I fell in love
I might get hurt, who knows?
I'M AFRAID but anyway . . . here goes!

After I had finished penciling in the lyric, I hurried out front and sat at a table. I never wanted to miss Duke's entrance at the Hurricane. I have never seen anything else quite like it in a nightclub. The band would be onstage first, warming up the audience with a few of Duke's more popular numbers; then Duke would descend from the ceiling on a platform that was operated hydraulically, dressed in white tails, smiling that I-love-you-madly smile and playing his mood of the moment on the piano that accompanied him earthward.

I don't know exactly how it happened, but there was a lady who kind of approached me, a young, fine-looking gal. The first thing I knew, she was sitting at the table and having a drink with me, and sure enough we wound up together. We had a couple of real swinging dates and went through all kinds of changes. It was fine. She knew what she was doing. She was a tremendously sensual, multitalented lady who brought a great amount of personal charm to everything she did. One day she said to me, "Look, I've got a girl friend. A real beautiful little blond girl. I tell you what. Why don't the four of us get together? You and Duke and this girl and myself?"

We got together, but we were looking for a place to go. Duke was living with Evie, and we couldn't go there. There was noplace where I could take the four of us. But Duke as usual solved the problem. Up in Harlem there's an area called Sugar Hill, where the better-off blacks—legitimate businessmen, mob guys, number bigs, successful pimps and anyone else who could afford the area—lived. Duke knew a lady there who rented her apartment for just such occasions. He called it his buffet flat. On the way uptown we stopped the cab to buy some pretty flowers for the pretty ladies. When we got there everything was fine, everything was great. There were separate bedrooms, and I put the bluish orchids with lots of petals in a handy vase. Duke was in his room, and my lady friend had

35

worked it so that she was with Duke and I was with the blond girl. My friend confessed when the four of us were together that the reason she had been swinging with me was so that she could get with Duke.

I had been telling Duke how great she was and how wonderful she was, in her presence. She turned to me and said, "Don, those were just preliminaries."

"Really," I said, vividly remembering the lady's capabilities. "What do you use for the main event, dynamite?"

Duke and I soloed with our ladies in our separate bedrooms, then we all got together in Duke's room, going through our paces and changes. Finally Duke and I put on our shorts and went to another room, where the lady had some food fixed for us. On the way out I noticed the vase where we had put the flowers when we came in. The plants were still there, now completely devoid of anything but the stems. I smiled, reminiscing on what we and the girls had done with the petals.

We wound up good friends. The little blond disappeared in time, but my lady friend remained as a very staunch friend of Duke's and mine—me for my shoulder, and Duke for the rest of him.

When we heard she was getting married, Duke's only comment was, "It's a shame she's going to confine all that great stuff to just one man."

Al Hibbler

DUKE USUALLY HAD THREE OR FOUR SINGERS WORKING WITH THE BAND. He had Kay Davis and Joya Sherrill, and he had picked up Marie Ellington,* who eventually married Nat Cole. She had been working at the YWCA in Chicago as a secretary for thirty-five dollars a week when she auditioned for Duke as a vocalist with the band. Duke really didn't need another girl singer but he said, "She looks so pretty up there in her white gown, I'm going to put her on anyway."

There was no male vocalist with the band because Herb Jeffries, who had been with the band for quite some time and had been featured in Duke's musical *Jump for Joy* and had cut a

*Because of the similarity of names Duke gave her billing as "Marie," omitting her last name.

smash hit record on the song "Flamingo," had left to go out as a single and was doing very well.

Betty Roche, who had been working with the band singing things like "Rocks in My Bed" (a big standard song written by Duke), heard blind Al Hibbler sing at a Saturday-night neighborhood gig. She loved his voice and she brought Al to the attention of Ray Nance, who played trumpet, violin, danced and sang in the band.

Little Ray was an all-around performer who was very much favored by Duke because Duke appreciated his great talent. Ray kept telling Duke about Al Hibbler, and Duke kept saying, "We have enough vocalists. We don't need any more vocalists."

Ray kept on pitching, saying, "Well, we don't have a male vocalist."

Duke insisted, "We don't need one: we have all these chicks sitting up here singing their songs. They sing everything we need."

Finally, in desperation, Betty Roche and Ray Nance got together one night at the Zanzibar and they set it up with Billy Strayhorn, Duke's arranger and musical amanuensis, to play piano, with Sonny Greer on drums and a couple of other guys from the band. While the people were in the restaurant and Duke was in his dressing room between sets, they had Al Hibbler come on and sing. He sang a couple of things and clean broke it up. Duke heard all the applause and came out to see what was going on. He saw the incredible impact that Hibbler had on the audience. They were actually standing and applauding and some were cheering, with even a few bravos here and there.

When it was over Ray and Betty approached Duke and said, "Come on, man, how about hiring Al?"

Duke looked at them, smiled very sweetly and said, "I thought you knew. Al has been working with the band for the last two weeks." He turned to Al, "The band manager will give you your money."

Duke worked out a great MO with Hibbler. When Hibbler was to sing, Duke would stand at the microphone and Hibbler would be in the wings. Duke would keep talking, and Hibbler, guided by the sound of Duke's voice, came to the microphone, put one hand on the microphone and did his performance. When he was coming off Duke stood in the wings and kept talking to him, his voice guiding him off.

Duke really watched out for Hibbler. It was a treat to see them walk down the street together. Hibbler never used a cane; he just seemed to be strolling along with Duke. What really happened was that Duke was making occasional shoulder contact, a thing he developed to keep Hibbler walking correctly and looking like everything was fine. He would just touch him with his shoulder every so often to guide him or steer him or slow him down.

One time, in the Deep South, in Florida, Hibbler proved he had learned his lesson well. The band was playing, and Hibbler was singing "Don't Take Your Love from Me," when two gangs who had a beef with each other pulled guns and started shooting it out on the floor. Naturally, everyone ran for the dressing rooms. When Duke got back to his dressing room he found that Hibbler, who was blind as a bat, had gotten there first—had beaten him to the dressing room.

Hibbler, who was known to imbibe more than just a little, had one additional, incredible talent. He could be driven to a strange area in a strange town and, without faltering or deviating from his purpose, make his way directly to the nearest bar.

The band was playing at a club on Forty-eighth Street in Manhattan, next to a luggage store. Hibbler was standing at the bar when Duke came to get him. He said, "Come on, man, it's time to go on," and led Hibbler to the stage. The band started playing "My Little Brown Book," which Herb Jeffries had recorded before Hibbler joined the band.

While Hibbler was singing, Duke walked up behind him and whispered in his ear, "The next song is going to be 'Flamingo.' Shake your head if you know it. If you don't, nod your head. But I know you know it, because I heard you sing it a long time ago."

Hibbler shook his head yes. The band played it and Hibbler sang it.

As soon as it was over, Duke grabbed Hibbler and took him offstage during the applause. He said, "Come on, man, I got

38

somebody I want you to meet." He walked Hibbler over to a table where Herb Jeffries and Lana Turner were sitting. Duke said, "Hey, Herb, don't you think Al Hibbler sings 'Flamingo' better than you?"

Jeffries didn't say a word, but Lana Turner reached up and kissed Hibbler on the cheek and said, "Yes, I think he sings it much better than Herb."

Duke did things like that. He liked to play games.

Duke had an unusual method of teaching Hibbler a new song. Whenever the band played a theater, he had one of the other singers perform the song and he'd say, "Hib, go out in the audience and learn the song." Hibbler sat out there in the double dark, listening. Duke got him backstage and asked, "You sure you know it well?" Then he'd rehearse him some more and eventually tell him, "Tomorrow we're going to record it, but don't tell anybody."

Once Duke called a special recording date for Hibbler in the CBS Studio, where they once had the Lux Radio Theater. Duke called out, "Hey, Hib, come on over here. I want you to meet somebody. I want you to meet Jayne Mansfield."

She had heard about Hibbler and the Braille system, so as Hibbler started reaching out, she just took his hand, saying, "Here it is. Right here," and put his hand on her well-publicized breasts.

Chant of the Clitoris

DUKE WAS DOING A RECORD DATE WITH THE BAND FOR COLUMBIA RECords at the old church on east Thirtieth Street, which Columbia often used because of the great sound that seemed built into the carved wooden walls and the high ceilings. (Frankie Laine and Johnny Ray had recorded their greatest hits there. Harry James and Xavier Cugat looked forward to coming to New York because of the crisper sound of the records produced there.) The usual entourage was present: the wives and girl friends of members of the band; some hangers-on; Joe Morgen, Duke's PR man; the band manager.

Sweetpea was sitting at a table off to one corner, squinting through his hornrim glasses, finishing up the instrumental arrangements that were to be recorded. As he finished each

39

page, Tom Whaley, the copyist, extracted the individual parts for each member of the band. Ray Nance was belligerently drunk, and Paul Gonsalves was staggering around. It was a normal record date.

Duke sauntered in wearing his porkpie hat with the brim turned up in front, his wraparound camel's hair coat, which he nonchalantly tossed on a chair, and his lucky sweater. After greeting everybody with the customary four kisses apiece (one for each cheek), he sat down at the piano and looked casually around. His right hand went into action and hit the chords he always used to summon the band. They came flying, floating and crawling into their places. School was in session. They didn't want Duke mad at them. He was a father who loved his children very much, who took care of them, who gave them a great deal of latitude, but only up to a certain point. Now he demanded respect and cooperation.

(Joe Ferrer once said to me, "Don, it was incredible the way he could cope with that zoo that was his band; when you think of Johnny Hodges with his kiss-my-ass attitude and Paul Gonsalves in the same band, to say nothing of Tricky Sam and some of those other wild men that he traveled with. But his greatness was so lasting and so flexible that if they were there, fine. If they left for a while, as they sometimes did, he understood them. They always came back to the fold. No matter how rude they were to him, as Johnny Hodges was time and time again, or how combative, as Ben Webster was, or as spaced out, as Paul Gonsalves was, they knew that Duke was home, and he could handle their bad manners and their irresponsibilities with tolerance and affection.")

After the microphones had been set up and the recording engineer got the sound balance he wanted in the control room, the date started. The first tune was a walking-tempo instrumental with a sixteen-bar introduction by Duke on the piano. The engineer's voice rang out over the loudspeaker, "Take one," and off they went. Ray Nance fouled up two takes banging around, and once somebody knocked over an ashtray. They finally got what they wanted on the ninth take. Duke played each intro differently. He was the only musician I have ever heard who could embellish himself while he was creating. After the date Duke hung around in the studio for over an hour, talking with the engineer, to make sure everything was perfect. Then we headed over to Reuben's on East Fifty-eight Street for the cheese blintzes that he loved so dearly. Polly Bergen and Luther Henderson were at the next table, so we joined forces and lied to each other till almost sunup, when it was safe for Duke to go to bed.

Two days later Duke called me on the phone, saying, "Don, you're real good at titles. Do me a favor."

I said, "Of course, how can I not?"

He explained. "Columbia called me. They want titles on those two songs we cut the other night."

"Don't worry about it, Duke. I'll take care of it."

"Thanks, Don. I knew you would."

I called Columbia and got somebody's secretary on the phone in the department that controlled record releases and said to her, "This is Don George. I write with Duke Ellington, and he asked me to call in a couple of titles for the two instrumentals he recorded night before last."

The girl asked me, "What are they?"

I forget the other title, but one I gave her was "Chant of the Clitoris."

She said to me, "How do you spell *clitoris?*"

I looked at the telephone in utter disbelief and thought, wow, maybe I'll get away with this. I spelled it for her. "*C-l-i-t-o-r-i-s.*"

She spelled it back to me and I said, "That's great, that's wonderful."

Columbia at that time was pressing records up in Bridgeport, Connecticut. Pressing records is a three-way process: there's a master, then a mother, then a stamper. The stamper comes down and finally presses the record. An inspector with a magnifying light comes around and checks the grooves on the records. If the grooves are a little fuzzy, they get rid of that stamper and use a different one. This one fellow was inspecting the records and he happened to glance over at the label and saw the title "Chant of the Clitoris" and he raised a holy howl. If it wasn't for him we would have had some wild collector's items with that label on it.

About ten days later Duke called me. (I was waiting for his call. I was sure Columbia had gotten back to him about the title

41

by that time.) He said, "Don, did you ever call in the titles on those instrumentals I asked you to call in to Columbia?"

I was properly horror-stricken. "Oh, my word, Duke, I'm so sorry. I forgot all about it."

A New Act

LAWRENCE BROWN HAD A TREMENDOUS ARGUMENT WITH CAT ANDERSON and chased him across the stage in full view of the audience. Duke announced to the people, "Ladies and gentlemen, you have just seen part of our new act."

Afterward Duke told the fellows, "Look, if you're going to do these things let me know, and I'll write the music for it."

Duke Reminisces

I ALWAYS LOOKED FORWARD TO CATCHING DUKE IN A NOSTALGIC MOOD. IT was in those moments that we discussed beginnings, reasons for being, the people and circumstances that brought us to where we were. On not-too-frequent occasions Duke would lift a corner of the veil that he used to prevent his privacy from being invaded. It was at those times that we really looked at each other.

Once I reminded him of an evening in Toronto. "Duke, what did Sonny mean when he said you'd been a dishwasher?"

Duke [reminiscing]: That was way back; in the teens. At the Plaza Hotel in Asbury Park. Sonny played the hotel with his school band, but he didn't know I was alive. I didn't tell him about it until years later. I used to be a soda jerk, too. In D.C. I even wrote a song called the "Soda Fountain Rag."

[Duke paused to reach up and scratch his hairdo exactly in the center with one vertical finger. Then he continued]: I used to play piano all the time. I idolized James P. Johnson and Lucky Roberts and all those fellows. I could play their piano rolls, note for note. Sonny Greer was playing at the Howard Theatre. He talked me into coming to New York with a band where he was the leader. I didn't want to go at first because I didn't have much money, but Sonny's a fast talker and he started throwing around names like Fats Waller and Willie "the Lion" Smith and all those great people, so I finally said okay.

42

Sonny got Wetzel and Snowdon and Toby Hardwick and we went up to New York. Sonny and Toby and I stayed at Toby's aunt's apartment while she was out of town. Nobody was working, and things were rough. Sonny would make a buck here and there, hustling pool, and share it with Toby and me. Sonny used to play pill pool, where the pills are numbered from one to fifteen and kept in a leather receptacle. The dealer shakes it and then throws out one pill each to the players. Sonny had a thing set up with the dealer in this one poolroom, so he won pretty often. [Shaking his head and laughing.] Sonny sure was something!

[Duke was going great, really flowing, and I didn't want to interrupt him. I confined my contribution to, "He still is."]

Duke [continuing]: I remember one rainy night Sonny made a killing at the poolroom, and he was heading home when down the street came a hooker. A white hooker. She said to Sonny, "How you doing, man?" And Sonny said, "All right, everything's fine." She said, "I ain't doin' so good." Sonny said, "Hey, I got an idea. You come with me." She thought Sonny was propositioning her, but he said, "I got a pal. I want you to meet him."

So Sonny came to the apartment, opened the door, walked in with this beautiful chick and said, "There he is, entertain him." He turned to me and said, "I had a little luck tonight. Here's a present for you."

Duke [continuing]: The chick was fine, and I locked Sonny out.

ME: You locked him out in the rain?

DUKE: He kept banging on the door saying, "Man, I paid the bill. I paid the tab. Let me in." I said, "I'll see you tomorrow." He said, "I won't pay for your dinner." But I just ignored him.

ME: What happened?

DUKE [chuckling]: He got over it.

ME: How did you guys make it all the time you were waiting for gigs that didn't happen?

DUKE: Every Saturday night we played the rent parties. We got a dollar for playing and all the food we could eat and all we could drink. Some cat would be trying to make the rent money and it was during Prohibition, so he'd make some gin in the bathtub and his old lady would cook up some ribs and greens and stuff and sell them while the musicians played and the people got drunk and laughed and had a good time.

ME [remembering]: My brother and I had a cordial store during Prohibition on Fifty-first and Ninth Avenue in Manhattan, right in the middle of Hell's Kitchen. They just called them them cordial stores. We really sold whiskey and beer. We'd take the near-beer that was legal in those days, remove the caps from the bottles, put in about a tablespoonful of pure alcohol, recap it and sell it. It used to give you a hell of a headache, but you could get drunk on it. The cops would come in every week and shake us down. They only took the good whiskey in the sealed bottles, with the labels still on. They didn't want any of the stuff we made.

[That was when the big mobs got started; during Prohibition. They were running whiskey down from Canada, by boat and by car, mostly in the middle of the night. They had their territories and they showed no quarter when any other mob encroached. They made their own alcohol and beer, sometimes dumping wood alcohol that crippled and killed people on the illicit market. They controlled the nightclubs and houses of prostitution and practically everything else where liquor was sold. Anything for a buck. Legs Diamond hung out at the Club Abbey and always took his lawyer Dixie Davis's advice. "Don't leave any witnesses alive." Dutch Schultz (Arthur Flegenheimer) was blasted in a men's room in New Jersey after he got too greedy. Vincent "Mad Dog" Coll was cut down by machine-gun bullets in a telephone booth in the drugstore adjoining the Hotel Chelsea after kidnapping a rival mob chief and holding him for ransom. It was the Wild West all over again, but the society people loved it. They went out of their way to fraternize with "the boys."]

DUKE [continuing]: In New York the gigs were few and far between, but we could always count on Saturday. We could get all the food we wanted and take some home, and a dollar besides. We all went along. Me, and Fats Waller and Willie "the Lion" and Sonny. We played the house rent parties every Saturday night. [Getting up and walking around the room.] That was home sweet home.

ME: Willie "the Lion" told me how you both played stride piano together at those parties.

44

DUKE: I learned a lot from Willie. From Sonny, too. [Shaking his head.] He was something else. Half the time his drums were residing with "Uncle,"* and he'd show up with a suitcase and drum on that with some brushes and sticks and play the gig.

ME: How did you get to the Kentucky Club?

DUKE: We played at Barron Wilkins's club first. It was a basement club, up in Harlem. We ran into "Bricktop" [Ada Smith] one day. She was singing at the club, and she got us a job there. We played there from June through August, when Barron was wiped out by some dudes with unfriendly guns, so we were out of a gig. A man named Leonard Harper, who produced the shows at the Cotton Club and Connie's Inn, had heard our band and liked it; in fact I had a room at his house. He said, "I got a job for you guys. A new club opened, the Kentucky Club at Forty-ninth Street and Broadway. Would you be interested?" So we went down there and we stayed four years. That was for the "boys"!

ME: We still call them the boys. What was the club like?

DUKE: It was a small club. No room for dancing, but it became the rendezvous for all the professional people. It was a hangout, a late-hour spot for everybody. Paul Whiteman and Red Nichols and all the bunch would come in to hear us play. We opened at eleven o'clock and we never closed as long as somebody wanted a taste. It was during Prohibition, and they had to be careful who they served, but they never had a beef.

ME: Was that when you started fronting the band?

DUKE: That happened up at Barron Wilkins. Sonny didn't want to be responsible to all the guys, and he felt more comfortable laying back on the drums. The Kentucky Club was great for me. That's where I started writing all my songs.

[He looked up. The sunlight shining through the open window bathed his face. He rose, stretching and yawning.] It's my bedtime now. Good night, Don.

ME: Good night, Duke.

When he awoke late that afternoon and had his usual breakfast of steak and chopped liver and lettuce and tomatoes and hot water and lemon juice and vitamin pills, after spending an

*The hock shop.

45

inordinate amount of time in the bathroom ("Don, I always get my best ideas in the john"), I pursued the conversation that had temporarily ended that morning when he went to bed. I was anxious to know why he left the Kentucky Club, downtown in the heart of all the Broadway action, to go back up to Harlem again.

"What in the world happened, man? There you were right in the middle of everything. Right around the corner from Lindy's and Dave's Blue Room and Reuben's. You told me yourself Reuben's had the best cheese blintzes in New York. They were open till four or five in the morning, and the greatest people in the world fell in. You could just about always run into Damon Runyon at Lindy's, and Mark Hellinger. Those fellows loved you and wrote about you all the time."

Duke shrugged. "We didn't have much of a choice, Don. The 'boys' said to go to the Cotton Club, and when the 'boys' say you go to the Cotton Club, you go to the Cotton Club.

"The guys hated to leave a soft thing like the Kentucky Club at first, but it eventually worked out for the best. We changed the name of the band to Duke Ellington and the Cotton Club Orchestra and enlarged the band from six pieces up to twelve, and after we settled in it turned out to be just great. We were on the air coast-to-coast from six to seven in the evening, and Ted Husing was one of our announcers. We played for the finest artists in the world, and the greatest songwriters in America wrote the scores for the shows. Ethel Waters sang Harold Arlen's 'Stormy Weather' in the show, and we were the first band to play it on the radio. (Looking up into his head.) We were the first band to play 'Stardust' on the air. Hoagy Carmichael was a good friend and brought it to us. (His eyes lit up.) Ted Koehler, Dorothy Fields, Jimmy McHugh—there were great writers doing the Cotton Club shows in those days."

Me: I hear you were doing pretty well yourself in the song department at the time.

Duke: Some of my songs were starting to get a little attention. I played them on the air, and occasionally Irving Mills got us a recording date and I mostly recorded my own things. Irving had his name on a lot of them.

46

Duke never forgot that summer evening in 1926 when Mills walked into the Kentucky Club and heard Arthur Wetzel, Toby Hardwicke, Sonny Greer, Freddie Guy (who later committed suicide) and Duke playing "St. Louis Blues." That night Duke played the "Black and Tan Fantasy," and Mills said, "This is it. This isn't just a Tin Pan Alley songwriter but a real composer at work, weaving different themes, creating compositions, not only thirty-two-bar songs."

(Duke, though he was still married to Edna, was at this time living with Mildred Dixon, a Cotton Club dancer.

He was a great whist player, and many nights after the club closed, Owney Madden, Big Frenchy, George McManus and Mike Best, some of the biggest mob guys of the era, would start a game in the back room with Duke standing in for Mike Best or Owney Madden, who owned the club.

Duke saw to it that he always won a little for the fellow who backed him but never enough to arouse the ire of the rest of the players.)

Duke continued, "Polly Adler would call Sonny and me once in a while after our gig at the Cotton Club to come downtown and entertain some of her more illustrious clients.* After everyplace else was closed, they'd wind up at one of her houses for a party. Polly would call up and say, 'Get hold of Sonny and come on over.' She was a petite, gregarious lady, with great charm, whom everybody loved, and she got along great with all the mob guys except one dude called Pretty Boy Amberg (who got his nickname the same way a bald man is called Curly), who used to get his lunatic kicks by hanging the naked girls out the window, swaying them back and forth by their ankles before he pulled them back in. Being aware of all the notches on his forty-five, it was considered discreet not to cross him."

Duke went on, "When we finished playing, Polly would hand us each a hundred-dollar bill and say, 'Thanks, boys, here's cab fare.' We'd take the money and go back uptown and spend it at Ivie's Chicken Shack, or Small's Paradise, or Dickie Wells, where the girls would pick up folded dollar bills from

*Polly Adler was the number-one madam of New York.

47

the tables by raising their skirts and exercising their personal magnetism."

In later days Polly enrolled at UCLA for a course in journalism and wrote a smash-hit book titled *A House Is Not a Home*. She had everyone pulling for her.

Jack Robbins

DUKE HAD GONE OUT ON ONE OF HIS TOOTS AND SPENT TOO MUCH MONey. He didn't have enough left to pay the band. He figured he'd go downtown to his publisher Jack Robbins's office, see Jack and get the fifty dollars he needed to meet the payroll.

On the way down in the subway, he started figuring out, well, he's Duke Ellington, how can he ask for fifty dollars? Fifty dollars would be bad for his image. Duke Ellington would need five hundred dollars. He walked in to Jack Robbins's office, put his hat on the desk and said, "Jack, I'd like you to loan me five hundred dollars." (In those days five hundred dollars was a lot of money.)

Jack placatingly said, "Just a minute, Duke. I don't really see how I can do that. That's an awful lot of money. You're a very wonderful man and everything, but I just don't know how—"

Duke interrupted him. "I'll give it back to you at six o'clock tomorrow."

Jack capitulated. "Duke, you've never lied to me. You've always been a perfect gentleman. I'm going to trust you."

He sent for his bookkeeper, got five one-hundred-dollar bills and gave them to Duke. Duke went home, put the bills in his shirt drawer under the shirts, had dinner and went to work that night. The next day he got up, went to rehearsal, came home, shaved, dressed, reached under the shirts, got the five one-hundred-dollar bills and took them back to Jack Robbins. At exactly five minutes to six he handed him the five hundred dollars.

Jack fell out. "Jesus," he cried. "Nobody ever did that. That's phenomenal. What a man you are, Duke. You're truly a man of your word. You can have anything I've got."

Duke said, "Jack, lend me five hundred dollars."

Herb Jeffries

DUKE AND THE BAND WERE WORKING IN *JUMP FOR JOY*, A SHOW DUKE HAD created the music for, in a theater in Los Angeles. Herb Jeffries was the vocalist with the band. Part of the deal was that the band played for about an hour after each performance, from a platform that rose up until it was practically in the audience. The vocalist came face to face with whoever was seated in the first row.

Every night Jeffries sang his big hit, "Flamingo." The band played a dynamic, exciting intro as the platform rose, and Jeffries really opened up. He was a trouper, a seasoned performer. He had sung the song thousands of times with ease and poise almost amounting to bravado. He was tall, light-skinned and, with the razor-slash scar on his face, handsome in a buccaneerish sort of way. The song was a smash hit wherever he appeared.

One night the platform rose and he found himself looking into the beautiful face of Hedy Lamarr. He froze completely. The band played the intro, and nothing happened. The whole audience was waiting, and Duke was looking at this lovely lady. Duke started the intro again. Jeffries was still frozen. He couldn't make a sound. Duke tried once more, starting the intro for the third time. Nothing. Duke looked at Jeffries standing there glued to the stage like a tongue-tied schoolboy, finally turned to the band, gave the cue and they blasted out with their theme, "Take the A Train."

Taft Jordan's Pistol

THE BAND WAS PLAYING A ONE-NIGHTER IN ASHVILLE, NORTH CAROLINA. Kay Davis, Laura Hibbler,* Russell Procope, Taft Jordan and Al Hibbler got off the Pullman (the way the band traveled in the South at that time) and decided they were going to walk into town from the yards where the Pullman was parked to get something to eat at a barbecue place they had heard about that stayed open all night. It was about four o'clock in the morning,

*Hibbler's wife.

and they were walking down the quiet street when Taft Jordan remembered he had his pistol with him.

He said, "Man, I have never shot this thing. Maybe I ought to shoot it and see what kind of action I get."

Kay Davis said, "No, I wouldn't do that if I was you."

Procope came on, real loud, "Man, give me the gun, I'll shoot it."

Taft handed it to him. Bam! Procope shot it. It was a real quiet night, and the gun sounded like a cannon going off.

A few minutes after he shot it, here come the police from both directions. They pulled to a halt, tires screeching, and jumped out of the cars, guns drawn, shouting, "All right, you niggers. What are you doing out here in the street? Get in the cars." They loaded them in the cars and took them down to the police station and told them to get out. Everyone did but Hibbler. He was still sitting there. One of the cops came over and pointed a flashlight at Hibbler and yelled, "Get out. Get out of the car."

Laura intervened, "Leave him alone, sir. He's blind. He can't see."

The cop said, "Godamnit, I shined that light in his eye. Why did he blink?"

Later the guys gave Hibbler hell. He could have gotten them all killed. He was sitting there and wouldn't get out of the car; and just when the man shone the light in his face, he happened to blink. The police held Taft because of the pistol, but the next day Duke got him out.

Clothes

DUKE WAS A CLOTHES HORSE. A REGULAR DUDE. AS A CHILD HE HAD PRE-dicted the nickname Duke for himself, and as an adult he much more than lived up to the title. He loved clothes because that was part of his theatrics, but he also loved the originality of what he could create in clothes. It gave him another area to shine in. He was the first performer to wear white tails onstage (with a white turn-down collar instead of the traditional wing). He was bored with the tuxedo jacket, so he sent out to an upholsterer for swatches of all kinds of damask and stripes. Everyone thought he wanted things made for his home, but he proceeded to order sport and tuxedo jackets from the upholstery material.

Duke hated ordinary ties so he went to a shirtmaker and designed some combination bow-and-string silk affairs that he called kissy-poos, which he wore whenever the situation demanded an adornment for the royal neck. When he was ready for action, he would stand in front of a mirror, chuckle and say, "How about that, Don?" He would see what he wanted to see.

He was the first man to wear ballet slippers with a tuxedo. The band was working in Basin Street, and Duke had a swollen foot. He asked Ralph Watkins, the proprietor, to send someone out for a pair of bedroom slippers. Ralph reminded him that the stage was high and the bedroom slippers would be visible to the audience and would hardly complement the image of the dapper Duke Ellington. Duke said, "Fine. Send someone over to Capezio's and get me a pair of ballet slippers." Duke wore the black ballet slippers with his tuxedo, went onstage and started a whole new fashion.

He was like a proud little boy showing off his new Sunday clothes to the little girl who lived next door, or the little girl who lived down the street, or the little girl who lived around the corner or any little girl he could entice to stand still long enough for an indeterminate (and usually temporary) period of time. He was like a butterfly; he was like a bumblebee that would land on a flower and take out the sweetness, then drift away and go somewhere else. He would touch someone's life long enough to make his little mark, and then, after checking his wardrobe and coiffure, blithely meander on to something or someone else: to the next song, or the next town, or the next movie lady or the next slightly slutty waitress. ("Don, everyone has to dig a little distortion once in a while, in order to lead a rounded life.")

People were richer when he left them. He contributed something to everyone he touched. One reason Duke loved to travel was that it was the best way to meet new people. He loved people. He was an incredible devourer of relationships. In whatever country we traveled, the president or the prime minister invariably sought him out. Kings, queens, and princesses bowed to him.

Another reason was the stimulation that travel brought to his writing, his work; the tight association with the band, not only when they did the gig but on the bus or train; the road rehearsals, the shows in different places; the opportunity to have the band play the melody that he had written just the night before. He was so stimulated by the thought of travel that there were times when we weren't supposed to go any-place that he would get up and start walking around as though we were leaving for another town. Duke had a time clock built within him. If we had to catch a plane or a train or drive some-place on a time schedule, invariably Duke, without rushing or hurrying, would arrive at the airport or the train station and casually stroll to the mode of transportation just as they were calling "all aboard." He never looked at a clock or carried a watch, but he had a built-in sense that told him what time it was; how much time he had left to do what he wanted to do before moving on.

But every day came to an end. And with it came the utmost delight. With a sigh of relief he would remove the corset he almost always wore, gently massage the relieved areas with his fingertips and the palms of his hands, reestablish the sanctity of his stocking cap, put on the much-lived-in cotton robe and turn to his ladies and his music. That done with, he would wave good night (or good morning) and in what seemed like seconds be snoring softly in the quick sleep of those who are blessed with a clear conscience and faith in tomorrow.

I'm Beginning to See the Light

JOHNNY HODGES, AFFECTIONATELY KNOWN AS RABBIT TO EVERYONE, DID look something like the kind of milk-chocolate bunny that parents buy for their cnildren every Easter in a little straw basket filled with snredded paper and assorted jelly beans.

His alto saxophone poured forth the sweetest, roundest tones this side of the Angel Gabriel, and his renditions of Strayhorn's "Passion Flower" and Duke's "I Got It Bad and That Ain't Good" literally had them standing in the aisles whenever he played his solos in front of the band.

Johnny used to segue between songs and occasionally be-tween choruses with a melodic phrase that kept haunting me.

It wasn't much—usually about four bars that he kept repeating. Finally it really got into my blood. One night I said to Duke, "That's a hell of a phrase, man. It sounds to me like it could be a hit."

Duke replied, "Really? He's been playing that thing for a long time. He just keeps noodling around with it." Then, getting involved, he said, "If you like it that much, let's get with Johnny and finish the thing."

Johnny, as usual when it came to writing a song, was all for it. "That's great. We can leave the first two lines the way they are, then do a third line ending up a half-step; what's your title, Don?" I reassured Johnny. "Don't worry, I'll get a title." I kept racking my brain but came up empty. It's not easy to get a good title anytime you want it.

A few afternoons later, killing time, I walked down Broadway to the Paramount Theatre on the corner of Forty-fourth Street. Live shows played there at the time, accompanied by a major film and usually a short. (The Paramount was where Frank Sinatra got his big send-off when the fertile brain of George Evans, his public-relations man, came up with the breakaway suits and the kids cutting school and screaming for Frank and really breaking it up in the theater and at the stage door.)

I got there about five minutes before the short. It didn't take much time; just fifteen or twenty minutes about a Holy Roller revival meeting in the Deep South, in a tent church with an all-black congregation.

The black preacher was incredible. He raved and ranted and exhorted the people, stomping back and forth, doing things to get the people going. Wild things. Screaming about religion. "God is good! Jesus is the father of the world! We've got to believe! We must have faith. Faith will carry us through!" Finally he got his flock real crazy, chanting and singing and shouting along with him, when a great, big, fat lady in the rear of the congregation rose up in that tent church. Her eyes rolling up in her head, she stood up straight, her hands raised in supplication, her fingers spread wide open. She was shaking all over, and she screamed, "I'm beginning to see the light." Then she fell to the ground in a dead faint . . . and I got up and ran out of that theater to the Hurricane, where Duke was

53

rehearsing the band. I grabbed Duke and Johnny and I yelled, "Hey, fellows, we've got a title." I wrote the lyric, and we finished the song.

Little did I realize at the time that "I'm Beginning to See the Light," which eventually turned out to be an important standard, would cause me to embark upon an odyssey that would take me thousands of miles and taunt me with many, many months of frustration.

Of all the songs we had written, this one kept walking back and forth through my mind, talking to me, saying, "Me, me, I'm the one. Do something about me." Its voice was so persistent that I had no choice but to embark upon what eventually turned out to be a crusade. I showed the song to everyone I was able to contact on the East Coast: the music publishers, the record companies, the band leaders—Tommy Dorsey, Isham Jones, Russ Morgan, Sammy Kaye and, as Yul Brynner said in *The King and I*, et cetera, et cetera, et cetera.

The song was neither a ballad nor a rhythm song, but it had a lyric with picturesque imagery laid on a melody in walking tempo. No one seemed to know what was happening. I couldn't get arrested here. So I borrowed traveling money from the shylock who hung out in the Brill Building. He was a great guy, not like one of the mob shylocks who get six for five, 20 percent every single week, and if they don't get it, you're in trouble. You pay the vigorish every week and you still owe the principal. He gave me the money. Eventually, whenever I might be able to pay it back, no matter when, all I had to do was give him one dollar extra for every five I borrowed. It was great because I didn't have the feeling I was trapped, that I might get my legs broken if I wasn't able to pay on time.

I bought a ticket for a milk train on the Pennsylvania Railroad that went to Chicago. It took a little longer than overnight, from six in the evening to approximately noon the next day. It was wartime and there was practically no transportation from Chicago to the Coast. I finally made a connection with Charlie Strom, the theatrical passenger agent. For twenty dollars he got me on the Champion, an all-coach train to Los Angeles.

I left the Pennsylvania train in the morning and crossed

town to the Champion, which left about 6 P.M. There were a lot of service people on the train going out to the Pacific theatre—nurses and soldiers who had been on leave, sick leave or R and R (rest and recreation).

I was sitting up front in the railroad car, where most of the action was located around the drinking fountain; fellows and girls drinking whiskey, getting water for chasers. They were grabbing each other like it might be their last day on earth.

The Champion was an all-coach train, no roomettes, no sleepers. We finally got to Los Angeles. The muscle in the calf of my right leg was pulled. It had gotten twisted under the seat in front of me while I was sleeping.

As I got off the train, it started to rain like hell. I was standing under an overhang for protection. In about five minutes the rain stopped and the sun was shining.

I hailed a cab, and not knowing where to go, I told the driver to take me to Hollywood and Vine. There I was sitting on my suitcase on the corner of Hollywood and Vine with about seventeen dollars in my pocket. I didn't know where to go or what to do. Then I remembered that a man named Taft Schreiber, who was a big wheel at Music Corporation of America, owned a small hotel on Wilcox near Sunset.

It wasn't far, so I limped over and spoke to the clerk at the desk, saying, "I'm Don George. I guess Mr. Schreiber called you about me."

He leafed through some papers and looked up. "No."

I said, "Mr. Schreiber told me to come here and check in. He said if you wanted to, to call him at the office and check with him."

The clerk took me at face value and worked out a deal. Sammy Kaye's band was staying at the hotel. His two arrangers had separate rooms, and one of the rooms had twin beds. The clerk doubled them up and gave me one of the rooms. I had very little money, so I went out and hustled up a piece of special material to write and made a little more, and started making the rounds with "I'm Beginning to See the Light."

I showed it to Johnny Mercer, who had just started Capitol Records with Buddy de Sylva and Glenn Wallich. Johnny told me it was a cute title with a monotonous melody and, "Come on, Don. How about that lyric?" (After the song became num-

55

ber one on the Hit Parade, we met in the Key Club on Vine Street and he asked me why I had never shown the song to him.)

Morris Stoloff, music director at Columbia Pictures, told me, "I can't put it in an important film, but maybe I can use it in something if you rewrite the lyric."

I showed the song around just the way I had on the East Coast, with the same lack of success. I began wondering what the fuck was going on in the music business. Here I am with a song I bet my shirt on, written with a great and well-known writer like Duke Ellington, and after all these months I still can't get arrested with it.

There was one shot left. Harry James, who led the top band in the country, was playing at Casino Gardens, a huge barn of a ballroom owned by Tommy and Jimmy Dorsey, out at the beach in Santa Monica. I bummed a ride out. Harry's dressing room was beneath the raised bandstand. The band manager came to the door when I knocked and had me wait while he took the lead sheet in.

Harry came to the door and said, "Come on in." He picked up his cornet, a concert horn, and ran the tune down a couple of times, then started singing the lyric. He said, "Leave it with me, Don. Check me in about a week." I asked him for his phone number.

"It's in the book. Under Harry James Orchestras. That's the home number."

I called him in a week. He said, "What's your name? What's the name of the song again?" I didn't know he was putting me on.

He asked me to call in another week. I figured I'd blown that one, too. But when I called a week later, he said, "Meet me at Columbia Records in an hour."

At Columbia he played the record for me that he had cut a few days earlier. It was great. I was bouncing. I couldn't get to a phone fast enough to call Duke, who had continually been cautioning me against spending so much time and effort on one song.

Johnny Thompson deservedly received the Downbeat Award for best arrangement of the year.

Because of the war and the shortage of shellac, and jealousy among his more important recording artists, Manny Sachs, head honcho at Columbia Records, limited the sale of any one single recording to 300,000 records. Because of this the Harry James record, which broke the song wide open, ran a poor second in sales to the recording by Ella Fitzgerald and the Ink Spots, which was released when the song became number one on the Hit Parade and sold well over a million records.

We had mixed emotions upon learning that "I'm Beginning to See the Light" was the record being played on every loudspeaker on every PT boat that carried our boys to the attack on the beaches of Normandy.

I'M BEGINNING TO SEE THE LIGHT

I never cared much for moonlit skies
I never wink back at fireflies
But now that the stars are in your eyes
I'M BEGINNING TO SEE THE LIGHT.

I never went in for afterglow
Or candlelight on the mistletow
But now when you turn the lamp down low
I'M BEGINNING TO SEE THE LIGHT.

Used to ramble through the park
Shadow boxing in the dark
Then you came and caused a spark
That's a four alarm fire now.

I never made love by lantern shine
I never saw rainbows in my wine
But now that your lips are burning mine
I'M BEGINNING TO SEE THE LIGHT.

San Francisco

IT WAS HOT, HOT, HOT. IT HAD BEEN A STIFLING, HUMID, THREE-UNDERSHIRT day. Now, looking out the window from the living room of the suite in the Hotel Fairmont, the lights of San Francisco twinkled like the biggest Christmas tree in the world. Funny, thinking about Christmas on a hot summer night with the air conditioning turned off and the windows closed. With Duke sitting at the piano wearing a sweater—which was typical. Duke would wear a sweater in the warmest temperature. People would sit around perspiring, sweat just pouring down their faces, and Duke would be very comfortable. He liked all the warmth he could get. He was noodling around with some chords with his right hand. The remains of his recent breakfast sulked on the room-service wagon near the door; a steak bone, a wilted lettuce leaf, a lonely forkful of chopped liver.

Duke was bitching more than just a little bit. He hadn't been involved with a woman for almost forty-eight hours. Not even peripherally. Even now he was late for his opening at the Macumba, one of the newer clubs, and he wasn't even dressed.

"You'd better get shaking, Duke. You're hanging up a lot of people."

"Where the fuck is Jonesie? He's never around when I need him."

"You're a big boy, Duke. You're old enough to dress yourself. Besides, you just sent Jonesie down for another pack of cigarettes. It's about time you quit smoking; those damn things aren't doing you any good."

Duke said bitingly, "Since when did you become the Lord Almighty?"

"Cool it, Duke. There's bound to be some pretty ladies there. You'll be all right when you get out where the people are."

Duke lit one of his many too many cigarettes and started to dress, still tying his tie the way his left-handed father had shown him so long ago. He was starting to relax.

"Call downstairs for a taxi, Don."

"You're not ready yet. Do you want the taxi now?"

"Sure, tell them to get a taxi and tell the man he'll get double the meter for waiting."

In the taxi I studied Duke. He was becoming his usual charming self. Something somewhere within him invariably rose to rescue him from bizarre situations, usually created by himself. He was his own most talented accomplice. But here it was

58

his first night on a new gig and he was almost an hour late. What will he come up with this time?

When we got to the Macumba, the band was playing, and as we looked around, the people were obviously discontented; some of them were audibly griping that they had paid to see Duke personally and there was no Duke, although they had been tapped for both a music and a cover charge. When Duke walked up to the stand, we even heard some boos from the crowd.

Duke looked at the people crowding around the bandstand, smiled benignly as though they were his wayward children, crossed to the microphone, looked around roguishly and said, "Ladies and gentlemen, if you had seen her you would understand."

There was a split second of silence; then a sharp intake of breath; and then a roar of approval and an explosion of laughter. He owned them, lock, stock and barrel.

They all belonged to him. Every person in that room was his ally for life.

He sauntered to the piano, sat down, casually leaned toward Johnny Hodges and inquired, "Hey, Rabbit, what's the next number?"

Between sets we adjourned to the men's room, through the kitchen and down a flight of stairs. Afterward the attendant, a dispirited, white-jacketed, combination shoe shiner-and-whisk broomer who brightened visibly when he saw Duke, turned on the faucets, handed us each a small bar of Ivory soap and a laundry-clean towel and whisk broomed us for the second time.

"Good evening, Mr. Ellington."

"Call me Duke."

"Thank you, Mr. Duke. It sure is nice to have you here. We've sure been looking forward to your coming. Would you like a shine? I won't charge you for it. I'm so glad to see you, this one's on the house."

He was really going.

Duke (stepping upon the shine stand): "You're not supposed

59

to give this stuff away, man. You're supposed to sell it. How are you going to get rich working for nothing?"

"That's just the point, Mr. Duke. That fellow who closed here last night doesn't feel like you." (The singer who had closed the night before was one of the top performers in the country, with one smash hit record after another, whom Duke had helped at the start of his career and who had a reputation for miserliness greater than Rudy Vallee's.)

"He came in here twice a night for two weeks, used all my towels and soap—and just left without a word."

"Maybe he left something for you upstairs."

"No, I checked. He even stiffed the waiter who brought him his dinner every night."

Duke staked him to a couple of dollars and went up to play the next set. After the set I saw him heading back to the men's room. Curious, I followed and eavesdropped on his conversation with the attendant. He was apologizing for forgetting to give him the twenty-dollar bill the singer had supposedly given him to pass along.

"I'm sorry, man. I don't know how I could have forgotten it. I've had so much on my mind lately."

"God bless you, Mr. Duke."

I got upstairs before Duke saw me, and later that evening, just before closing, I watched him do the same thing with the waiter.

I couldn't help but remember something Tony Bennett once lovingly said about Duke.

"Therein lies one side of him. In addition to being the greatest American composer, the most prolific one, was the human side of him which was so human it became absolutely mystic. I observed through the years that he was doing that over and over again, to everybody that he'd meet. Either on a given second, or a four-month plan, or a six-month plan, whatever it took to get certain things done. He had his antennas out there, he'd just look for people and try to help them, right until the day he died."

Duke liked Harry Carney to drive him between playing dates except when there was a string of one-nighters and then

60

it was bus time for everyone. Harry played great baritone sax. He had a trick of being able to inhale through his nose and exhale through his mouth at the same time, fascinating thousands of audiences by holding a note without breaking it for a full three or four minutes using this gimmick. He was a very relaxed, gentle man, and Duke would usually sleep soundly when Harry was the driver.

The band had put in its two weeks at the Macumba, and after closing on the final night, Harry and Duke and I headed down the coast road toward Hollywood with Harry at the wheel. It was a beautiful, moonlit night, and we could hear the waves breaking on the shore above the hum of the motor. Still I kept getting the feeling that something was wrong.

"Harry, something's bugging me. I don't know what it is. The moon's up there, the ocean's out there . . . Man, I'm telling you, there's something wrong. I'm going to ask Duke what's going on."

"Don't wake him up, Don."

"He won't mind. He's going to sleep all day, anyway."

Harry shrugged. "Go ahead. Ask him. He knows everything."

Duke was sleeping peacefully, using his porkpie Joe College hat for a pillow.

I shook him. A grunt.

We were somewhere between Big Sur and Malibu. The feeling persisted. I shook him again. He stirred.

"What's happening? Are we there?"

"No, Duke. There's something strange going on. I keep getting the feeling that everything's mixed up."

Duke looked around and shook his head. "There's nothing strange. You were brought up in New York on the East Coast, right?"

"Yes."

"When you drove south along the East Coast, the ocean was on your left. When you drive south here on the West Coast, the ocean's on your right. It's simple. The ocean's on the wrong side."

He leaned back and went to sleep again. It was daylight when they dropped me off at my place and went on to his manager's house on Hightower Drive, where Duke was staying.

Bowling Alley Building

THE BOWLING ALLEY BUILDING ON VINE STREET IN HOLLYWOOD MIGHT, with a large stretch of the imagination, be called the kid sister of the Brill Building in New York City. Its two stories consisted of a coffee shop and bowling alley on the street level, with the upper area being occupied by major music publishers: Mayfair-Morris, Shapiro-Bernstein, The Big Three (Robbins, Feist and Miller) and the like. It was a hangout where songwriters would meet to write and to peddle their songs. Just north of the building, on Vine Street, was the Club Morocco, which was closed for nonpayment of taxes, throwing the beginning singer Frankie Laine out of work, which situation Duke immediately rectified by talking to Billy Berg and getting Frankie a job in Billy's club by promising to come in a couple of times weekly with a few friends.

Billy later helped Frankie with his first record date, which produced "That's My Desire," the record that catapulted Frankie to stardom. The King Cole Trio was working at Billy Berg's when somebody stole Irving Ashby's guitar. I mentioned it to Billy, who shrugged and said, "I heard about it." I told him there was a fifty-dollar reward.

The next night one of the "boys" who hung around the club approached the table where I was sitting and said, "Where's the fifty?"

I said, "Sit down and have a drink. I'll be right back." I went backstage and found Ashby. "Give me fifty dollars."

"What for?"

"To get your guitar back, man." He gave me the fifty, which I exchanged for a key to a locker in the Greyhound Bus Station on Cahuenga Boulevard, and Ashby retrieved his guitar.

Duke, Nat "King" Cole and I were in Billy Berg's when a man came staggering out onstage with a knife protruding from his chest while Ella Fitzgerald was singing. Between the cigar-smoking hoods sitting at a front table, blowing smoke up in her face, and the blood spattered on the stage, Ella was getting much the worst of it, but great lady that she is, she stuck it out and finished the set. The club was closed shortly thereafter.

Close by the Club Morocco was the Columbia Recording Studio, where such great artists as Frank Sinatra, Harry James and Duke cut their records. Just opposite was the NBC Building, home of the lady censor who okayed song lyrics before they were broadcast and who made Herb Magidson change a line in a song, claiming that using the name *Rembrandt* would make people think of nude women.

A new owner bought the Bowling Alley Building, gutted the alleys and built a brand-new nightclub in the entire lower area of the building, booking Woody Herman for the opening show.

On opening night Duke and I drove down to pay our respects to Woody, who was an old friend. As we pulled up to the curb, Sam Weiss, the general professional manager of the Mayfair-Morris Music Companies, who had been standing on the sidewalk, approached the car.

"Hi, Duke; hi, Don. It looks like a swinging night."

Duke smiled and shook hands. "Just visiting some old friends. What's been happening with you, Sam?"

Sam replied, "Same old thing. Listening to songs. Running around trying to get records." His eyes lit up. "A fellow came in this afternoon with a good song; great title."

I egged him on. "Was it really that great?"

Sam nodded excitely. "Listen to this! 'I Fell and Broke My Heart.' "

It was an incredible coincidence. Just that day Duke and I had begun work on a song with the same title. I said to Sam, "You might not believe this. It's a million-to-one shot, but Duke and I started writing that title this afternoon. Our first line is, 'When you pushed me out of heaven, I fell and broke my heart.' "

Sam looked disappointed. He shrugged and said, "Well, I guess I'll pass on mine. Have a nice evening, fellows."

(Shortly thereafter Duke recorded our song, "I Fell and Broke My Heart," on Columbia Records, with Woody singing the vocal.)

Sam turned and walked away, Duke raised his eyebrows,

63

cocked his head at me and we entered the club and joined Woody, who was sitting in a semicircular banquette outside the main room.

An important singer we knew came over and joined us. We were talking about old times when a man whom I knew very well came in. He was a narc, a narcotics cop. (In California at that time if a narc busted somebody of stature, like Gene Krupa or Harry James or Woody Herman, for marijuana, which was a horrific thing in those days, he would automatically get promoted to sergeant.) I knew the singer blew pot and I knew that chances were that he had some on him. When the narc came over to the table, I stood up and started the introductions. I tried to get the singer's eye, without much luck. I introduced the narc to Duke and to Woody, and when I came to the singer, I took the narc's hand in a firm handshake and held it as tightly as I could and said, "Oh, by the way, my friend here is on the narcotics squad."

The singer finally got the message. He got up and started slowly toward the men's room, which was about fifteen or twenty feet away.

Duke caught my eye. He was slowly shaking his head from side to side (No! No! No!), but I was committed and held onto the narc's hand in what looked like a handshake, but I was really holding on for dear life. I wanted the singer to make the john and flush what he was holding. I knew he had to be carrying something. The narc glared at me. I held onto him as long as I could without making an obvious thing of it.

The singer got to the door of the men's room. I saw the door close behind him, and I knew this guy would never make it in time to grab anything he had, so I let go of him. When I let go of his hand, his right hand went inside his jacket and under his left armpit where he carried his gun. I said to myself, halellujah. I thought it was my end. His eyes were blazing, and I could see that he realized he had just lost his promotion. He knew it, and his hand went in very slowly and came out very slowly, and there was nothing I could do. I couldn't make a move, because it might make him more nervous. His hand came out empty. Thank God, it came out empty.

He stared at me for what seemed like a lifetime, then turned slowly and walked away. Duke heaved a deep sigh. "I don't think you ought to do anything like that again."

I was still shaking. "Please order me a drink, Duke."

Duke patted my shoulder. "At my time of life, I'd hate to lose my favorite lyric writer."

I ran into the narc on the street a couple of days later. He said, "Hey, kid. You know I almost killed you the other night?"

I played it straight. "What are you talking about? I just don't understand."

He said, "You know what I mean."

I said, "Really, I don't." Fortunately I never ran into him again.

The Gold Lorgnette

WE WERE IN THE LIVING ROOM OF MY APARTMENT AT THE ALTO NIDO IN Hollywood. The dark green walls formed an exotic background for the baby grand relaxing in one corner, with the flame-colored gladiola sitting in a vase on top. Through the window we could see the huge, famous HOLLYWOOD sign lighting up the hills just above the Pilgrimage Pass.

The Murphy bed was down, and a Lena Horne album was playing on the Magnavox.

Sonia, my number-one romantic sparring partner of the moment, who had just returned from her job at Earl Carroll's Theater Restaurant on Sunset Boulevard, was alternately teasing me and her blond girl friend Linda, who had recently acquired a gold lorgnette and was not relinquishing her grip on it, come hell or high water.

Eventually they joined forces and ganged up on me. Their combined talents were such that it was only a matter of time before it became obvious that I needed help.

SONIA: You're writing with Duke Ellington, aren't you?
ME: Yes.
SONIA: Well?
ME: Well, what?
SONIA [petulantly]: Well, call him, man.

65

Duke was staying at his manager's house on Hightower Drive, near the Hollywood Bowl, with the ubiquitous Evie, who had insisted on making the trip. Duke and I had a code. Whenever he wanted to shake loose, I would phone and if Evie or the manager's wife answered, I would say that I had a great idea for a song that wouldn't wait. It invariably worked.

I dialed the number. "Hello, Evie? This is Don, Is Duke there? I've got a fantastic idea for a song. No, it can't wait."

Pause.

"Duke, is anybody on the extension?"

Pause.

"Okay. Listen, I have these two gals here . . ."

The line went dead.

About seven minutes later when Duke walked in, the ladies and I were au naturel. After happily perusing the assembled, accessible architecture and putting a couple of breath mints in his mouth, Duke smiled at Sonia.

DUKE: I Know you're an angel.

SONIA: How do you know that?

DUKE: I can see your halo reflected on the ceiling. [Turning to Linda.] Ah, tidbits to be served with tea.

[Between enthusiastic interludes Duke was seated at the piano emceeing the festivities, with excerpts that were suited to the occasion, from among our numerous songs ("The Wonder of You," "To Know You Is to Love You," etc.), when there was a loud banging at the door.]

DUKE [frowning]: I Hope that's not Evie.

I opened the door and in floated one of the country's top bandleaders, a good friend of ours, with two more ladies. He had just finished a recording date at the Columbia Studio on Vine Street and obviously felt in need of some relaxation.

I said to Duke, "Talk about the Roman emperors. Looks like we've got our own little orgy right here."

Duke [reprovingly], "This in no orgy, man. This is therapy."

Our bandleader friend greeted us, "Hello, you bastards, where have you been hiding?"

I said, "We were here waiting for you, man."

Duke kept on playing the piano. Our friend and his ladies proceeded to light up. They were blowing pot and drinking whiskey at the same time, a murderous combination, but it didn't seem to bother them. If anything, it worked like an aphrodisiac.

The piano playing had stopped. I turned to see what had happened.

Linda had thrown a pillow on the carpet, had knelt and was concentrating on Duke. During the intricacies of her maneuvers (and they were wondrous to behold), the chain on the gold lorgnette, seemingly with a life all it own, encircled the closest, and needless to say, the most vulnerable area of Duke's anatomy. During the ensuing disentanglement we all became hysterical with laughter. After things calmed down, our friend floated out the door with his ladies, and Sonia and Linda repaired to the dinette to rustle up some food.

Without bothering to get dressed, Duke and I sat down at the piano and started writing a song.

Later I couldn't help thinking about our friend. He was married to a beautiful girl, yet there he was balling with a couple of chicks not even remotely in the same league with the lady who was waiting for him at home. Oh, well . . . *penis erectus non conscientum.*

Blue

DUKE LOVED THE COLOR BLUE. ANYTHING BLUE; EVERYTHING BLUE. ONE OF his all-time-favorite arrangements, which the band played constantly, was of the Irving Berlin song "Blue Skies." The color blue soothed him, stroked him, nursed him. Baby blue, cornflower blue, French blue and royal blue, his favorite. (Anything royal was always at the top of his list.)

As often as possible he wore blue silk, pleated, slip-on shirts with very few buttons. (He would never wear clothing that had lost a button.) He called them kissy-blue shirts. The originals were designed by him and made in London. He occasionally wore sleeveless V-neck blue sweaters as undershirts. Once someone brought him a dozen blue undershirts from a shop on Madison Avenue. He spent the day telephoning people and describing them. He was utterly delighted. He had never seen blue undershirts before.

The smaller, converted bedroom in the apartment on West End Avenue had the gorgeous navy blue enameled furniture that Duke had personally designed and shipped from Sweden.

The fantastic chifferobe had separate areas for blue cashmere socks, shirts, underwear and sweaters. He had literally dozens of sweaters, all blue cashmere. There was never any problem about what to give Duke for a present; one always gave him blue cashmere sweaters.

In his travels he missed all the great places—the beaches, the museums, the historic sites. He never did any sightseeing. He did not come out in the daytime. He said it was not for him; he was a night creature who only came out when dusk fell. He never had the blinds open in any of his hotel rooms or apartments. They were always closed and heavily draped, and he covered the lamps with blue cashmere sweaters to help darken the room. Once one of the lamps got so hot that a sweater caught fire, and the concierge insisted that he change hotels.

Every time Duke worked at the Rainbow Grill, a fresh coat of powder blue paint was added to the walls of his dressing room. It was ludicrous that he worked in a grand place like Rockefeller Center and had such a tiny dressing room. But when you walked in, it was as though you were walking into the royal suite at Buckingham Palace. It couldn't be more elegant, because Duke was there, regal in his blue cashmere robe, fingering his crucifix, smiling, welcoming you.

Duke loved his mother dearly and treasured his memories of her. He described to me how, when he was a little boy, she always dressed him in a blue suit to go to church on Sunday. His parents were of different faiths, so he went to two different churches, one for his dad and one for his mother. The day his mother died he was wearing a brown suit. He never forgot it and became very superstitious about brown. Once someone gave him a sweater flecked with brown. He turned away, saying, "It isn't blue."

He disliked the color green because it reminded him of grass on graves, and he refused to face death. He would never discuss it or even remain present during a conversation about death. It saddened him to the soul when, through remembered love, he often retraced his steps to the cemetery where his parents were buried, to pay homage to their memories.

Brown was sorrow; green was sadness; but blue was joy.

Blue was Jan Peerce singing "Bluebird of Happiness."

Blue was Elvis Presley's record of "Blue Suede Shoes."

Blue was an acquiescent lady with blue eyes.

Blue was the blue telephone, resting on the blue chifferobe in the blue bedroom of the West End Avenue apartment, waiting to spring into nocturnal action.

Blue was the wailing hunger of the twelve-bar basic blues that he loved so much he would sit at the piano for hours, improvising.

The ultimate in blue was being onstage, bathed in a blue spotlight, wearing blue socks, a kissy-blue shirt, smiling his come-and-get-me smile and playing his favorite of all the songs we had written together, "I Ain't Got Nothin' but the Blues."

When Duke was surrounded by blue, he knew that God was in His heaven, all was well with the world.

I AIN'T GOT NOTHIN' BUT THE BLUES

Ain't got the change of a nickel
Ain't got no bounce in my shoes,
Ain't got no fancy to tickle
I AIN'T GOT NOTHIN' BUT THE BLUES.

Ain't got no coffee that's perkin'
Ain't got no winnings to lose.
Ain't got a dream that is working
I AIN'T GOT NOTHIN' BUT THE BLUES.

When trumpets flare up—I keep my hair up
I just can't make it come down.
Believe me, pappy—I can't get happy
Since my ever lovin' baby left town.

Ain't got no rest in my slumbers
Ain't got no feelings to bruise
Ain't got no telephone numbers
I AIN'T GOT NOTHIN' BUT THE BLUES.

Jaywalking

IT WAS A LOVELY DAY. ON MY WAY TO MEET DUKE, I STROLLED CASUALLY along Hollywood Boulevard, catching up on my window shopping. It was early December, and the boulevard was alive with Christmas decorations strung from one side of the street to the other. The people were always more relaxed here than in the East, and there was a welcome lack of hustle and bustle as I passed the Broadway-Hollywood department store and crossed Ivar Street. When I reached the opposite curb there was a policeman waiting there, with his summons book and pencil poised at the ready, blocking my path.

He said, "I'd like to see your identification."

I looked around, thinking it was some kind of put-on. I asked, "Why, what's happening?"

He said, "You were jaywalking."

I said, "How fast was I going?" When I saw the look on his face, I added, "I'm from the East. I didn't know anything about that."

He smiled, disbelieving. "Everybody tells me that."

When I showed him my New York driver's license and other identification with my New York address, he relaxed a little, explaining that under California law pedestrians waited until the light changed before crossing the street even if there were no cars in sight.

"Be careful," he said as he wrote out the summons.

When I told Duke what had happened, he said, "That's nothing. You'll probably be fined a few dollars. There's really no problem."

I folded the summons, put it in my wallet, put the wallet in my pocket and proceeded to forget all about it. Shortly afterward we went out on the road again for a series of one-nighters. One night Duke, Harry Carney and I headed out from Denver toward Salt Lake City, with Harry driving. To get there we had to drive across the top of the Great Divide, and it was really blowing. The wind was so strong that the snow, instead of coming down vertically, was being blown across the road horizontally. There were just a few feet of shoulder on each side of the road, then a hell of a drop: hundreds, maybe thousands of feet. Harry Carney was sensational. The car's brights didn't help any, we couldn't see the road, yet he stayed right in the middle of it.

70

Coming down from the top and heading for Salt Lake City, we were going through farm country. After the scare we had had, we all had to go to the john. We passed a number of out-houses close to the road, but it was so cold we didn't dare stop the car to get out. We reached Salt Lake City, and Duke and I checked into the Hotel Utah. The band, which had arrived the day before, was checked into a nearby motel.

Duke and I and the band manager were sitting in the hotel room when the phone rang. Duke, as always the phone freak, grabbed the phone first. He listened for a minute, then handed it to the band manager, saying, "This is for you."

The manager listened intently for a while, then left hurried-ly, throwing a "See you guys later" over his shoulder at us.

We later found out that the band had been so happy to get to the motel that they were celebrating. Some of the guys drank whiskey, some blew pot: unfortunately there were a couple on heavier stuff. They were really having a wingding. Some of them had gotten rooms exactly opposite each other with a hall-way in between. They opened the door of each room wide so they could see from one room across the hall right through into the other. They had taken a sheet from the bed in one of the rooms and taped it on the wall across the windows and marked big red circles on it with the lipstick of one of the ladies they were entertaining. One of the fellows had an air gun. They were in the far side of one room, shooting pellets out of the air gun across the hall, through the other room, hav-ing target practice. The sheet caught fire, and they started yell-ing and throwing water. It was a devil of a mess. The phone call had come from the manager of the motel. It was eventually straightened out, and after a few more one-nighters we headed back to Hollywood.

The second day that I was back at my apartment in the Alto Nido, there was a loud banging on my door at six thirty in the morning. Those were my drinking days, and I had rolled in at about three A.M.. I fumblingly opened the door, and there was an officer of the law, in a khaki suit with a hat that looked like the one Nelson Eddy serenaded Jeanette MacDonald in, and a Sam Browne belt on the outside. He asked, "Don George?"

I said, "Yes, what's the problem?"

He pulled a paper out of his pocket. "I've got a warrant for your arrest."

I stared at him. "For what?"

He said, "There was a summons issued to you that you failed to answer."

I said, "Come on in."

He held back, "Now, just a minute."

I insisted. "Come on in, man. It's six thirty in the morning. I don't want to stand in the hall talking; we'll wake people up."

He came in, and I made some coffee and we got kind of friendly. I said, "Look, I'm hung over like mad. I can't make it downtown today; I've just had a couple hours' sleep and I'm in no shape."

He agreed. "You seem like a nice guy. I'll give you a break. If you promise me faithfully that you'll be in court tomorrow morning at nine o'clock, I'll let you go back to bed again."

I assured him that I wouldn't jeopardize him in any way, and he left. The next morning I was in traffic court. The judge was just slugging everybody. One fellow had driven through a crosswalk that had pedestrians in it. The judge said, "Fifty dollars or ten days." He was really sending it in.

I was starting to get worried. I caught an attendant's eye. "What's the matter with this guy? He's being awfully rough."

He whispered behind his hand, "His son was killed by a hit-and-run driver, and he's murder on anybody with moving violations."

I finally got up before the judge. He looked at the papers and said, "Don George?"

I said, "Yes."

He took off his spectacles and looked closely at me. "Why didn't you answer the summons?"

I replied, "I would have answered it, Your Honor, but to tell the truth, I forgot all about it. After I got the summons I went out on the road with a band, and in the course of events I forgot all about having the summons in my wallet."

He said, "What were you doing with the band?"

I replied, "I write songs with the bandleader."

He asked, "Did you ever write anything that I might know?" He was loosening up a little bit, so I fell back on the good old standby.

"Yes, we wrote 'I'm Beginning to See the Light.'"

He raised his eyebrows. "Who's we?"

I said, "Duke Ellington and myself." Duke's name, as always, was magic.

"You write with Duke Ellington?"

I nodded. "That's the band I was out with."

He kept murmuring, "Duke Ellington, hmm, Duke Ellington. Tell you what, Mr. George. I'm going to fine you two dollars for the jaywalking. What do you suggest I do about the warrant?"

I said, "When it comes to writing songs, I know what to do. But I don't know what to suggest about the warrant."

He said, "All right, because you write with Duke Ellington and you seem like a nice fellow, I'll charge you one dollar for the warrant. Good day, Mr. George."

The Cat

JERRY RHEA CALLED LONG DISTANCE, COLLECT, AND WANTED TO TALK TO Duke Ellington. Duke answered the phone.

The operator said, "This is long distance calling collect for Duke Ellington."

Duke said, "He's not in," and hung up.

Jerry said to the operator, "Come on, that was him on the phone. I've got to talk to him. Just call the number back and tell him that it's me."

The operator called back, "Is this Mr. Duke Ellington?"

Duke's sleepy voice answered, "No, no. He's not in."

Finally the operator asked, "May I ask who is this answering the phone?"

Duke said, "The cat," and hung up and went back to sleep.

Charlie Barnet's Monkey

DUKE CALLED AND ASKED ME TO MEET HIM AT MACINTOSH'S, THE CUSTOM clothier on Hollywood Boulevard who made most of

73

Duke's clothes. Their work was so great that Duke occasionally made trips out to the Coast just to get things from them. Duke asked me to meet him there at 2:30 and I showed up at 3:30, which meant I only had to wait a half-hour for him to arrive.

He had fittings for some suits and jackets and trousers, making sure the trousers had the four-inch cuffs that he liked so much. Duke had his barber with him. He paid a lot of attention to his hair and nearly always carried his own barber when the band was on tour, and whenever he was relaxing he usually had a stocking cap in residence to keep his coiffeur from wandering. His hair was gradually becoming a little more auburn, and he was starting to grow a pony tail.

Duke didn't drive. His barber was doing double duty as a chauffeur and drove off as soon as Duke reassured himself that I was there with my car.

When the fittings were finished, we stopped in at Musso Frank's for steaks. Duke had the night off and had picked up tickets for Ken Murray's *Blackouts* which starred Marie Wilson, the voluptuous precursor of Dolly Parton, and featured Peg Leg Bates, an old friend of Duke's. After the *Blackouts*, which broke about 10:15, we went backstage and revived some memories with Ken and Marie and Peg Leg.

Then we decided to take a run out and pay our respects to Charlie Barnet, whose band was playing at the Casino Gardens, Tommy and Jimmy Dorsey's ballroom. It was a pleasant evening, and we drove with the top down.

Charlie was between sets, and we sat around talking with him and Rita, who was either his fifth, sixth or seventh wife. It got to be one o'clock and the music was over, the dancing stopped and the Gardens closed. Charlie said, "Why don't you fellows come out to the house with us? We have some people out there now. We'll have some drinks and a little food, and a lot of conversation. It'll be fun."

Charlie lived in a big old house on Sunny Slope, surrounded by shade trees, with a swimming pool lying snuggled behind it. In the living room he introduced us to his pet, an ambidextrous monkey, who was continually having a romantic affair with himself, to the amusement of the onlookers. Later we were all sitting around the pool, having a drink, when one of the girls came out of the house and said, "Charlie, there's something the matter with the monkey."

Charlie went in to check, and he came back a moment later carrying the monkey's body. He said, "The monkey's dead."

We were all pretty well juiced by that time. I had belted quite a few. Charlie was a pretty good drinker. The other people were fairly well loaded. Duke, as usual, drank very little.

We solemnly debated the situation and decided that the monkey was entitled to a decent burial. We got flashlights and candles and utensils for digging and carried the monkey up on the hill behind Charlie's house. We performed a funeral service, starting with "Our Father, who art in heaven . . ." Charlie orated a touching eulogy, and after paying our last respects, we returned to the pool for another drink.

After a little while we heard the noise of sirens, and there was a loud banging on the front door. Charlie opened the door, and the local constabulary, with their best paramilitary attitude, charged in with drawn guns and backed us against the walls and frisked all of us, not being too gentle about it, as though they were auditioning for a Humphrey Bogart movie. They recognized Charlie and Duke, but that didn't seem to make any difference. They accused us of burying a body on the hillside and wouldn't believe us when we said it was just a monkey that had died. It seems there was a lady who lived nearby who had been unable to sleep and was watching the house through binoculars, and she had seen the procession going up the hill and the digging, so she called the police and told them about the body that she had seen buried. She swore that she had been a witness to the disposal of a corpse.

The cops still wouldn't believe us. We had to go back up the hill, still covered by guns, dig up the monkey's body and show it to them. We buried the monkey again, performed a ritual with a much shorter service and only a perfunctory eulogy. By this time the cops who had come in so belligerently were slightly hysterical with laughter. They stayed long enough to have a drink.

Much later, about five o'clock in the morning, a young gal

who had come out from the Casino Gardens with us appeared at the top of the stairs. She was stark naked and weaving around stoned to the eyeballs. She tripped and fell down the stairs and must have hit every step on the way down. She got up as Charlie and Duke and the rest of us all ran over to see what had happened to her.

She drew herself up, looked at Charlie very solemnly and said, "Mr. Barnet, I want to thank you for the most beautiful night of my life."

By this time Duke and I had been involved with a couple of ladies, and we were ready to go. It would be light soon, and Duke would be able to sleep. I looked at Duke, he nodded, we said our farewells, went out to the car, put the top up and drove peacefully away.

Lena and Lennie

LENNIE HAYTON WAS MUSICAL DIRECTOR AT MGM PICTURES WHEN HE MET Lena Horne on the lot. Lena at the time was sort of a protégé of Arthur Freed, the great songwriter who was then the executive producer of musical films at MGM. Freed cast Lena whenever possible, invariably in singing roles in nightclub scenes, so her performance could be cut from the film when it played the South, where the intolerance was so heavy.

Lennie in his way was very avant-garde. Socially he was ing a lot of things in the late twenties and early thirties that weren't overly fashionable; he realized before many others did the importance of what black Americans had contributed to this country. Lena once said that he taught her more than any of her own people ever did about black American music; he had more records, more knowledge, more education and more understanding in that area than anyone she had ever known. They lived together, they worked together and they loved each other dearly. Lena and Lennie were married in 1947. It was a marriage made in heaven.

Now here we were, Duke, Sweetpea and I, on a lovely, sunny, southern California morning. The trees were smiling, the birds were swapping octaves and the bougainvillea was winking at us as we convertibled through the nicer areas of town toward Nichols Canyon, where the ever-gracious Lena and Lennie had invited us for a late breakfast. We were happy at the thought of seeing our beloved friends again.

As we pulled into the driveway, we were profusely greeted by Lena and Lennie and the great bassist Red Callender. Lena, if anything, was even lovelier than when we had first met in the early days at the Capitol Theatre in New York City. Lennie, smiling pleasantly above his gray-streaked Vandyke, wore the yachting cap which was his inevitable trademark and which I had once accused him of wearing to bed. The tremendous affection that existed between Duke and Lena and Sweetpea soon became apparent. (They had been close since before the war, when together they used to visit Kelly's Stable in New York City, where Billie Holiday was singing, accompanied on the piano by Nat "King" Cole. Billie, with her many problems, wasn't always able to make it to the club, and the three of them were there on the historic night that Ralph Watkins, the proprietor, faced with a large crowd and no Billie, said to Nat "King" Cole, "Either you sing or you're fired," thus starting Nat on his illustrious career.)

We went inside and started talking about old times, just clowning around. Lena served a sumptuous breakfast; orange juice and prunes and bacon and eggs; and Lennie's mother had sent over a gallon jar of gefilte fish, which we put an almighty dent in. We were almost through breakfast when the phone rang. The maid answered, and Lena said, "Ask them to call back in a little while when we've finished eating."

The maid hesitantly said, "Miss Lena, I think you should take this call."

Lena went to the phone and returned with her eyes blazing. A neighbor of Lena's had phoned to tell her that she had seen some other neighbors plant something on Lena's property in an area that wasn't visible from the house. We felt quite a bit of trepidation, because Lena was the only black living in all of Nichols Canyon. Usually the only other black people that could be seen there were butlers, chauffeurs or some other form of servant.

We decided we'd better go out and check on it, and sure enough we found a place where the earth had been freshly turned. We dug up the ground and uncovered a can filled with marijuana. We immediately sensed that it was a setup and that whoever planted it had already called the police. We took the marijuana back to the house and flushed it down the toilet, then sat back down again to finish our interrupted breakfast and wait for what we felt would be the inevitable visit from the police.

Perhaps it was not only because Lena was black but because they had seen these two other black fellows arrive with me, and Red Callender also was black. Perhaps the event occurred because of the added attraction of Duke, Sweetpea and Red. In any event, a short while later, without any fuss or fury, a constable's car pulled up and two marshals stepped out and knocked on the door. They had a search warrant. Lena said, "Go ahead, you can search the house." They didn't look inside the house. They started searching the property and went right to the spot where we had dug up the marijuana. Naturally there was nothing there. Without a word they climbed back into their car and roared away.

Later, driving back to town, Sweetpea and I were discussing the events of the day. Duke's only comment was, "The birds sounded happier this morning."

Sweetpea

HOMOSEXUALITY WAS AS NORMAL FOR SWEETPEA AS ANY OTHER AREA OF life, heterosexuality or whatever, was for anybody else. He was a sweet, wonderful, nice person. Every once in a while he had his little uproars. He didn't pout, but he might get up and yell about something. Especially if he wasn't getting his royalties from a publisher, he'd scream and yell and howl and go through all the changes, but basically he was one of the great people in the history of the music business. He had an incredible musical talent. He was Duke's musical equal, with all the musicality and all the great classical knowledge he brought to Duke. For example, on many pieces that appear with Duke's name, occasionally Sweetpea gets credit, but so many others were written with Duke doing part, then handing it to Sweetpea, saying, "Here, man, you finish it."

78

Duke, seeing some of the things Sweetpea started, would take them from him in the middle, saying, "Hey, man, I'll finish that thing." They had gotten into each other's minds and musical areas so completely that when it came to anybody being able to discern who wrote what, very often they themselves didn't know what part each had written. They were incredibly close musically.

I myself had a tremendous affection for Sweetpea. We used to sit sometimes and talk for hours—on the road, in strange towns, in godforsaken places. We'd be out on one-nighters, the band would be playing a gig and Duke would be sweet-talking some dame, often with half-hearted efforts at mild seduction, merely to stay in practice, and Sweetpea and I would be off in a corner talking.

We settled all the major problems of the world. We left the smaller problems like unemployment, foreign affairs, the economy and all those minor areas to be settled by other people. We settled all the important problems like where we were going to have dinner, where the band was going to play next, when were we going to get our royalties from publishers, why songs had to be written in thirty-two bars. (I remember Duke griping to me one time as we were riding in a car and a Cole Porter song, "Begin the Beguine," came on the car radio. Porter seldom adhered to the current thirty-two-bar pop limit. Duke griped about it. He said, "Jesus Christ, anybody could write those goddamn good songs if they took all the time he did. Man, look at all the time he's taking to write a song.")

I've been with Duke at a band rehearsal when they were rehearsing one of Sweetpea's arrangements and the band was lackadaisical. The fellows moped in late, whenever they were ready. Duke usually handled these situations with aplomb, but this time he was really bitching. He belted out with his voice going up a decibel with each repetition, "Let's go back to letter *E*, gentlemen. *E* for Edward, *E* for Ellington, *E* for elegant," each time his voice getting higher until he yelled, "What the fuck do you guys think you're doing anyway? Letter *E*, *E*, *E*." All the while Sweetpea just sat there calmly, smiling patiently.

When we were out on the road playing one-nighters, split weeks, nightclubs or whatever, even when we were in Hollywood for weeks at a time, wherever we were, Sweetpea never worked the neighborhoods, never cruised. Most homosexuals I've known cruise. If they don't cruise, they keep their eyes open for somebody to make it with. Sweetpea wasn't like that. Sweetpea was faithful, sincere with his friend. He had the same friend for years. He never cruised or rampaged around, not even when he had had a few drinks. He ls always the most gentlemanly fellow in the group.

Sweetpea has never been shown to be the great companion, writer and co-writer, arranger and co-arranger he was. His own compositions, "Take the A Train," "Lush Life," "Chelsea Bridge" and "Passion Flower," were among the most beautiful and exciting the Ellington band ever played.

Sweetpea was tight with everybody. Everybody loved him. He was only about five feet one inch tall and occasionally looked like a small, slightly burned, whole-wheat-toast owl. Yet somehow I feel somewhere deep within his soul he must have resented the fact that Big Brother Edward got all the accolades, all the hosannas, for creations that he was at least partially responsible for.

Sonny Greer

DUKE, SWEETPEA AND I WERE SITTING IN DUKE'S DRESSING ROOM IN THE Million Dollar Theater in downtown Los Angeles. This dressing room was no different from the hundreds of others we had huddled in from coast to coast in the various theaters, nightclubs, fairs, festivals and what-have-you's the band had played. The same pipe rack for wardrobe, sink in the corner for instant relief, naked light bulbs circumnavigating a mirror that pleaded for resilvering. There was seldom any air conditioning backstage. That was usually reserved for the front of the house, to soothe the paying guests. The only truly human dressing room we had ever had the privilege of enjoying was the one at the San Francisco Opera, with its beautiful carpet, full-length mirrors, indirect lighting and chaise longue to relax on.

It was intermission. The first half of the show had been played without a drummer because Sonny Greer was missing. Duke didn't know whether to feel concerned or angry when Sonny came staggering in, blind drunk, weaving from side to side. Duke started eating him out, cussing him, using some words I'd never heard before. He went all out of character, clean forgetting his natural, relaxed self. I had always respected him as a great writer and composer, but here was a talent I had never suspected.

Duke finally paused for breath, and Sonny gazed at him sorrowfully through his stupor and said, "Duke, if you knew where I was today, you wouldn't raise your voice to me, and you wouldn't swear at me, and you wouldn't say those terrible things to me."

It stopped Duke for a minute, and I wondered what Sonny was going to come up with. Duke asked, still steaming, "Well, where were you today?"

Sonny looked at him forgivingly through his alcoholic haze and said, "Duke, today is Rosh Hashanah, and I was at the shul davening all day."* It was so ludicrous that we just broke up.

Finally Duke told Sonny to straighten himself up for the second half of the show, and Sweetpea and I headed for the rehearsal room downstairs, below the stage. I had written a lyric for one of Duke's tunes, and Sweetpea was playing it back for me to make sure I was happy with the way the lyric fit, when there was a big crash over our heads and the plaster dust started settling slowly down from the ceiling. Sweetpea said, "Hey, wait a minute, the band is right over there. That's the corner where Sonny sits."

We ran upstairs just in time to see them carry Sonny off the stage. The way the stage had been set up, the band was sitting on three tiers, with the top one about six feet above the ground, and Sonny had been placed way up top with his drums and his cymbals and his chimes all around him.

During the intermission the stage manager, a real young fellow, had been showing Sonny's heavy cathedral chimes to

*At the synagogue, praying.

someone. There was a brake on the wheel, and somehow they released the brake. Dusty Fletcher was onstage doing a rendition of his smash hit song, "Open the Door, Richard." Sonny had to catch his cues and really work, especially when Dusty came to the title phrase. Sonny was still drunk as a lord, and when he leaned back, the whole bloody mess started rolling. One of the chimes caught on his jacket, and he grabbed at the rest to try to save himself. Sonny fell back and went ass over tea kettle down onto the stage, with the chimes landing on him as he lay there, pling, plong, pling, plong.

When Sweetpea and I got there, the audience was applauding. They thought it was part of the act, it was so funny. Duke was happy Sonny wasn't hurt badly, but he had to laugh. "I knew that whiskey would catch up with him one of these days."

After a couple of days Sonny got his wind back and went right back to his drinking routine, but from that day forward, drunk or sober, he insisted on playing with both feet on the ground. ("Oh, no, man, not me. You're not going to get me up there.")

Later that week I was sitting at the top of the outdoor fire stairs working on a lyric for a song. It was a pleasant evening between shows. Al Hibbler, the blind singer, was standing in the stage doorway taking the air, when I heard him screaming, screaming. I ran down to help him. Some freak had ground out a lit cigarette in blind Al's face. By the time I got there half the band had come tearing out. These were my gentle friends, my sweet brothers; but they weren't so gentle now, a pistol here, a knife there. They fanned out, looking for the maniac, but there was no way they could find him. Al, being sightless, couldn't describe him.

Nat "King" Cole

DURING THE SECOND WORLD WAR RALPH WATKINS OPENED A CLUB called Kelly's Stable in New York City. He hired Nat "King" Cole as accompanist for Billie Holiday, the great blues and jazz singer. Watkins got upset because Cole continually came in and rehearsed and practiced on the piano. He com-

82

plained, "What does this guy think he's going to do? Play in Carnegie Hall? He's hired to accompany Billie if she shows up, but he comes in and practices three or four hours every day."

Eventually, when Billie failed to show up once too often, Watkins billed Cole as a singer, starting him on his vocal career. Nat stayed at Kelly's Stable long enough to build up a vocal repertoire, then headed for Hollywood, where he added a guitar and a stand-up bass and became the King Cole Trio, recording on the new Capitol label, which had just been formed by Johnny Mercer, Buddy de Sylva and Glenn Wallich.

He was an immediate success with such record hits as "Straighten Up and Fly Right," "Nature Boy," "Mona Lisa" and "Calypso Blues." By that time Duke and Nat and I had become close friends. Nat was not only a brother music man and a brother writer, he was a great guy. And the ladies loved him.

One star-studded evening Duke and I decided to ride over and visit with Nat, who was singing at the Flamingo Club on the other side of town. The top was down and the night-blooming jasmine filled the air with a scent that was so beautiful it was almost unbearable. We pulled into the parking lot and parked next to another convertible with an attractive gal sitting behind the wheel. As we got out of the car she called out, "Are you friends of Nat's?"

I recognized her immediately. She was one of the top movie stars of the day. There was no way she could hide that face and that voice. I answered, "Yes."

"Would you take a note in to him?"

"I'd be glad to."

She scribbled a note on a piece of paper and handed it to me. I followed Duke, who was already in Nat's dressing room. On the way I read the note, which stated very directly, "If you want any of this redhead, you'd better get your black ass out here."

I handed the note to Nat, who read it without a change of expression. I asked him, "Is there any answer, Nat?" He shook his head in the negative and went out to do his show.

On a trip to New York, Nat met Marie Ellington, (no relation to Duke) who was singing with Duke's band at the Zanzibar. He fell madly in love with her, and when he returned to California he divorced his wife, Nadine, and married Marie. They bought a beautiful red brick house in Hancock Park, one of the wealthiest and most exclusive areas in the heart of Los Angeles, but they soon found out they weren't being received with open arms in the all-white neighborhood. After the dog had been poisoned and rocks thrown through the windows, they received an offer to sell at a profit. Nat wanted to accept, saying, "I don't want to live anyplace where I'm not wanted," but Marie prevailed upon him to stay. The neighbors held a meeting in a neighborhood public school, chaired by a female federal judge, discussing means of getting them out of the area. Eventually the IRS slugged Nat with tremendous tax penalties and fines that were questionable, to say the least.

But they stuck it out, and there I was one morning having breakfast with Nat and Marie. It was being served by the white, live-in couple that so ably fulfilled the functions of housekeeper, cook, laundress, butler, chauffeur, gardener and all-around handyman. Between the eggs and the coffee, the morning mail arrived and was brought to the table. Nat thumbed through it perfunctorily until his attention was riveted by the contents of a large manila envelope.

He motioned to me. "Come on, Don. I want you to hear something," and led the way to the upright piano that waited patiently in an alcove off the living room. He played and sang a song called "Lush Life" that I was hearing for the first time. He turned to me. "What do you think?"

I loved the song. I said, "It's just great."

He nodded enthusiastically. "I'm going to record it on my next date."

I wanted to know, "Who wrote it, Nat?" He handed me the lead sheet on which was written, "Words and music by Billy Strayhorn." I asked him, "How long have you known Billy?"

He looked at me quizzically. "I never met him, Don. Isn't he the little guy that works with our friend Duke?"

I nodded. "Yes. By the way, Duke is opening at Ciro's shortly and Strayhorn is coming out for the opening. You can give him the good news then."

The song Duke and I had written, "I'm Beginning to See the Light," was the all-time favorite song of Herman Hover, who owned Ciro's, a nightclub on the Sunset Strip midway between Hollywood and Beverly Hills. Duke was booked to open at Ciro's. His was the first black band to ever have been booked there; in fact, no black person had even been served there. (In Hollywood, much as in the rest of the country, many places were closed to blacks.)

The opening night was going to be fantastic. The papers were playing it up, and the radio was blasting away. Because "I'm Beginning to See the Light" was such a heavy favorite of Hover's, I naturally was the fair-haired boy as far as he was concerned. He loved Duke and he loved me. He was booking a guy in who had the number-one song in the whole world at the time, and everything was fine.

Sitting in Carlos Gastel's office one day,* I heard Carlos call Hover at his home and ask for a reservation for two for Nat and his wife Maria for Duke's opening. From what I could hear, I gathered that Hover was giving him all kinds of apologies from the other end, that it was sold out and there was no way of getting in. I felt kind of funny about it.

I felt certain that the reason Hover had turned him down was because Nat was black. I spoke to Duke about it. And Duke said, "Well, maybe they *are* all sold out. After all, Ellington is opening!" (Here's Duke playing games again, the devil's advocate.)

I looked at him and sensed what was going on in his head. I said, "Hey, wait a minute; let's stop all the bullshit. We know why Herman gave that story to Carlos—it's because Nat's black. There's never been a black guy sitting at Ciro's or the Mocambo or the Trocadero; the rope is always up when they show. Come on, man, it's the black bullshit all over again."

I shook my head. "Duke, we've known Hover for years. We know these aren't his own sentiments. He's in a bind. He's a businessman, and he has to cater not just to the opening-night crowds like the show people, who won't come back again until the next opening, but to the people who come here night after

*Gastel was Nat "King" Cole's manager.

night after night; the California first families with the old money, the real estate money, who won't even talk to a Chicano or a black man." I shrugged. "The reason Hover said there was no room for Nat was because he couldn't help himself."

Duke looked at me and said, "Don, I'm sure you'll know how to handle it."

I replied, "How do you mean?"

He said, "As long as you're discreet, I'm sure you'll think of something." (Putting me on again.) "I have the utmost faith in you. After all, you're Don George."

I called Nat on the phone and I said, "Hey, man, how would you like to go to Duke's opening at Ciro's?"

Nat said, "Fine."

Nat was playing downtown at the Orpheum Theatre. I asked him what time he got through and he replied, "About twenty to eleven, Don."

"How long will it take you to drive uptown to Ciro's?"

"About twenty minutes."

"Okay, Nat. Tell you what. At ten minutes past eleven sharp, I'll come to the door and meet you and bring you in, okay? You'll be my guest."

In the meanwhile I had called Herman Hover and said, "Herman, I have some very important people coming to Duke's opening."

He knew Duke and I were together, and we had written his favorite song and he loved us both. He said, "Fine. How many people?"

I said, "Oh, about eight or ten."

Herman said, "Okay. Because it's you, and because your friends are important, I'll put a table on the dance floor." (The dance floor was pretty small to begin with.)

I said, "Great, wonderful," and thanked him very much.

When opening night arrived, I went to the door at ten minutes past eleven (my date was sitting at the table; all the other seats were empty) and picked up Nat and his wife, Marie, and we walked inside.

The red velvet rope was up. The maitre d' saw them and he said, "I'm very sorry, Mr. Cole. We're all sold out."

I said, "That's all right, they're my guests," and took them each by an arm and walked them inside. There was no way he could stop us. Nat and his wife sat down at the table next to my date and myself. That made four of us, which left six empty chairs. I invited the people in the band: the singers—Al Hibbler, Kay Davis, Joya Sherrill—Johnny Hodges, Harry Carney and the other key guys in the band. Duke, naturally, had helped cook up the deal. I said, "Anytime you're between sets or you feel like a drink, just come on over, sit down and have a drink."

We had a pretty good thing going. Except for my date and myself, we had an all-black table all night long for the whole world to see. During the course of the evening everybody who had come to Ciro's for the opening came over to get Nat's autograph and Duke's, when he was at the table. Joan Crawford came over and Lana Turner and Ava Gardner and Mickey Rooney and Buddy de Sylva and Johnny Mercer and Manny Sachs and many, many other stars came by to shake hands and sit and stop for a chat. Everybody crowded around the table because here was a parlay of two men, Duke and Nat, whom these people loved and might not see together ever again.

A Wildly Attractive Gal

IN BOSTON AT A PARTY AFTER A CONCERT, DUKE LATCHED ONTO A WEIRDLY dressed, wildly attractive gal and disappeared with her. The promoter asked me, "What's Duke going to do with her?"

I replied, "The usual thing, I suppose."

He shrugged. "I wonder if he knows her right leg is a prosthesis."

Every Hour on the Hour

I PICKED UP THE PHONE ON THE FIRST RING. THERE WAS A FAMILIAR VOICE ON the other end. "Hello, Don?"

I replied, "This is he."

"This is Sam White, over at Paramount."

"How've you been, Sam? Everything all right?"

"Everything's fine. By the way, are you still writing with Duke?"

"Sure. We're practically married as far as the songs go."

"I'd like to talk to you about a picture I'm producing. Can you make it over to the studio this afternoon about three?"

"Sure thing, Sam. I'll see you then."

During our meeting at the studio, Sam filled me in on the film he was about to shoot. It was called *People Are Funny*, after the hugely successful radio show that featured Art Linkletter. The cast included Linkletter, Rudy Vallee, Frances Langford and a young singer they were promoting named Bob Grabeaux. They needed a middle-of-the-road ballad for Grabeaux, and Sam, being an old friend, had sold the powers that be the idea that Duke and I would be just the team to write it.

After thanking Sam, I drove out through the front gate, past Lucey's, the restaurant where all the stars hung out, made a right turn and was stopped at the corner by the traffic light turning red. Glancing idly around, my eyes fastened on a huge billboard advertising the Santa Fe Railroad. The sign read: EVERY HOUR ON THE HOUR A TRAIN LEAVES FOR SAN FRANCISCO. A light bulb exploded in my brain. Voilá! There's our song title: "Every Hour on the Hour (I Fall in Love with You)." Duke loved the title and so did Sam, who got a fast okay on the song. Duke left to fulfill an engagement in Chicago shortly before Sam called to say that the contracts and checks were ready. I drove over to Paramount, and he asked, "Where's Duke?"

I said, "He's on the road."

He looked puzzled. "Well, somebody has to sign these contracts."

I replied, "Sam, you know me pretty well. Tell you what we'll do. You give me the contracts and the checks, and I'll see that the contracts are signed and returned to you and I won't deposit my check or give Duke his check until after he signs the contracts and the contracts are in the mail."

Sam said, "Fine. I know you well enough. Everything's okay."

I put the contracts and checks in my pocket and headed for Chicago and Duke. Travel was tight. There was no chance of getting on a plane, but I was fortunate enough to bribe my way into an upper berth on the Super Chief, which was the fastest train between Los Angeles and Chicago.

Those were my drinking days, so the first thing I did was head for the club car and find a seat next to the most attractive, unattended young lady in sight, who was wearing slacks that looked as though they'd been put on from the inside. After a few drinks we were rapidly becoming close friends. We happened to glance out the window as we were passing a long shed set back about a hundred yards from the track, with just three boastful words painted in large letters on the low, sloping roof—MIKE'S TOOL WORKS. We drank a toast to Mike's ability to function and soon headed back to the sleeping car.

It was a tight fit for both of us in the upper berth, but we made it. During the night I had the feeling that something unusual was going on, but I was so loaded that I didn't realize what had happened until the next morning, when I was washing up in the lavatory and caught sight of my lacerated back. My lady friend had practically ripped me to pieces. When we got to Chicago I tried to duck her, but she reminded me that I had promised to introduce her to Duke.

We took a cab to the Stevens Hotel, where Duke and the band were playing. I called Duke on the house phone and he said, "Hey, baby, what are you waiting for, come on up."

We got off the elevator and had just reached the door of Duke's suite when an evil-looking black man with a gun in his hand slammed me up against the wall and snarled, "Where do you think you're going, white boy?"

I remonstrated, "Hey, what is this? I called Duke from downstairs. He told me to come right up." The man was frisking me and doing a good job.

"What's your name?"

"Don George."

"You wait right here."

I wasn't going anyplace, not with that gun looking at me. He opened the door to Duke's room with a key he took from his pocket and disappeared inside. He reappeared almost immediately and said, "Okay, my man. Come on in."

When we got inside, Duke said, "Say hello to Willy Manning."

I replied, "What's it all about, Duke? This guy really shook me down."

Willy Manning explained, "We got word that somebody was trying to kidnap Duke. A couple of guys cowboying around."

"But you saw me with a lady."

"I'm not taking any chances."

Duke intervened. "Never mind that now, Don. Who's the pretty lady?"

I turned to Manning. "Would you keep her company while I talk to Duke in the bedroom?"

When we got inside I took off my shirt and showed Duke my back. Returning to the other room, Duke smiled sweetly at my erstwhile companion.

"It was so nice meeting you, but we have a rehearsal now, and Mr. Manning will get you a taxi."

It was obvious that Duke wanted no part of the possibility that his Johnson's Baby Oiled, talcum-powdered, golden hide might be damaged by the flailing claws of an orgasmic female.

After they left I told Duke about the contracts and the checks from Sam White. He wanted to know if I had spoken to any publishers yet about the song. I told him I'd probably work out a deal when I got to New York, where Duke was opening the following week at the Four Hundred Club, and suggested that we sign the Paramount contracts.

Duke said, "There's no hurry, Don. Let's take care of it in New York. Right now let's get something to eat. I'm hungry, and the chef is a good friend of mine."

After we ate the usual (steak, lettuce and tomatoes, chopped liver and ice cream), Duke left some of the steak on the bone, wrapped it in a napkin and left it on his plate.

We went downstairs and I sat through the band's performance till one A.M., when the ballroom closed for the night. It was the middle of the day for Duke. He said, "Come on, Willy, let's take Don to the Club de Lisa."

I said, "What's that?"

"Just a club over on the South Side."

When we got there, I fell out. It was huge, with every kind of entertainment possible. There were tap dancers and cooch dancers and belly dancers. The windows were painted black so you couldn't tell day from night. I was the only white man in the place, and after a while I got separated from Duke and Willy.

There I was, surrounded by a few hundred big, bad Leroy Browns and their income-producing ladies, all offering me drinks and telling me what a great guy I was. I was having a grand time with my new friends when Willy Manning rushed up to me excitedly.

"I've been looking all over for you, Don. [Looking around anxiously.] Are you all right? Is anybody bothering you?"

"No, everything's fine, Willy. What's the problem?"

"Duke is worried about you. He sent me to find you." [Taking my arm.] "You shouldn't be roaming around by yourself in a place like this."

The sun was up when we hit the street. We had spent the night and part of the day at the de Lisa. Back at the hotel, just before heading for New York, I asked Duke once more to sign the contracts, but he stalled again.

"We've got plenty of time, Don."

By the time Duke got to New York, I had made a deal with a music publisher and I was walking around with two sets of contracts and checks in my pocket.

Duke had a great opening at the Four Hundred Club on Fifth Avenue, near Forty-fourth Street. Lots of celebrities, paparazzi, noise, hullabaloo. It was a downstairs club, a big, big room. I went there with the contracts—I had both the contracts from Paramount and the contracts from the music publisher—and I brought them to Duke and said, "Hey, Duke, we've got to sign these things. I've got the checks, and as soon as you sign these contracts, I'll put them in the mail and give you the checks."

He smiled. "It can wait, Don. I have a lady I want to talk to right now."

I shrugged and said okay, again recognizing the irrefutable fact that Duke was the greatest procrastinator in the world and hated to write anything down or sign anything. Lead sheets, letters, wills—everything was usually discussed and finalized on the telephone, often at three or four o'clock in the morning.

Besides, I got a kick as usual just sitting around listening to the great music the band played, chatting with Lena Horne and Cab Calloway, who occasionally got a little salty when he was in his cups until Lena sweet-talked him out of it, and of course, Sweetpea, the perpetrator of most of the arrangements I loved so much.

The second night I went back with the contracts and repeated, "Duke, let's sign these things."

And he said, "Well, I'm kind of busy now; let's do it tomorrow night."

The next night I went back and he stalled again. On the fourth night I went in and as he started stalling once more I pulled the papers out of my pocket and started ripping them up and cussing and swearing, and I said, "Duke, let me tell you something, man. This is the end of us. We're not going to write together anymore. You're not my brother any longer. You're not even my cousin. This is the last time you pull this bullshit on me, you son of a bitch."

I was screaming at the top of my lungs, the perspiration building up on my forehead, trying to look as ferocious as possible. The people standing around were horrified. I tore up the contracts and threw them in his face. Half of the pieces landed on the table and half landed on the floor.

Duke was shocked. He said. "Don, how can you do that? [Placatingly.] Please don't talk to me like that. You know I'm your buddy. I was going to sign those contracts tonight."

I said, "You were."

He nodded. "Yes, I was."

I said, "Okay, here they are."

And I laughingly pulled the real contracts out of my pocket.

He was slowly shaking his head from side to side as he signed the contracts.

EVERY HOUR ON THE HOUR

You needn't carry a watch
Or gaze at the sun in the skies;

You can always tell what time it is
By the look in my eyes.

EVERY HOUR ON THE HOUR
I fall in love with you.
Every minute on the minute
Another dream comes true.

Every second that you're near me
The thrill is still the same.
As the first time I kissed you
Before I knew your name.

We don't have to be together
For me to feel your touch,
Just the thought of you
Can make me want you so much.

Every second, every minute
You're in my heart and then
EVERY HOUR ON THE HOUR
I fall in love again.

Grist for the Mill

DUKE AND I WERE TEAMMATES, TWO BUDDIES IN THE OLD SENSE; THE REAL way. The way it is in novels, in movies. A real all-American way of relating to each other. Like Mutt and Jeff. A black boy and a white boy; except that the black boy was a golden boy. We were banging around all over the hemisphere—Toronto, Hollywood, Canada, Mexico. Duke would look at me and shake his head. He'd see me with a chick once or twice and then he'd see somebody else with her, and he'd say to the fellow, "Hey! How did you meet her?"

And the fellow would say, "Don introduced me to her."

Duke said, "Wow! That Don rustles up so much stuff, he's got to give some away."

We had that relationship in addition to the writing. But the relationships he had with other people were just incredible. He had a need for drama that at times became Machiavellian. If

93

there wasn't a drama existing, he would create one. He would divide and conquer by rubbing people together in the band, or by getting Paul Gonsalves when he was at his lowest, when he could hardly stand, to do solo after solo and walk around the room, while Duke would sit by like the cat that ate the canary, meek as a lamb, when he started the whole damn thing himself. Basically he was complex and contradictory and really a man of the 1890s.

He learned all that he learned and made something of himself within a very short span of time. In the tapes of his interviews and stage raps from 1933, he sounds stiff and nervous, young and very inexperienced and frightened. But listen to him in 1963 and he's the suavest, most articulate guy in the business. The whole thing turned in the mid- to the late forties; this new dude was sophisticated. This dude was it. A lot of his ways he got from his dad, who was very courtly, very well spoken, the kind of man you see in movies but don't think you'll ever meet. Like Ronald Colman, he had just everything: meticulous manners, beautiful timing—he was enviable.

Duke would be sitting at a table at the Cotton Club and a couple he knew would approach, and (subliminally imitating his father) in dulcet tones he would ask, "Won't you join me?" To a single lady he would say, "My mother always told me to gravitate toward beauty, so I had to come and see you." That all came from his father, James Edward; J.E.; Uncle Ed, who could talk the paint off the wall: He looked suave and he was the biggest ladies' man in his area. He used to go to a place called the Bird Cage and just make love to everybody. It was the old Victorian thing; his lady was at home, not supposed to know. Duke became Victorian through his father. He loved his dad, who died when he was only fifty-eight, and Duke was only thirty-eight. They were more like brothers than father and son. They don't make men like Duke's father anymore. There's no climate like that today. There's no respect for people. People don't know how to dress anymore.

Duke's only concern was getting the next eight bars straight in his head. He was totally involved in his craft and used people to their own good as fuel for his music. He used them as grist for his mill. Especially women. Like a painter. Picasso was the same way. He would go through women just to get the flavor, just to taste it all, to check it all out and then work from that. Different sizes of women, different sizes of breasts, different sizes of hips; men like them revel in that, because it goes right into their music or their art. Making love to them is a means to an end, because they're so deeply into their art. Music really was Duke's mistress. There was an interrelationship between Picasso and Duke and their wholesaling of women as grist for the mill, just to end up in a picture or a tune ten days later. If Duke made love to a lady in Ohio one night, in Utah ten days later he thinks of her and puts her all down on paper and has the band play her the following day. You'd have to know him real well to know that tune was inspired by that lady, or perhaps the lack of a lady. There's another thing: the blues. He might miss a chick like hell; he might have screwed up in a relationship and she put him down; and he's missing the hell out of that chick he knew in Chicago in 1930 or '40, or '50 and he feels wistful. It's all in there, and that's what makes it great. I don't think we know what caused it all. His richness of experience is what gives the music its potency. Nobody wrote music and had a band that colorful and that tragic and that swinging, with all the other things in there, because nobody lived a life like Duke Ellington.

He was very large physically; he was born strong. He had big bones and big shoulders and strong legs, and he could hack it. These other fellows, like Fats Waller, screwed up and were played out at thirty-nine because all they did was drink, drink, drink. Fats just drank himself into oblivion. One of the things that saved Duke was his lack of alcoholism. He stopped drinking regularly in 1940. In the days of Prohibition he always drank with one eye open. Sonny and those fellows would drink till they got stoned and wet their pants, but Duke would always pace himself. He knew how to drink. His dad taught him.

His dad had had a still in the house in Washington. Duke told me his dad made moonshine—corn liquor—just for his friends; and he had the most expensive canisters from Europe in the family larder, in the pantry, for guests. Duke said, "If you think that was wild, I used to go to our neighbors who lived across the state line in Virginia, and those families had casks of moonshine dated like champagne. This one is 1895, this one is 1890, this one is 1870, this one was made by grandfather; they really took it seriously. To those Southern families their liquor represented pride." Most middle-class families made their own booze. For those who could afford it, rye whiskey was very popular before Prohibition. Duke said, "Rye whiskey, rye whiskey, rye whiskey I try. If I don't have rye whiskey, I surely will die."

When Prohibition came they had to import bourbon and Scotch from Canada. (When Duke was graduating from the eighth grade, his high-school-freshmen friends took him to a drugstore where the man gave him some corn liquor, and he got sloshed on his graduation day on the stuff the kids bought him as a present.)

Duke's father really was something. He would say the damnedest things, and he was successful with more chicks out of the chorus than Duke. At one point it was a kind of competition. At the Cotton Club they would vie for the attention of the girls, and J.E. apparently won out more often than Duke. He was a man of experience, and Duke was just a kid in his twenties. In those days the chicks would go for Pop because Pop was a man of the world. He'd been around. A chick would look at Duke and look at J.E. and say, "I'm going with this one. I like his story."

Duke didn't create all the bullshit he was credited with. He just followed in the footsteps of the creator. His father started out being a butler in the White House for Grover Cleveland, then worked in the navy as a draftsman. When he came to New York there was a constant tournament between Duke and his father—maybe playful, maybe not. But Dad wore fancy vests with a gold chain and a diamond ring. Duke had been running the show while Pop was in Washington, but when Pop came up North he knocked 'em all dead.

So many of Duke's attributes—the great charm, the wonderful gregariousness, the consummate and sincere appreciation and adoration of women, the immovable loyalties—were all fostered and nurtured in Duke by his love of and proximity with his father.

Johnny Ray

I SET UP A DATE FOR JOHNNY RAY TO CUT TWO SINGLE SIDES WITH DUKE ON Columbia Records. Duke and I wrote both the songs. One was called "To Know You Is to Love You" and the other was called "The Lonely Ones." Two really good songs. I suggested Johnny's arranger for the date but was overruled by Johnny's manager in favor of preserving the Ellington "sound."

Came the time for the session, which was to take place at the church on East Thirtieth Street in Manhattan, which Columbia used as a recording studio. Billy Strayhorn, Duke's arranger, was sitting in a corner just finishing the arrangements, despite the fact that he had had weeks to write them. As he was writing the arrangements, Tom Whaley, Duke's copyist, was extracting the parts from the score, copying them and handing them to the musicians one at a time.

Strayhorn saw me and said, "Don, we're going to need some more lyrics here."

I said, "Which song?"

He said, " 'The Lonely Ones,' " which was a ballad in a slow tempo, and a chorus and a half would be more than enough for a single side.

I asked, "How is it laid out now?"

He said, "I've got two and a half choruses."

I said, "That's pretty long. Are you sure you want more lyrics?"

He replied, "Yes, I think we ought to continue on with it."

I said, "No way, let it go at that, Billy."

Shortly thereafter Johnny Ray walked into the studio with Dorothy Kilgallen and an entourage of eight or ten people.* Duke played them in with a few bars from "Cry," Johnny's hit record, and there were embraces all around. Johnny was a Scotch drinker and slightly up on it, but not too much; just enough to be convivial. He was an easygoing guy, and right

*Kilgallen was a popular gossip columnist who not long afterward failed to recover from an unfortunate combination of whiskey and sleeping pills.

then he was at his peak. He had just had two smash hits, "Cry" and "The Little White Cloud That Cried." It was really a coup, a wonderful thing, that I had been able to put him together to do the vocals with Duke, who was sitting there noodling away on the piano waiting for the engineers to set up the microphones and get the sound balance.

Johnny got up on the stand with his copy of the song in his hand. He was a pro and had rehearsed the songs and knew them well. The first song they were running down was "The Lonely Ones." Johnny was singing and the band was playing . . . Johnny was singing and the band was playing . . . Johnny was singing and the band was playing . . . and they still hadn't come to the end of the arrangement. Johnny stopped singing, looked around and held up his hand for silence. Duke hit a sustained chord on the piano. The music stopped, and everyone gave Johnny his complete attention.

He said, "Gentlemen," and paused. Raising his voice a number of decibels, he yelped, "What the fuck *is* this, an LP?"

To Know You Is to Love You

To Know You Is to Love You,
To see you is to care,
To hear you and to touch you—
Is to walk around on air.

To kiss you is to preview
What heaven holds in store.

And darling, let me tell you
What I am living for,
To know you and to love you
A million mem'ries more.

98

THE LONELY ONES

You've seen them come and go
They walk alone where lights are low
And so they're called THE LONELY ONES.

You've seen their haunted eyes
The empty dreams they advertise
They know they're called
THE LONELY ONES

On rainy nights they rendezvous,
Wherever blue trumpets moan
There they wait and when it's late
They get the papers and go home.

Tonight I'm so afraid that
I will join that lost parade
My love why can't you see
Just you can set me free
Come back and rescue me,
From THE LONELY ONES.

Peter

"YOU LOOK A LITTLE PEAKED TODAY, DUKE."
"I let that chick give me some head last night. Now I'll be walking on my knees for the next three days." Shaking his head pensively, "Don, we're not children anymore."

I grinned in mock sympathy. "You can say that again. As the years go by my nose gets bigger and my peter gets smaller. If we could find some way to reverse the process, we'd be more famous than Madame Curie or Jonas Salk."

Duke replied, "You work on it, Don. I have the utmost faith in you." He was getting in the spirit of the thing. "We'll package it and sell it like instant coffee. Well get Sears-Roebuck and the A & P to distribute it." With a faraway look: "I'm sure William Morris will be happy to handle the merchandising. They'll probably package it with Rin Tin Tin and Clark Gable."

99

This was great. We were incipient millionaires. "Duke, we'll give Richard Burton and Laurence Olivier a piece of the action to do the television commercials." I remembered something. "Maybe we can get Allie Wrubel* to come in with us. They discovered plutonium on his property in Twenty-nine Palms. Nuclear power is sure to help us get over the top."

Broadening the horizon, I asked, "What about the foreign rights?"

Duke thought for a moment. "We can divide the world either into hemispheres or countries; maybe countries would be better. I'm sure the British will welcome us with open arms: the French have methods of their own. We'd better stay out of India until the Planned Parenthood Society gets a stronger foothold." [Bowing from the waist.] "The Japanese will probably want the picture-taking concession—"

I interrupted enthusiastically, "Half the women in the world will be grateful to us."

Duke reconsidered, "Don, on second thought, maybe we don't need any more grateful women just now. I'm going to take a nap."

The Band

DUKE WAS ELEGANT IN HIS HANDLING OF THE MEN IN THE BAND. WHEN Sonny Greer got drunk and fell off the bandstand, Duke didn't fire him. He sent him home till he straightened out and got well.

Sonny had pneumonia ten times in eight years. The doctor told him, "If you take another drink you're going to die." (At this writing Sonny is alive and kicking and well into his eighties.)

Ben Webster left and came back to the band six times. He just got drunk, called Duke a motherfucker and quit.

When Cat Anderson quit, Duke told him, "Look, man, I think you're tired. You need a rest. Why don't you take a couple of weeks off and get yourself together. Then come on back; everything will be all right." He told Ray Nance the same

*A noted songwriter.

100

thing when Ray quit the band. Cat quit because he figured he could do better with a band of his own. He got the band, went out with it and failed.

Johnny Hodges quit and came back more than once. Tyree Glenn quit at least three times. Every time someone quit, Duke told him to take a rest, take it easy and then come on back, come on home. "When you get tired of playing around out there, just come on home."

There never was anybody else who treated his musicians that way. Duke's greatness was so lasting and so flexible that if certain musicians were there, fine. If they weren't there, he understood them, loved them.

Duke knew his men well. He would give instructions to the staff at Basin Street and at the Rainbow Grill. "Don't put the lights on until I give you the chord." Then he'd be the first one on the bandstand, and he'd tinkle on the piano almost as though he were practicing, almost childlike, starting with one finger, then with one hand, then both hands. He'd stop, and the band would shuffle in one at a time. (The announcement to the audience had already been made.)

It might take five minutes before they were all in their places, but the lights weren't permitted to be turned on until they were all there. When he hit that chord and the house lights went up, those guys would wail and they'd kill themselves for him, no matter how sick they were. The kind of trust and faith he had in the men made them *want* to kill themselves for him.

But he could get angry. He was extremely intolerant of an inadequate performance, no matter what it was that had to be done, whether it was to type a letter for him, make a phone call, arrange an appointment or pick up a package. He could not understand that something could go wrong and it might not come out the way he expected. He hoped and expected that other people would be as professional and as thorough and as great as he was. And so few people were.

Duke and Jazz

DUKE DIDN'T MERELY PLAY JAZZ. HE PLAYED HIS OWN VARIATION OF WHAT he felt was the way music should be played. Just listen to the abstractions of jazz musicians and the flights of fancy that are seldom if ever repeated when the musicians improvise on the same tune another time. They go off and wander in a direction that makes sense in a jazz form but hasn't the cohesion of a written arrangement.

Most of Duke's performances involved arrangements. Everytime Hodges played "Passion Flower" or "Lush Life," he played it exactly the same way. Every time Carney played his solos he played them exactly the same way. When he held a note for three or four minutes, it was the same deep note on his baritone sax. This wasn't jazz, this was Ellington music. To label Ellington merely a jazz artist is not to give him the credit that he deserves. He was more than that. He performed songs in a manner that wasn't jazz, and wasn't a society tempo, and wasn't the way anybody else was playing or arranging or creating or composing or writing. It was essentially black music combined with an elaboration of expression. It had color, harmony, melody and rhythm. Duke was all by himself.

When an important event is occurring, it isn't easy to appraise it truly and evaluate its importance in the full span of the performing arts or any other art form. As time goes on there's a different evaluation, a different appreciation. When you shared an evening with Duke, you knew that you were in a presence that was extraordinary, but it wasn't till later, in retrospect, that you realized you had been in the presence of genius; not only genius as a creative composer, arranger and conductor, but absolute genius at handling an audience once he got up onstage.

He invariably came up with whatever was necessary to salvage any situation. He had the ability to be inventive. He toyed with his fellow man. We were all smitten by him and completely under his spell. And how he could weave that spell. It was something that was difficult to define. Ellington was contagious. Once you were exposed to him, you caught an incurable disease, Ellingtonitis.

He was the first to combine Latin and jazz.

He was the first to put jazz in a church.

He was the first to write jazz as serious music.

He was the first orchestra leader and composer ever to write music especially for an individual instrumentalist, like a Puccini might fashion an aria for an opera.

He had the sensuousness of a black artist, and the polish and savoir faire of what people wanted of a Ray Noble, a Guy Lombardo or a Benny Goodman.

He insisted on elegance in the presentation of his music. He was particular about the lighting and the scrim.

He appealed to the senses in a way that very few other musicians did. He was as sensuous with his music as he was with his women.

The Dick Cavett Show

DUKE WAS ON *THE DICK CAVETT SHOW* IN NEW YORK, WITH MEL BROOKshire and Cootie Williams. They were playing "I've Got It Bad and That Ain't Good." Cootie was singing along with Mel, and also playing his trumpet with the plunger.

At the end of the number, Dick asked, "Mr. Ellington, wasn't that a toilet plunger he used?"

Duke said, "Well, yes, it was a toilet plunger, but you see, it was made for the trumpet first and since then they've found other uses for it."

Prayer

THE HOLIDAYS WERE COMING. SWEETPEA WAS ANXIOUS TO GET HOME TO his friend, whom he hadn't seen for weeks. Kay Davis and Joya Sherrill, the girl singers with the band, were sleeping fitfully, huddled together like two weary kittens. We were playing too many one-nighters. Whoever booked the tour completely forgot to pencil in a stop for plasma. Play the gig till one A.M. Load all the instruments. Make sure everyone was on the bus. Tear Duke away from whatever lady he might be with, and if we were lucky, get moving by two or two thirty to the next gig, which might be three or four hundred miles away. Arrive about noon, never knowing in advance whether we'd wind up in some fleabag hotel, which happened as often as not. We were weary enough so it didn't really make that much difference as long as there was a clean bed where we could grab a couple of hours' shut-eye till it was time to rouse our weary bones and get under a shower in preparation for whatever band setup and rehearsal were necessary for our new gig. Those showers were like a blessing from heaven after a long night on the road. I would luxuriate under them, sometimes staying long enough for my fingertips to wrinkle like prunes.

Occasionally preparations had been made in advance for dinner for Duke and myself, but we often joined the members of the band, scuffling around a strange town, looking for some beanery that was willing to accommodate a motley assemblage of strange blacks.

(As Sammy Davis once told me, "Don, do the gig, get the bread and split.")

Even the ordinarily placid bus driver grew edgy while roaring through the night, manipulating our little community on wheels through countrysides we never saw. As usual I was sitting in the backseat of the bus, holding a lit flashlight in Duke's eyes, handing him a sheet of manuscript paper and a pencil.

"Come on, Duke, write the damn thing down. You can sleep later."

Duke was grumbling as he wrote the notes. For the first time ever, a voice from the front of the bus called out above the intermittent snores, "Put that goddamn light out back there." Hibbler was the only one who seemed relaxed; he was accustomed to the dark.

The next day, during rehearsal, Duke addressed the band. "The holidays are coming soon, children, and everybody gets time off from Christmas to New Year's." In answer to a question, "Of course, with pay." Mouths that had been turned down at the corners turned up. Faces lit up. Everyone grew perceptibly younger, looking forward to homes, families, nights off and various and sundry methods of personal wassail.

It was New Year's Eve. We were having a big party at the house on Riverside Drive. Ed Dudley, the borough president of Manhattan, was lining up all the girls to be kissed. "Come on, Don, you're first."

Our good friend Tony Bennett, singer and newly acclaimed painter, was dancing with his sister Mary. Blind Al Hibbler was telling everybody it was good to see them. Pastor John Gensel, who initiated the jazz vespers on Sunday afternoons at St. Peter's Church, was exchanging ecclesiastical anecdotes with Father Jerry Pocock of Montreal. They were Duke's foremost spiritual advisers and on occasion had accompanied him halfway around the world. (John once told me that Duke was one of the greatest quarterbacks that God ever had.) Pearl Bailey and her husband Louis Bellson, the great drummer, were there, mingling with celebrities from the theater, from the music world and from all areas of the arts.

The house was jammed full, and everyone was having a grand time, eating, drinking, singing and dancing. Midnight was approaching when we noticed that Duke wasn't around. We wanted him with us when the clocks struck, the chimes rang and the bells tolled. Everybody was asking for him. He obviously wasn't in the trophy room, so I started searching the house.

I went through all the offices, all the bedrooms, looked in all the johns, climbing the stairs from one floor to the next till I reached the top floor, with no luck. Duke was nowhere to be found. I wondered how a big, beautiful man with auburning hair and a burgeoning pony tail could completely vanish from view.

Giving up, I stepped into the ramshackle old elevator to return to the party, and in my haste inadvertently pushed the wrong button. The elevator opened onto a small room at the back of the house in an area I had never seen before. I opened the door.

There, alone in the small room, was Duke. He was kneeling, his eyes closed, his head bowed, his hands folded across his chest. He was praying aloud. I didn't move, not wishing to disturb him. I stood there, sensing his feeling, and his mood reached into me. He was thanking the Lord for all that he had, asking the Lord for strength in the coming year to overcome all the obstacles and to stay close to Him. Duke seemed to be in a state of being possessed, not in the sense of needing exorcism but a positive possession for good. His words were words of thanksgiving.

The vibrations and the power of his concentration and his communion with God not only involved him but reached out to involve me. He prayed for strength to keep him humble, to appreciate what he had, and to keep fame, money and women secondary to his love for God. He thanked the Lord for each of the musicians. He asked for the wisdom to be able to develop the very best musically in his individual musicians when he wrote a composition for them. For strength to write the right music for each man. He thanked the Lord for the community feeling between himself and the band, which was his instrument, his voice; for what he had and for guidance in the future. He prayed to be loving to everybody, and I remembered the time I was standing with him when a little boy came up to him and Duke said to the little boy, "When I grow up I want to be just like you."

As I listened to my brother kneeling there, a glorious feeling overpowered me, a feeling of great ecstasy. I fell to my knees beside Duke, and for the first time in my life I prayed.

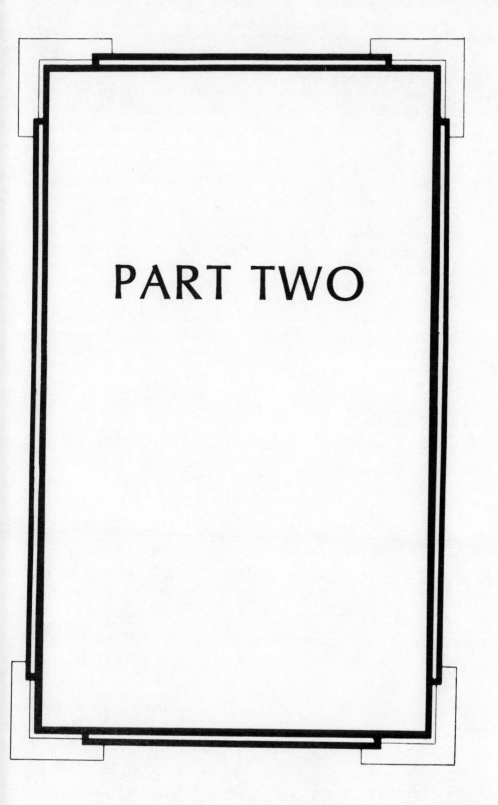

PART TWO

Hotel Rooms

THE FIRST QUESTION DUKE WOULD ASK UPON ARRIVING IN A HOTEL WAS, "Do you have king-size beds?"

If the answer was in the negative, he would proceed to manufacture his own. He would take the twin beds and push them together. Then he would take the mattresses on top of each bed and turn them horizontally at right angles. The two box springs would be going up and down, north and south, and the two mattresses would be heading east side, west side. Then he'd have the maids come in with the double sheets and hallelujah! There would be the Ellington bed.

Duke would check into two, three or four hotels, hand out keys to different ladies, then, later on, pick out the hotel room he wanted to go to. A lot of men who are womanizers don't like women, but Duke was a womanizer who liked them as well as loved them. And all the women ran after him. Duke would be with one woman, and there would be another woman waiting downstairs to go with him to the next town. Yet he felt very strongly about whichever woman he was with. He was not a Don Juan type, strictly out for sex. Duke possibly out-Gabled Gable and out-bedroomed Valentino and was certainly one of the great Lotharios of the twentieth century.

Duke was absolutely marvelous with women. He had an insatiable appetite. As soon as he finished eating, he wanted more. He was still hungry. But that didn't mean he didn't enjoy the menu. He didn't physically chase women. They chased him. His way of responding was very subtle. He was always ready. When he met a lady and she looked at him with those eyes, as they always did, he would join the chase by painting his standard verbal pictures of "I know you're an angel, because I see your halo reflected on the ceiling" or one of his other tried and true crotch warmers.

(Early on I had come to the inevitable conclusion that my beloved brother completely refuted the laws of physics and that his body, instead of being composed of 98 percent water like all other humans, was undoubtedly constructed of 98 percent bullshit. (Charming and lovable bullshit to be sure, but still bullshit.)

It was fascinating how he went from one hotel room to another. This was not a man who liked to go out. It was educational to watch him settle in with chick after chick after chick and piano after piano after piano. Always a piano and always a chick, each one competing for the same time. All his early life he had played and hung out in joints, at rent parties, at gigs. He had paid his dues, so it was understandable that he wanted to hang out in warm hotel rooms. It got so he didn't know one city from another. What was fascinating was that the world came to Duke. With all the devilment within him, he was the embodiment of Lucifer. In contrast to his spiritual side, he delighted in engineering machinations and intrigues between the band manager and the public relations man; between somebody's girl friend and somebody else's wife.

One couldn't expect a man like Duke to be judged in relation to the ordinary. Genetically, biologically, cerebrally and in terms of the emotions, Duke was a superior being. There was a sense of not just the four sides of a square but an extra dimension that he possessed. Duke was an alternate universe. He was a court unto himself. He was a kingdom unto himself. His kingdom was always a hotel room, his throne was a bed, his magic wand a piano. In every hotel room there was a piano. The piano had three legs, the girls had two legs. Duke practically lived in five-legged hotel rooms. Occasionally, when he had more than one female guest at a time, he luxuriated in seven-legged hotel rooms. Duke never lacked female companionship. He was Casanova, Lochinvar and the White Knight all in one. When I marveled at his infallibility with women, he smiled at me, crossed himself and said, "Don, when God shuts the door, He opens the window."

The Turtle Hotel, Akron

WE WERE AT THE TURTLE HOTEL IN AKRON, OHIO. I HAD TWO BEAUTIFUL chicks in the room with me. It was Saturday night, and we couldn't get any whiskey. Duke was right across the hall. He said, "Those are two pretty chicks," and he was trying to get to

110

one of them. I had them both in the room and I was getting ready to work out like mad. Duke wanted to get in there so bad.

He knew I didn't have anything to drink. He knocked on the door and said, "I've got a pint of whiskey," and held it up to the transom where I could see it.

I let him in.

The Blackstone Hotel, Chicago

IN CHICAGO THE BAND HAD PLAYED FOR A VERY FANCY, RITZY DEBUTANTE ball at the Blackstone Hotel. As Duke was leaving the Blackstone to return to his own hotel, two very lovely young ladies approached him and asked for his autograph. He obliged them, and they chatted for a moment, telling him they had come up from Alabama to attend the ball.

One of the young ladies asked, "Mr. Ellington, which hotel are you stopping at?" Duke told them, then got into a taxi and went back to his hotel.

About an hour later he received a phone call. "Mr. Ellington. Guess what? I don't know if you remember us, but we just got your autograph back in the lobby of the Blackstone Hotel, and we have just moved into your hotel, and we would like to know if you would come up and join us for a drink?"

Duke, being a gentleman, said, "Yes, I'd be glad to," and went right up to their suite. There they both were, dressed in elegant negligees. They invited him into their boudoir and things began to happen.

Meanwhile one of the girls thought it was a great idea to call Mother in Alabama, so she called Mother, who just had to talk to Duke Ellington, because she adored him so. Duke told her how charming she was and how lovely the daughters were; that they were in good hands, because Mr. Ellington was taking care of them. One of the girls told her mother, "We're fine because we're with Mr. Ellington and he's such a perfect gentleman." (In our lexicon a gentleman was a man who rested at least part of his weight on one elbow.) Meanwhile the other girl was investigating Duke. They finished the conversation and went on with the party.

111

Duke, in telling me the story, said, "Don, those girls were really well brought up. Wasn't it nice of them to call their mother?"

Meeting Martin Luther King, Jr.

MARTIN LUTHER KING, JR., FLEW FROM ATLANTA TO CHICAGO, WHERE Duke was rehearsing the musical *My People*, which he and Billy Strayhorn had written. The police and reporters met King's plane, and King left in a limousine with a police escort, sirens screaming, tearing down Michigan Boulevard.

Marian Logan, who was in the car, mentioned, "Duke Ellington is staying at the Blackstone."

King said, "Why don't we stop there. I'd like to meet Mr. Ellington."

They pulled up to the hotel and sent someone in to get Duke. He wasn't up, of course, it being daytime. The assistant manager went up to the darkened room and told Duke, "Dr. King is downstairs. He'd like very much to meet you."

Duke was excited. "What'll I wear? What'll I wear?" and eventually grabbed the same old pants and things he always wore, because he never dressed up except when he was going onstage. He just put on whatever junk was hanging around, including a white bathrobe with blue lining, and put his pork-pie hat on over his stocking cap, and they came down the elevator. When they got outside the hotel, the wind was really blowing down Michigan Boulevard.

King jumped out of the car, and they were introduced. "Dr. King . . . Dr. Ellington." Just as they embraced like old friends, a great gust of wind blew Duke's hat off, and Duke was standing there with his arms around King, wearing only his stocking cap, his bathrobe fluttering in the breeze, while the policemen chased his beat-up old porkpie hat down the street.

Politics

DURING THAT FIRST WEEK AT THE CAPITOL THEATRE IN NEW YORK CITY, when we immediately recognized each other as brother alley cats, I had said to Duke, "Hey, man. Dig everything that's happening in this country. There are black guys getting lynched; black guys getting beat up; black guys getting sent to jail for life for nothing. They're even putting dogs on people down there. There are a lot of people standing up and being counted. How come you never say anything?"

He replied, "Don, at the Capitol Theatre people come and pay seventy-five cents to see me. They're not paying to see a politician. They come here to be entertained, not politicized." Shrugging, he added, "That's it. That's the way it is."

At the time he had already written "Echoes of Harlem," "Black and Tan Fantasy," "Black, Brown and Beige" and "New World A'Comin'." Being the new boy on his block, I thought it best not to press the issue.

Many years later when the civil rights people were getting ready to march on Washington, where Martin Luther King, Jr., made that great "I have a dream" speech that roused half a nation, Dick Gregory came to Basin Street East, where Duke was working. They sat and talked over lo mein and ribs and various and sundry other goodies. Gregory told Duke he was leading the march on Washington with Sammy Davis, Jr., Lena Horne and Sidney Poitier, and asked Duke to join them.

Duke said, "You know I'm not a marcher, I'm a lover. If there's any kind of sweet sounds that you want to make for this event, you can call on me and I'll make sure that I'm in the neighborhood. But you know I never did care for walking a lot." Duke felt that Gregory was a great humorist and might be hurting himself. He said, "You can do more good for the people if you're the best at what you're doing and you conduct yourself admirably."

Bobby Kennedy, who was attorney general of the United States at the time, came in to Basin Street East to talk to Duke about the march. Without his cooperation there would be no march. He promised Duke that it would be peaceable and well protected. He told Duke that President Kennedy had been working with Joe Glaser, Duke's agent, who was helping finance the jet that was taking Lena Horne and Sidney Poitier and Sammy Davis, Jr., and a number of other artists to Washington, D.C. Duke said to Bobby Kennedy, "I'd love to go, but I've got sore feet. I can't walk that far."

Duke told me later, "I'd never get involved in anything like that. It would be daytime and hot as hell, and the sun would be

113

up and stay up all day, and besides, it would be in Washington, D.C., where I have no intention of going."

It was marvelous how tactfully Duke could deal with the most controversial issues. He could have been a politician himself. He could double-talk anybody into anything. He could charm you right out of an argument that you came prepared to give him, and make you feel so self-conscious that you apologized to him when you really wanted an apology from him. When someone asked him to play for a presidential candidate, he said, "One of the exquisite privileges, and the only moment I enjoy being alone, is when I can go into the ballot box and privately vote for the man of my choice. Once he's in that White House he's my man, whether I voted for him or not. The rare privilege that I enjoy, placing my vote as an American in private, is something I'm not going to give up."

He never got involved in any campaigning. He was asked to do an Adlai Stevenson affair when Sammy Davis, Jr., was working for Stevenson. He didn't say no, he just said he was busy.

Duke adored America. He loved everything about America, particularly the recognition he got in America wherever he went. But intellectually he didn't agree with the way the civil rights situation was being handled. He didn't really believe in the marching and the suffering and the killing. He watched it on television sometimes and said, "Those cats are crazy." On the other hand, he had such admiration for Martin Luther King, Jr., that he wrote the song, "King Fit the Battle of Alabam."

Dr. King was always calling Marian Logan (Duke's doctor's wife and one of King's foremost assistants) to come down South somewhere and do something for the cause. She was going to Mississippi on her first trip. She felt a great deal of trepidation and nervousness, despite Ramsey Clark's and Bobby Kennedy's assurances of protection. Duke called her in the middle of the day.

She said, "Arthur's not here; he's at the office."

Duke replied, "I didn't call to talk to my doctor, I called to talk to you."

She was concerned. "Oh, what's wrong?"

He said, "What in the fuck are you going to Mississippi for?"

114

He was really serious. He thought she was crazy to go. He shouted, "You've got to be out of your goddamn mind. I want you to stay here and take care of my doctor. You don't need to go to Mississippi. Let somebody else do it."

She went anyway. A bomb was thrown into the church in Mississippi where she was speaking, but fortunately she escaped without injury.

Miss Fitzpatrick

MISS FITZPATRICK WAS A JEHOVAH'S WITNESS WHO APPEARED WHEN THE band was playing at the Apollo Theatre in New York City. They looked around one day, and she was just there. She was a little old lady in her sixties who started traveling around with the band. A soft-spoken woman who read the Bible with Duke, she sat in the various dressing rooms of the members of the band and preached her litany to them. She went out to California on the train with the band.

She didn't go on the one-nighters but always showed up for a couple of weeks or a month whenever the band sat down anyplace.

She came into Hibbler's room one time when he had a horrible hangover and said, "I want to talk to you about God."

Hibbler said, "Get out of here, I don't want to talk about that shit."

Duke, who was passing, came in and said, "Did I hear what I thought I heard?" He put both his legs across Hibbler and pinned him down.

Hibbler shouted, "Will you tell her to get the fuck out of here! I've got no time to talk about God. I've been out there drinking and carrying on. I've got no time to be fucking with that woman."

Duke said, "How do you know she's not God? Have you ever seen God?" Hibbler admitted that he hadn't. Duke persisted, "Well, how do you know she's not God?" Hibbler got to thinking about it and thought maybe Duke might be right. Duke made him promise never to say anything like that again.

Sonny Greer used to tease her. "Come on in my room. I want to beat on your tom-toms. I want to make miracles. I want to make love to you."

She'd just laugh and say, "Get away, Sonny."

Everybody in the band respected her, gave her all the respect they could, unless somebody made somebody else real mad and a "motherfucker" would slip out. But as a rule they'd cool it when she was around.

Miss Fitzpatrick married Paul Black, Ted Lewis's shadow, and disappeared as softly and gently as she had originally appeared.

Yehudi Menuhin

BOB BACH WAS PRODUCING A SUMMER-REPLACEMENT TELEVISION SHOW featuring Stan Kenton on CBS called *Music '55.* He booked Duke and the band, who were playing at Jones Beach at the time, on the show. Bach, who had worked with Duke before, was casting around for an idea to make the show look a little different. At the same time Yehudi Menuhin, the great classical violinist, was coming back from Europe. Columbia Artists, who handled Menuhin, informed Bach that he was available. Bach decided to put Ellington and Menuhin, two giants, together on the same show. Menuhin, who didn't fly, sent a cable from the ship: "I will arrive on the sixteenth. Come to the Drake Hotel and we will go over what we will do."

The day after Menuhin arrived, Bach was shown up to his suite at the Drake and found him sitting cross-legged on the floor in the lotus position. There was a Steinway concert-grand piano relaxing in the corner. Bach walked over to the piano and suggested, "I think you'll stand in the curve of the piano here with your violin, and Mr. Ellington will be sitting on your right at the keyboard of the paino."

Menuhin stopped dead. He wore a puzzled expression as he enunciated in his elegant British accent, "The piano . . . He plays the piano? I thought Mr. Ellington played the trumpet."

The performance was a smash. Duke and Stan Kenton had fun with Duke's theme, "Take the A Train," as a two-piano duet. This was followed by Menuhin and Duke fraternizing on a few choruses of Duke's "Come Sunday." There were huge montage drawings on the set in the background that had been done by some young unknown named Andy Warhol.

Newport Jazz Festival

WHEN GEORGE AVAKIAN FIRST MET DUKE ELLINGTON, HE WAS EIGHTEEN years old and had just graduated from the Horace Mann High School for Boys. Duke and the band were playing a one-nighter at a country club in Scarsdale, where the family of one of Avakian's classmates were members. They arranged for Avakian to attend the performance, which took place in the swimming-pool area of the club. Duke didn't condescend to the crowd but played his full program, the same way he might at the Paramount Theatre.

At intermission Avakian went to the john and found himself standing right next to Duke in the urinal. After reading the sign on the wall—PLEASE DO NOT THROW CIGAR OR CIGARETTE BUTTS IN URINAL AS THEY BECOME VERY SOGGY AND EXTREMELY DIFFICULT TO RE-LIGHT—he took a big gulp and introduced himself. He told Duke that he admired him a great deal and collected his records; then he took another deep breath and said, "I notice that you're remaking a new 'Black and Tan Fantasy' and things of that type. Are you going to continue doing that?"

Duke replied, "We will to some extent."

Avakian continued. "How about 'Misty Morning,' 'Saratoga Swing' and some of those others?"

Duke said, "Well, it depends on whether the band that I have right now would really sound good doing those tunes. I have to think about each one of them carefully. But it's interesting that a young fellow like you knows those records."

Avakian said, "I think they're just as great as the ones I'm hearing today. How do you feel about it?"

Duke thought a moment. "You know, I don't think too often about the old records, although they sure were good, because I've got to think about keeping ahead of all these young fellows coming up. If I don't watch out, somebody's going to overtake me and I'll wonder what happened. My eye is always on the future, and I'm thinking about the next piece I'm going to write, not about the piece I wrote yesterday or the piece I wrote ten or fifteen years ago."

By this time Avakian was through urinating and Duke was replacing himself and buttoning up. (In those days they didn't

117

have zippers.) Duke took the time to continue the conversation while he was washing and air-drying his hands.

When I commented upon the fidelity of Avakian's memory, he said, "You know, you don't forget the first time you ever spoke to one of your heroes, especially when it's under such peculiar circumstances. I was just eighteen years old. He didn't have to talk to me."

Seventeen years later George Avakian was Duke's producer at Columbia Records. Duke had been booked to play at the Newport Jazz Festival, and Avakian thought it a good idea to record there. No one had ever recorded a music festival of any kind up to that time. Avakian made a proposal to the festival, which at the time was being financed by Louis Lorillard and run as a nonprofit organization. It was accepted over the protesting bodies of the people at Columbia. They went ahead, anyway, and Avakian suggested to Duke that since he was always writing something, "Is there something that you can call the 'Newport Jazz Festival Suite'?"

Duke said, "Sure, there always is."

Avakian said, "Good. Let's make that the centerpiece, and we'll pick a program to go around it. Let's try to get more than one LP if possible."

Duke called the band together and delivered a speech reminiscent of a football coach's halftime pep talk, something like Vince Lombardi exhorting the Green Bay Packers to even greater efforts. He had obviously been preparing everything, because he and Avakian had been talking on the phone while the band was on the road, and he had become very excited about the idea.

He admonished the band, "We've all worked very hard for this, and George has stuck his neck out. We only have one shot, and I know we're all going to get out there and give it everything we've got. Let's go out there and get them." Just before he hit them on the tail, he said, "Oh, incidentally, let's try something a little different. Let's play something we haven't played for a long time. We're going to do 'Diminuendo and Crescendo in Blue.'"

There was silence for a moment. Then Gonsalves said, "You mean I get up and play a lone solo? What is it? What key?"

Somebody said, "Oh, you remember. It's a change into B flat. All you do is blow the blues."

118

Duke said, "I'll bring you in and I'll take you out. That's all you have to do. Just get out there and blow your tail off. You've done it before."

Someone remembered, "Oh, yes, we've done that tune once."

Gonsalves said, "Okay, fine."

What happened then became incredible history. The reporters and critics agreed that Duke's performance of "Diminuendo and Crescendo in Blue" was one of the most exciting performances any of them had ever heard.

Duke opened with four introductory choruses on piano; by the second, the rhythm section had already laid down a rocking beat and Duke had served notice of what was to come. Three minutes later, following the long series of ensemble choruses, Duke took over for two more rocking choruses that kicked off Paul Gonsalves playing one of the longest and most unusual tenor sax solos ever captured on record.

Gonsalves played for 27 straight choruses. . . . At about his seventh chorus, the tension, which had been building both onstage and in the audience since Duke kicked off the piece, suddenly broke. A platinum-blonde girl in a black dress began dancing in one of the boxes (the last place you'd expect that in Newport!) and a moment later somebody else started in another part of the audience. Large sections of the crowd had already been on their feet; now their cheering was doubled and redoubled as the inter-reacting stimulus of a rocking performance and crowd response heightened the excitement.

Throughout the rest of the performance, there were frequent bursts of wild dancing, and literally acres of people stood on their chairs, cheering and clapping. Yet this was no rock 'n' roll reaction; despite the unbridled enthusiasm, there was a controlled, clean quality to the crowd; they were listening to Duke as well as enjoying the swirling surge of activity around them . . . (at least 7,000 were still there about midnight of the last night). Halfway through Paul's solo, it had become an enormous single living organism, reacting in waves like huge ripples to the music played before it.

Out of sight of the crowd was an unsung hero who is quite possibly the person most responsible for this explosive performance. No one will ever know for sure, but perhaps the Ellington band might never have generated that terrific beat if it weren't for Jo Jones, who had played drums that night with Teddy Wilson. Jo happened to be in a little runway below the left of the stage, at the base of the steps leading up from the musicians' tent behind the bandstand. From this vantage point, hidden from the crowd by a high canvas, but visible from the shoulders up to the musicians, Jo egged on the band with nothing more than appreciation and a rolled up copy of the 'Christian Science Monitor.' As Duke . . . drove the band in the early stages of *Diminuendo and Crescendo*, first the reed section and then the trombones and finally the rest of the band picked up on Jo, who was shouting encouragement and swatting the edge of the stage with the newspaper. . . . The saxes began hollering back at Jo, the rest of the band joined in, and by the time Gonsalves had sprung the dancers loose it seemed that bassist Jimmy Woode and drummer Sam Woodyard were playing to Jo as much as to anyone else. Even the superplacid Johnny Hodges, who will probably not raise a half-masted eyelid come millennium-time, smiled and beat time back at Jo.

Gonsalves dug in harder and harder, and when he finally gave way to Duke, the release was electric. But only for an instant, for Duke himself was swinging, and when the band pitched in with the low-register clarinets plumbing the depths, the tension built anew. With Duke and Jo still whipping up the band from opposite sides of the stage, the last choruses climbed to a climax topped by Cat Anderson, Duke's high-note specialist, who booted everybody home after the 59th chorus.

The management and the police, unable to sense the true atmosphere of that crowd, grew more apprehensive with every chorus. Fearful of a serious injury in the milling crowd, which by now had pressed forward down the aisles (the open area between the boxes and the elevated stage was already jammed with leaping fans), producer George Wein and one of the officers tried to signal Duke to stop. Duke, sensing that to stop now might really cause a riot, chose instead to soothe the crowd down with a couple of quiet numbers, with Johnny Hodges winding up the evening playing *Jeeps Blues*. George Wein shouted, "That's it," and the program was over.*

Everybody was very excited. The band knew they had done something big. Everybody was kissing everybody else. We were all throwing our arms around each other. Duke looked drained but happy. Everyone was smiling, smiling, smiling.

The Newport Jazz Festival album, from whose liner notes written by George Avakian we have quoted profusely, is the most memorable and bestselling record Duke ever made. Joe Glaser, Duke's manager at the time, said it did wonders for him on his personal appearances. Public interest in Duke perked up tremendously, and he got more work at higher prices.

*Reprinted by courtesy of Columbia Records and George Avakian.

As an eighteen-year-old boy in the mens' room at the country club when he first met Duke, George Avakian suggested that he redo some old tunes; then, as a grown man and Duke's producer at Columbia, Avakian was talking him into a new composition, the "Newport Jazz Festival Suite," when out of nowhere Duke pulled the old tune, "Diminuendo and Crescendo in Blue" from the period when they first met, a move that catapulted Duke back to the top of the musical heap.

A Waitress in New Orleans

IN NEW ORLEANS THERE WAS A RESTAURANT WHERE DUKE AND LOUIS ARMstrong hung out. There was one cute little waitress who went the other way when she saw them coming because of the teasing she always got from them. One day they came in, and she went over to the table and said, "Mr. Ellington, Mr. Armstrong, I just scratched what y'all like."

Armstrong replied, "That's all right, baby, just go back, wash your hands and bring us some cheeseburgers."

Washington, D.C.

I HAD SPENT A FEW DAYS IN D.C. WITH DUKE WHILE HE PLAYED THE CARTER-Barron Stadium, with Ella Fitzgerald and Oscar Peterson as his supporting performers. On the closing night, when it started to rain, he decided he would leave early instead of staying for the final bows with Ella. On the way back to the hotel, we stopped off at the Shoreham to trade a few jibes with Louis Armstrong, who was playing there.

At first the maitre d' wouldn't let us in because Duke was wearing one of his blue sweaters. He looked down his nose at Duke. "Sir, nobody is permitted in without a jacket . . . " Then he he recognized Duke. "Oh, I beg your pardon, Mr. Ellington." They rolled out the red carpet and room was made for us.

It turned out to be Louie's birthday. As he spotted Duke he announced, "Ladies and gentlemen, there's guy in the audience who's been my favorite since I was a kid. He's been my man since I was a little child."

Duke, nothing loath to join in the game, retaliated with, "When I was on my mother's knee, she told me how wonderful Louis Armstrong was."

Many people came to the table for autographs while Duke

was eating, and he was most charming to them. One man said excitedly, "Duke, do you remember me? I met you in 1937 in Miami, Florida."

Duke replied, "How could I forget you?" which pleased the man and his wife enormously.

After the show Louie invited us up to his suite for a birthday party. We were introduced to Louie's doctor, who traveled with him a great deal. At one point Louie opened a suitcase filled with vitamins, saying, "I'm the happiest hypochondriac there is." He showed us a laxative called Swiss Kriss and gave it credit for keeping him healthy and in good shape. He was excited and happy to have Duke there with him, especially on his birthday. (Ella and Duke's band were still back at the Carter-Barron performing in the rain.)

We cut the cake, which Louie didn't eat, and then Duke said, "We hate to do it, Louie, but we have to split now. We've got to finish packing and drive back to New York."

We got a cab back to the Washington Hilton, and Duke went to his suite to see if the Countess had finished his packing, while I went to my room to put the final touches on mine. I was really zonked by that time. I'd been drinking at the Shoreham, then at the birthday party, and topped it off with a few in my room.

My bags were ready, and I was waiting for a bellman to come get them and take them to the car when there was a knock on the door. I expected it might be Harry Carney, the great baritone sax player and buddy of Duke's, who always drove whenever Duke was making one of his jumps, but it turned ut to be the band manager, instead, who brought a message from Duke. "Tell Don that he's not going to ride back in the car with us, that he can take a cab to the airport and take the plane back to New York."

I was loaded. I got a picture of myself. Instead of throwing stuff into the car and whoosh! off we go, I'd be getting a cab to the airport, getting on the plane in the middle of the night without a ticket, getting off in New York, getting another cab, then getting to where I had to go in New York. I said to myself, "What kind of shit is this?" Then I went over to Duke's suite and I romped and I stomped and I yelled, "You motherfucker, you're not my brother anymore, you're not even my cousin." I tore out of the room and took the plane back to New York.

A few days later I felt remorseful. This is my buddy; how can I call him a motherfucker and tell him he's not my brother anymore. I called him at the hotel in Boston where he was working. He got on the phone. I said, "Edward?"

He said, "Don," as though nothing had happened. "Are we cousins again?" A few days later I received a box of Pfaelzer steaks that he sent me from Chicago.

Europe: 1933

DUKE WAS VERY CLOSE TO THE KINGS AND QUEENS AND RULERS OF MANY countries throughout the world. He not only loved them, they loved him. He was proud of his honors, starting with the French Legion of Honor. He received awards from every country in Europe, Asia, Africa and Australia. He received an award from Wales that even Richard Burton, the greatest living male actor, had not as yet received. He was awarded more doctorates than anyone else in the world, black or white.

I'm so glad he smelled the roses while he was here.

One cold bus-riding night, between Denver and Salt Lake City, I cajoled him into telling me the story of a trip the band took to Europe in 1933.

Duke leaned back and relaxed. "I wouldn't fly in those days. I believed in Louie's [Armstrong] famous saying, 'I don't want to be on the plane when the pilot's number is up,' so we sailed on the *Ile de France*. It was a beautiful ship; hand-carved woodwork and marble all over the place, and the greatest food impeccably cooked by at least a squadron of French chefs. I had a stateroom way up top. Man, I could see a million miles of ocean through that porthole." (Later Duke confessed to me that in 1912, as a child of thirteen, he had read about the *Titanic*. He had never forgotten it, and on this first trip across the Atlantic, he spent every night on deck, fearfully watching out for icebergs.)

In Paris the band played a concert at the Palais Chaleux. They played the first half, and then there was an hour interval—intermission, we call it—during which there was a fabulous buffet on a great long table laden with delicious foods and cognac, champagne, wine and that rarity in Paris . . . Scotch. The people, aristocrats and servants, some on their hands and knees, were busily searching for something on the floor. A duchess, who was one of the hostesses, had lost one of her larger diamonds, and the chances of her having it returned in that crowd were about equal to your chances of getting your watch back that was borrowed from you by somebody during the rush hour on the New York subway. The duchess finally got bored seeing people looking all over the floor for the ring. She looked around haughtily, then took Duke by the arm, saying, "It doesn't mean anything. I can always get diamonds, but how often can I get a man like Duke Ellington?"

She disappeared with Duke. The band started the second half by themselves, and eventually Duke smilingly reappeared to finish the concert.

Later, gathering up Sonny Greer from the Crazy Horse Saloon, they made their way to London. In London Duke had a temporary problem getting into a proper hotel. The gossip columnists, as often happens, had a field day. The more repeatable questions were, "How black is he?" "Does he have thick lips and crinkly hair?" Eventually, through the good offices of Jack Hylton, England's premier band leader at the time, Duke was safely ensconced at the plush Dorchester, where Lord Beaverbrook, the newspaper mogul, and other social greats of the kingdom came to the rescue, making certain that he was socially as well as musically accepted.

Duke and the band were working at the Palladium when Duke was invited to Lord Beaverbrook's home and to the royal palace. At parties he played double piano with the King of England, who told him, "I have five hundred of your records." He taught the King the Charleston—"Come on, King, you can do it"—and became close buddies with the Prince of Wales. (In later years when the Prince came to the States, he was frequently in Duke's company. Wallie Simpson, the lady from Baltimore, wasn't overly enthused about the friendship between Duke and the Prince of Wales. It was hard for her to comprehend why they would spend so much time together.)

Duke spent most of his early A.M.'s cheerfully engaged in enjoying the delights of Jeanette MacDonald ("My mother Daisy taught me to gravitate toward beauty, so here I am") and Anna May Wong ("I picture you lying on a crescent moon, bathed in roses") and generally having a wonderful time.

From London the band went to Edinburgh, where Duke did

the town with an old buddy, Sir Harry "Roamin' Through the Glo'amin' " Lauder, who sang annually at the Winter Garden Theatre in New York. Duke smiled as he remembered. "He'd be wearing kilts and stockings with tassels and a hat with ribbons down the back and carry a knobby walking stick that looked like a shillelagh when he came to visit us at the Cotton Club in New York, bringing along his friends Lord and Lady Mountbatten, cousins of the King of England. [Duke was laughing now.] Some of the more sincere drinkers of Harlem looked almost ready to take the pledge when they first saw that little group."

AMAZING ELLINGTON
Editorial—London—July 1933

Ellington the Amazing. Ellington the Musician. Ellington the Showman. Ellington the Artist! How can I, in such a limited space, describe the unbelievable spectacle I have just beheld at the Palladium on the occasion of the Duke's initial performance in London?

We in England never see or hear such things. Picture the calm, collected Ellington, sitting at the piano, playing and directing his mighty band, without any ostensible effort whatever, yet all teams playing with the most bewildering precision ever heard from any dance orchestra. And a colossal array of coloured musicians in immaculate grey evening dress, playing a mighty collection of glittering gold instruments, not only with all that uncanny musicianship that you expect, but with showmanship never before seen in this country. The question arises: How is it all done?

It is the thrill of a lifetime to hear what must undoubtedly be the world's finest brass team, six of them (I said six of them!) and those four saxes, clarinets, and the big showman who makes Louis Armstrong insignificant—Fred Jenkins—whose solo work brought such applause that the Duke's piano solo was completely inaudible.

The house roared its genuine appreciation of what was the greatest spectacle in jazz that this country has ever seen. Ellington was always composed, always the gentleman, even to announcing his own compositions, to which he charmingly alluded as "our own composition."

125

With this wonderful orchestra, to which no gramophone record has yet done justice, are Bailey and Derby, a sensational dance team of two coloured boys whose footwork is as perfect as the band. Noticeably clever is the elimination of all rhythm while they dance, the band playing legato and pianissimo, leaving the rhythm entirely to the "hoofing" of this clever duo. This is another instance of Ellington thoroughness.

Ivie Anderson is a coloured lady who sings "Stormy Weather" as you'll never hear it again. Another valuable addition to the show is a dusky belle called Bessie Dudley, who shakes a hip with such style and personality that it makes you wonder if the British vaudeville stage could ever provide such talent without importing it. She danced to "Rockin' in Rhythm," an adequate title for her dynamic performance.

And high up on a rostrum, picturesque with his glittering array of percussion instruments, was greased lightning Sonny Greer himself, the perfect drummer, showman and vocalist.

"Tiger Rag" was another surprise, since it was played pianissimo. Never have I heard men play so perfectly together, with such thorough understanding and so perfectly effortless.

As I write this I am still under the spell of Ellington's show. I realise that these words are too perfectly inadequate to describe what I have just heard and seen. The house rocked in wild delight, showing an enthusiasm such as I have never before witnessed in a theatre.

The Duke has not only provided a musical thrill for musicians, but a show for the general public and his visit, to say the very least, must stimulate the most active interest in dance music in this country. Irving Mills must be truly proud of his Ellington.

Finally, a word of praise and many grateful thanks to Jack Hylton for making this historical visit possible. By bringing the Ellington aggregation to England he has given the entertainment industry something to think about and the public something to talk about. He has given us something we have never heard or seen before in this country, and never will again— Ellington the superb.

Renee Diamond

LIVING IN LONDON AT THE TIME THAT DUKE AND THE BAND MADE THEIR 1933 trip to Europe was a thirteen-year-old girl named Renee. She was already a big fan of Duke's, having listened to him by the hour on his recordings. She and her sister wanted to see Duke at the Palladium, but the show was booked solid for the two weeks it was there. Taking a chance, she called Duke from the lobby of his hotel, the Dorchester. He arranged for them to get tickets to the show for the first performance. At Duke's invitation, they went backstage afterward, thanked him and told him what a great time they had had. Duke suggested they come back for the second show, but they were afraid their father would be worried if they didn't get home in time, so Duke volunteered to call him and explain the circumstances.

The kids were tremendously impressed. This great, wonderful, tall, exciting, handsome muscial giant was their host for two performances and dinner. He introduced them to Ivie Anderson and Johnny Hodges and Sonny Greer and played some tunes for them on the backstage piano. When Renee heard Duke's magnificent "Rockin' in Rhythm," it opened vistas for her of a new and thrilling kind of music. It was a moving sight to see the great Duke Ellington, composer extraordinaire, comrade of kings, playboy of the Western world, consort musically with two teenagers, wooing them to his version of four beats to a bar. He sent them home in a taxi, deliriously and exhaustedly happy.

Duke and the band eventually went back to the States, and all through the intervening years he kept in touch with Renee by transatlantic telephone, constantly inquiring about her health, her school and her parents, promising to come to see her soon. He never wrote to her because he never wrote a letter to anyone, about anything.

It wasn't until 1948 that Duke returned to England, by which time Renee was married and the proud mother of a little girl. This time Duke returned with only Kay Davis and Ray Nance, without the big band. It was the first time Renee and Duke had had the opportunity to see each other in fifteen years.

Duke, except when he was performing, usually stayed holed up at his favorite hotel, the Dorchester, but once—wonder of wonders—he went to the Ascot races with Renee and her husband, Leslie, of whom he was becoming rather fond. The bright sunlight, however, and the out-of-tempo pounding of the horses' hoofs soon inspired him return to his hotel suite.

The following day, when Renee phone Duke at the hotel, she couldn't get through for hours. Both Duke and Frank Sinatra were in London at the same time, staying on the same floor of the Dorchester. Duke was there working, and Frank was in romantic pursuit of a titled lady. Frank, hounded by adoring fans (who had been goaded on by the gossip columnists) almost to the door of his own suite, hung out in his buddy Duke's digs, swapping stories and Jack Daniels until the coast was clear and he was able to resume the chase.

The next time Duke returned to London, Renee and Leslie and their daughter had just just moved to a new flat on the corner of Hartford Street and Park Lane in the posh Mayfair district, just across the street from the Hilton and close to the Dorchester. They had been there just a few hours and were deeply touched when the first phone call they received was from Duke. He said he was going to come by that night, bringing over a hundred guests from the big reception that was being held at the Phillips Recording Studio on Stanhope Place, to celebrate the completion of his latest album. The announcement caused Renee a bit of panic, but she told Duke she'd be glad to have them.

A short while later there was a knock on the door, and she opened it to find four big, husky men. She was a bit taken aback. "Yes?"

"Mrs. Renee Diamond?" questioned the biggest man.

"Yes?" she repeated.

He said, "We have a present for you from Mr. Duke Ellington." They carried in a Steinway baby-grand piano and set it in a corner of the room, where it fit as though it had been born there. Renee was excited beyond words. She knew that Duke was coming to play on her piano, the piano he had given them.

About an hour after the arrival of the piano, two huge cases of whiskey arrived. Soon afterward the house was filled to overflowing with guests.

Duke entered to applause and bravos, and after bestowing the four kisses on everyone (gentlemen included), quietly seated himself at the piano, upon which a small vase of roses rested. One single petal had fallen on the piano. The room was

Duke Ellington and Lena Horne, ca. 1940.

Duke and Don, 1943 *Collection of Don George.*

Duke and Billy Strayhorn (Sweetpea).

Marian Logan, Duke, and Dr. Arthur Logan, April 28, 1970. *Collection of Marian Logan.*

Evie and Duke. *Collection of Eve Ellis Ellington.*

Duke giving a concert at Odyssey House, 1972. Tony Miles, an ex-drug addict, and now Vice President for Human Services at Odyssey Institute, is at the right. *Odyssey Institute, Inc.*

Duke accepting an award for his Jazzmobile concerts, September 6, 1970, at 129th Street between Fifth and Lenox avenues. *John Canada.*

Duke Ellington and Louis Armstrong in Paris in 1969 while working on the motion picture *Paris Blues*. Sam Shaw.

In this picture mailed from Japan to his close friends June and Walter Read, Duke signed himself "Eddie," a name no one ever called him before or after. He was more than a little weary these days, and perhaps the childishness of the name evoked memories of a happy and carefree childhood. *June Read.*

S. I. Hayakawa, Shela Xoregos, and Duke Ellington, 1967. *By permission of the Collection of Shela Xoregos.*

Mercer Ellington leading the band, Ella Fitzgerald at the microphone; Mike Douglas on stool. Duke's grandson, Edward, in center background behind Ella. In 1964, to Duke's gratification, his son Mercer had rejoined the band, playing in the trumpet section and handling the band's finances. After Duke's death in 1974, Mercer assumed leadership of the band, thereby helping to perpetuate the Ellington legend. *Michael Leshnov, Photographer—Group W Productions.*

Duke Ellington and his protégé, the blind pianist Brook Kerr. *From the collection of Edith Exton.*

Don George and Lady Allison Assante outside the Cathedral of St. John the Divine after the funeral service for Duke Ellington, 1974. *Bert Smith.*

lit mostly by candles, for Duke intensely disliked overly bright lights. He sat at the piano, his fingers gently caressing the keyboard. After a few moments he played the most beautiful Debussy-like melody, which he later called "Single Petal of a Rose" and told Renee that he had written it for her.

Soon after that evening, at the Leeds Festival, Duke was presented to Her Majesty the Queen for the first time. He phoned Renee and said, "This is the most wonderful moment of my life. She's just so gracious, so beautiful."

About a month later, after he returned to the States, he phoned Renee and like a little boy said, "Renee, darling, don't be angry with me, but I loved the 'Single Petal' so much that I have decided, with your permission, to present this in a whole suite to Her Majesty the Queen, and I think I shall title it 'The Queen's Suite.'"

Later, while he was on another European tour, Duke invited Renee and Leslie to join him and the band at the jazz festival in Antibes, which is held during July. Afterward they drove at breakneck speed along the winding Riviera roads to the Galerie Maeght in the town of St. Paul de Vence, where they were due for a recital. Renee was frightened witless by the speed, but Duke gloried in it. The car could not go fast enough for him. Upon arriving at the galerie, they were greeted by a hysterical Frenchman who informed them that the Steinway concert-grand piano, which had been specially ordered for the occasion, was completely out of tune.

Renee threw up her hands in horror. Duke said, "Well, just a moment now." He put his arm through Renee's soothingly. "Let's just you and me go over to that piano and see; if it's out of tune at the bottom, we'll play it at the top. If it's out of tune at the top, we'll play it at the middle. I don't think these people know what terrible pianos I've played on during my life." The piano turned out to be superbly in tune, and Duke's playing was equally superb.

Whenever Duke said to his audiences all over the world, "I love you. I love you madly," he did really love everybody madly. This statement was never truer than at the Galerie Maeght, where he became engrossed in a model to whom he had taken a true Ellington fancy. Walking behind her on his way to the car, he tripped on the curb and fell forward, bruising his knees rather badly. While being helped to his feet by the solicitous members of the band, he half-ruefully, half-whimsically observed to Renee, "Maybe I'd be better off watching the curbs instead of the curves."

Duke and the band arrived in Paris one morning after playing a concert in Brest. They had taken the train in and arrived at about 7:30 A.M. On the platform stood Renee and Leslie, with champagne and toast. They looked like they had been partying all night. They shouted, "We're the Ellington Fan Club," acting like teenagers. It was such a lift for Duke. He loved it.

Duke had the capacity for so many different types of love— paternal, passionate, loving; as a lover, as a son, as a brother. And he expressed all of these different kinds of love in his music. Renee brought out the paternal side of his nature, in that she seemed to fulfill his need for the daughter he never had.

When she was asked about Duke, Renee replied. "I loved him. Duke Ellington was perhaps the calmest, most dignified personality in show business. Very few things seemed to upset him. He could improvise in any situation, but he did not like to be asked when he was going to retire, or even more he detested the question, which I once heard a reporter ask him, 'Duke, how do you rate Count Basie?'

"Duke looked at him in horror and said, 'Rate him? You don't rate a musician or an artist, you only rate a basket of tomatoes,' as he walked off in a great huff.

"Yes," she continued, "he is Duke Ellington. He lives only for today, and writes his music for tomorrow."

L'eau Chaude

DUKE DIDN'T DRINK COFFEE OR TEA. HE ONLY DRANK HOT WATER. HE WAS at a café on the Champs Élysées in Paris with his valet when the waiter came to take the order.

Duke said, *"S'il vous plaît, Monsieur, l'eau chaude."**

The waiter turned to the valet, who, eager to prove his sophistication, said, "I think I'll have some of that *l'eau chaude* too, man."

*Hot water.

130

Command Performance

THE BAND HAD JUST RETURNED FROM AFRICA, AND DUKE DID A COMMAND performance in London for Her Majesty the Queen, for the benefit of the Actors Equity Benevolent Fund. On the receiving line after the performance, Philip came by, looked at Duke and said, "My God, Duke, when have you slept last?"

Duke replied, "I don't know. I think I slept about three or four months ago."

Philip said, "The band sounds great, and it's always a pleasure seeing you, and say: Why don't we all go back to the Palace and put some eggs on. We can have a jam session."

Duke was all for it. "Let's go, baby."

Then the Queen came and extended her hand. Duke bowed, looked at her, and said, "Your Majesty, since I've last seen you, your beauty has compounded ten times."

She just buckled at her knees.

Back in the dressing room Duke was questioned about his incredible way with the ladies. He explained, "It's very simple. You just tell the Queen of England the same thing you tell little Paula who works down at the pool hall."

Dedication

DUKE HAD MARVELOUS DREAMS. HE WAS SO DEDICATED TO THEM THAT HE made them come true. Nothing frightened him. He wore the kind of face that children do who don't get frightened easily by things they decide they want—to fly a kite or climb a tree—who never deviate but stay on that one track until they get to where they're going. He was ageless. He never thought in terms of years. He thought in terms of things, of ideas, of feelings. He was tremendously dedicated to doing what he knew best, what mattered most to him. His greatness stemmed from his ability to overcome the most incredible obstacles.

From the start, from the time he was a kid in Washington, hustling gigs, and when he came to New York playing dollar rent parties, he was dedicated. He was so completely music minded and so creative that the creativity started as soon as he was big enough to get up to a piano and didn't stop until the day he died. Even after he became famous, nothing was laid out for him on a silver platter. He still had to get out there every day and prove himself.

Men like Duke Ellington are unique in that they give their whole lives to the public. Duke worked 360 days of every year, but he always tried to be home for Christmas and New Year's. He considered New York City his home. He loved New York City. He loved to walk on Fifth Avenue at four o'clock in the morning, heading for Reuben's. He loved New York taxi drivers. He enjoyed a tremendous conversational rapport with them.

Once there was a limousine waiting to take him to CBS to do a Mike Wallace show, and he was disappointed because he wasn't going to ride and chat with a New York taxi driver. He always said to me, "Don, give the man double the fare."

In some ways Duke was an unsung hero. His very success illustrated to the world what democracy was about. We sent emissaries to Russia and Poland to talk in the schools, and to their ambassadors and their heads of state, and the communication wasn't half as meaningful as a black man from humble beginnings coming there to perform and communicating without a knowledge of the language but with music and warmth, as Duke did, right to the people. Through the years he took the message of democracy unrehearsed to every corner of the world.

On one of his journeys Duke met Louis Armstrong in Paris, where they were both scheduled as guests on an Edward R. Murrow show. They had been circling the globe in different directions for the State Department, and as old and good buddies were more than happy to be together again. After chiding Murrow on the inordinate number of cigarettes he consumed, they cabbed to the famous cheese restaurant on the rue Amsterdam and compared notes.

Louis told Duke that when he went to Africa, there was a war on among the Mombassans, Somalians and Swahili, he wasn't quite sure which, but they called a truce and stopped fighting when he got there.

He shook his head, remembering. "I was dropped right in the middle of the jungle, and they carried me in on a beach chair on their shoulders. Man, don't let anyone tell you you come from Africa. I don't feel no way like I belong to those cats." Louis felt that there was nothing in the style of dress or the manner of speaking that made him feel that he had anything in common with them except the color of their skin.

Duke teased him. "You're a pretty important man, Louie. You stopped a war."

Louis shrugged. "As soon as I left they started all over again." Reaching for his fourth helping, he said, "Man, this is great cheese." Stretching, he added, "Well, I guess it's time for me to take a little vacation, Duke. How about you?"

Duke gazed off into the distance. "Louie, what would I do? Where would I go? In my work I go all over the world. There's no place for me to take a vacation. I'll tell you. I enjoy the whole thing just the way it is, because I have a band waiting. The day after I compose something, I can hear the music. Who can do that? A playwright has to wait for a producer to produce a play, but I have an immediate playback on what I've composed. That's what keeps me going. That's what interests me the most. It's not the gigs themselves, Louis. The gigs keep the band going. What keeps me going is to be able to compose and do the work."

Louis interrupted, saying, "Man, don't you ever stop?"

Duke replied, "Maybe I don't need a vacation." He smiled. "I have a complete change of pace every day, so at least I don't get bored. As long as something is unfinished, there's always that little feeling of insecurity. And a feeling of insecurity is absolutely necessary unless you're so rich that it doesn't matter."

Louis looked at the clock on the wall. "Well, time to split. I've got to make that plane." After paying the check, they kissed and started on their separate ways.

Duke looked back and waved to Louis. "So long, baby. See you around."

Flying

DUKE HAD A TREMENDOUS FEAR OF FLYING. HE KEPT COMING UP WITH THE same cliché we've heard many times. If God wanted man to fly, he'd have given us wings. He practically murdered another cliché. Somebody once said to Duke's buddy, Louis Armstrong, who absolutely wouldn't fly, "Well, Louis, when your

133

number's up that will be it," and Louie came back with the great line that's been repeated so many thousands of times. "Yeah, but I don't want to be there when the pilot's number is up." Duke felt pretty much the same way.

He was one of the earthbound legion of otherwise-daring and adventurous souls like Bing Crosby, Ralph Newcombe, Bob Newhart, Tallulah Bankhead, Jackie Jensen and so many others; performers, politicians, athletes, film and TV personalities, people who found it necessary to travel extensively, but who found it emotionally impossible to accept anything involving the atmosphere or the stratosphere as a means of transportation. Like them, Duke preferred conserving his celestial activities under the hereafter. Besides, he enjoyed going back and forth to Europe on the great transatlantic liners like the *France*, where he hosted incredible farewell parties that lasted for hours and hours, with all kinds of wonderful people and lots of kissing and hugging.

It was on one of those trips that he met a wealthy woman and her daughter from Baltimore, both of them extremely attractive. Before long they had a ménage à trois going in full blossom. In Paris they introduced him to the Sphinx, the most fantastic house of ill repute in the Western world, where they had box seats for the show. Afterward they all enjoyed themselves in supposedly private rooms with selected performers.

Duke was in West Germany. He had been booked into Berlin. To go from where he was in West Germany to Berlin, he would either have to drive on the Autobahn, which was in East Germany, or fly over it. The cold war between the United States and Soviet Russia, which controlled East Germany, was at its height. Duke was a little skeptical, wondering whether it would be okay to drive through there.

Strayhorn said to him, "Duke, what if they kidnap us on the Autobahn? You're a big, important American. You're known all over the world. If they kidnap you they can get all sorts of concessions from the United States government."

Duke really became upset. He asked, "Do you really suppose they might try to grab us.?"

Strayhorn continued, "We know what kind of people the East Germans are. They built that wall between East and West

Germany with barbed wire on top and tanks all around. If anyone tries to get out, they make no attempt to capture them, they just machine gun them to death."

Duke was worried. "What do you think we should do?"

Strayhorn replied, "Between the Russian ground and the American air, I don't think we have much choice, Duke. Besides, I heard the guys in the band talking. They'd much rather fly than take their chances of getting through Checkpoint Charlie [the exit on the Autobahn to Berlin] without an incident."

With the utmost trepidation, Duke finally consented to fly for the first time. He looked around nervously, and his hands were not completely under control as he boarded the plane. He refused a window seat but took one on the aisle, and through the entire, somewhat short journey kept his gaze fixed straight ahead, with his fingers curved tightly about the arms of his seat until the knuckles showed white. He was cajoled and stroked by the airline personnel and members of the band.

When the plane touched down in Berlin and Duke realized that he was safely on solid ground once more, a happy metamorphosis took place. He got off the plane all smiles, his usual wonderful, gregarious self, without a trace of the trauma he had felt during the flight. When the mayor of Berlin welcomed him, he responded cheerfully after bestowing the four kisses upon him, "Your Honor, that was the best flight I've ever had."

From that day forward he fell in love with planes. Whenever possible, he would travel no other way.

Books

DUKE WAS AN AVID READER AND COLLECTOR OF BOOKS. HE HAD DICTIONaries and thesauruses in many languages. English/French, English/Spanish, English/Italian. He had Webster's unabridged and *Language Usage*. He had Shakespeare and *Mother Goose*. He had almost every classic of mythology hibernating among his religious books. He had *A Mingled Chime*, the autobiography of Sir Thomas Beecham, with an inscription inside reading, "To Duke Ellington from his admiring colleague, Thomas Beecham, August 10, 1943."

Duke had always wanted to be a singer and to be an actor. In all his copies of the Shakespearean plays, he had underlined parts that appealed to him, not only to be set to music but to be performed by him. His library revealed Duke's love of the written word, his great longing for communication. It is not only proven in the songs he wrote but in the books he collected. Communication among people was very important to him.

He wanted to communicate with people of all ages and never really face reality. Once he looked out at the skyline of New York and said to me, "Don, you know why people don't want to die? Because this world is such a beautiful place."

Duke had two versions of *The Temptation of St. Anthony* by Gustave Flaubert. He wanted to learn about the different facets of a creative writer so he could get a true evaluation of him.

He had everything by Shakespeare, in many different versions. Someone had once told him there was an Ellington crest among the Scottish seals, and so he had the *History of the Scottish Seals*. He had the *Songs of Billitus*.

Passage after passage in his books is underlined, indicating that there were far more ambitions in this man than the average human being could appreciate by just seeing the orchestra leader and composer. He had the desire and the need constantly to learn, constantly to recharge his batteries and become a new source of energy for something different. He never wished to hit a sour note in communication. He was starving and thirsty for knowledge at all times. He was like a sponge; he could absorb whatever his eyes could see or whatever his ears could hear. He journeyed from Sartre to *The Adventures of Alice in Wonderland*, of which he had five versions. He adored *Alice in Wonderland*. He wanted to set *Alice in Wonderland* to music. Whatever the rabbit said absolutely gassed him, because he underlined everything the rabbit said.

Like the rabbit, he was always late for a very important date. That little song was doubly underlined in every version. He obviously fashioned himself after the rabbit, and he also thought of himself as Alice because he could be so many people. He could be as little as Alice when she was under a mushroom, or he could be a giant in whatever role he wished to play. He could do it. He could fit in anywhere. Duke was so together it was unreal. He was so evasive at the same time that you could never put your finger on any part of him. A lady could sleep with him and never really reach him and know who the real man was. There were so many Duke Ellingtons. He had the ability to be the man the person he was with wanted him to be. He was the Duke Ellington that he thought Sinatra wanted him to be; with Pastor Gensel, he became the religious figure who was doing sacred music. In England he could be as grand and as gallant as the Queen of England dreamed he would be. He could be whatever the occasion called for. He was Duke Ellington.

Evie

WHEN DUKE FIRST SAW EVIE ELLIS WORKING IN A CHICAGO CLUB, SHE WAS sixteen years old. She was breathtakingly exquisite, looking very much like a young Kay Francis. He liked her so much that he had his agent, Joe Glaser, the multimillionaire owner of Associated Booking, bring her to New York and book her into the Cotton Club as a showgirl. Shortly thereafter Duke, who had been living with Mildred Dixon, another of the Cotton Club showgirls, changed partners and Evie began to share the master's abode. Glaser had brought her to New York for Duke, but after she got here and started to blossom, she became the most outstanding girl in the Cotton Club line, and Glaser tried to romance her for himself. Evie wanted no part of him romantically, but they became very good friends.

When their Cotton Club days were over, Duke and Evie moved down to an apartment on Central Park West. Evie became a homebody. She had dinner parties for people close to Duke who had very little family life of their own before Evie came into their midst. There were Thanksgiving dinners, Christmas dinners, graciously prepared and served with love. She found pleasure in bringing life and warmth to their home.

Duke began to travel extensively with the band, both in this country and abroad. He had exquisite taste and brought Evie the most wonderful gifts—a diamond ring, matched jewelry, robes and nightgowns and lingerie all satin and lace. She liked Joy perfume, and he had it sent to her by the carton.

Duke was discreet in his affairs. His inner life and feelings were hidden behind a charismatic veil of charm. Publicly he was the most charming, most delightful master of ceremonies. Privately he was a romping, stomping alley cat. He could no more be faithful to one woman than he could be to one piece of music. When he finished the song or music he was writing, he went on to the next, to return occasionally to replay an old favorite. So it was with his ladies. But he was very gallant. He never completely finished a relationship with either a song or a lady, so he had a string of them just hanging on.

On the surface Evie seemed unaware of Duke's peccadilloes, but with all the rumors and gossip distilled by friends and strangers alike, she must have known at least some of what was going on.

Later on, when Duke wanted to live farther downtown, they moved to a three-bedroom, terraced apartment on West End Avenue that had a panoramic view of the lower city, the Hudson River and the Jersey Palisades. The bedroom with the upright piano was soundproofed so that Duke could play all night if he wanted to without disturbing anyone. The smaller bedroom contained the electric piano. One room was his writing room; the other room held all his books and shelves and shelves of manuscripts: work finished, work in progress, work about to be started. The writing room was blue—blue walls, navy blue furniture, blue bedding.

Evie made a personal island of the apartment for Duke; a haven; a port in a storm. She handled everything like nobody else could . . . sent vitamins to St. Louis on such and such a date, called the hospital to get a prescription, called John Popkin at the Hickory House to send the steaks. . . . When I teased her about it, she laughed good-naturedly, saying, "I've got to earn my keep."

As time went on Duke became more careless about his in flagrante delictos, and they came more and more to the attention of Evie, who was a lady of deep passions that were impossible for her to subdue at all times.

One evening Duke was at the Logans, noodling around on the piano, when the phone rang.

Duke said, "If that's Evie, don't tell her I'm here."

Logan's wife picked up the phone. "Yes . . . Yes, Evie." [Pause] "No, he's not here." [Pause] "Yes, yes. Well, all right, if

138

you want to." She hung up and turned to Duke. "Evie said she's coming right over."

There was a demijohn, kind of a powder room, right off the kitchen. They put Duke in there to hide him. A few minutes later there was a banging on the door, and they let Evie in. She had obviously been involved with a bit of the grape. She was wild-eyed and bushy-tailed and loaded for bear.

She demanded, "Have you seen Duke?"

Logan said, "No, we haven't seen him. Here, let me take your coat." He was startled. "Hey, what are you doing with a gun in your pocket?"

"It's for that bastard, Edward. Every time I turn around, he's with another woman. This time it's a countess. He's really swinging with her."

Logan repeated, "Duke's not here."

They were standing on the landing that led to the upstairs bedrooms.

Evie pouted. "I've been to his barber looking for him, and I've been to his tailor and earlier I went over to his dentist. I can't find him anyplace." Belligerently, she said, "When I find him, by Christ, he's going to know it." If she had seen him she probably would have pulled the trigger.

Marian pleaded, "Evie, it's probably all gossip. You don't really believe it, do you?"

Evie was there for nearly an hour before they could convince her to leave. When he was sure she had left, Duke came out of the john, walked over to the piano and resumed playing at the point where he had been interrupted.

Duke spent more and more time traveling with the band, in the States and around the world. He was seldom at home. Evie very often went to the theater. She went to openings with Peggy Lee. She spent evenings with Lena Horne and weekends in the Hamptoms with the Edmund Andersons. She went to Saratoga. More and more she lavished affection on Davy, the miniature poodle that Joe Glaser had given them. (Barbra Streisand got Davy's sister, which in some way made them distant relatives.) But she took nothing away from Duke. She was always there when he needed her.

One night she got a phone call saying that the Countess was staying with Duke at the Statler Hilton Hotel in Detroit while the band was playing across the lake in Windsor, Ontario. She constantly heard stories about Duke and the Countess being seen together and began to brood about the situation. She found out that they were together in Japan. She needed someone to talk to and went to Marian Logan, her confidante, saying she was going to fly to Tokyo to confront them. Marian spent two days trying to talk her out of it, meanwhile telling her husband, whom Duke called every day, to warn Duke to be on his guard.

Three days later Logan phoned Duke and said, "Evie's not coming. Marian called her this morning and she's still here."

Duke, feeling safe, moved the Countess back into their suite.

Without saying a word to anyone, Evie took the plane and flew halfway around the world to Tokyo. Arriving at Duke's hotel, she announced to the man at the desk that she was Mrs. Ellington, and he sent her upstairs without checking. Entering the suite, she was greeted by the Countess's little dog barking and jumping all over her. She opened the door to the bedroom, and there were the Countess and Duke in bed. Pandemonium ensued, with Evie screaming and waving a gun around, demanding that he make a choice between them, which of course he was unable to do, and the Countess's dog barking and the Countess hightailing it out of the room for parts unknown.

Duke didn't know what to do. He just couldn't face the fact that he had to solve a problem, so he called Bobby, the band boy, and said, "Bobby, take Evie downstairs and get her some coffee."

That was his solution. As she was leaving the room, Duke said to her, "I'll have somebody talk to you about it."

Duke wasn't cruel or vindictive. He was no monster. He didn't have a mean bone in his body. He was emotionally constructed in such a fashion that there was nothing else he could do. He was just completely incapable of existing with turmoil or negativeness or uproar. It was just that Duke was Duke. He lived where the roses lived, where rainbows were born. He walked wth the gods, his head in the stars. He could no more resist loving romance and beauty than he could resist breathing.

Evie eventually came to understand all this, and they remained together.

Years later, when Duke was dying in the hospital, Evie came early in the mornings when no one else was there. She brought some fancy ice cream or the strawberry cheesecake he liked, some manuscripts that he could run down on the piano he had installed in his hospital room or whatever else he wanted. Jim Lowe, Duke's man, would phone her and say, "The boss wants his blue pajamas," and she would bring them. She went to Alexander Shields, Duke's favorite shop on Park Avenue, and ordered a cornflower blue, terry velour caftan with butterfly sleeves, and another one made of a magnificent blue silk. The silk one was to be Duke's birthday present, but that box was never opened. She had a two-way-radio cab service called Interboro Radio that would take her to the hospital and sometimes wait for her. Evie was a grade-A, stand-up, loyal lady. Duke had bet on the right lady when he bet on her. He knew that she was his friend. No matter what happened he knew he could count on her. He had put her through every test. He had cheated on her, neglected her and put her through the wringer like no other woman. But she was always there when he needed her. Even though the intense sedation kept him alternating between periods of pain and euphoria, to the very end he called her two or three times every day to say to her, "I love you, doll. Honest, I love you," and send her flowers and the four kisses.

The Countess Fernanda de Castro Monte

THE COUNTESS FERNANDA DE CASTRO MONTE WAS A VERY ELEGANT LADY, a very mysterious lady. She reminded one of a cat. I have seldom been privileged to meet someone who looked like she did, or spoke so many languages, or was as bejeweled. When she appeared on the Ellington scene, she was working in Las Vegas as a singer—a fabulous singer. One night she came in to see Duke and was so overwhelmed that she came in every night and was eventually fired from the Tropicana, where she was under contract. She said, "I became his slave," and gave up her singing career.

From that time on they were together all over the world. She was strong and cunning in maneuvering for herself and the things she wanted, and for the things she wanted to get for Duke. She was a tall, strikingly handsome, blond lady who stood bold, with her boots and her suede pants and suede suits with slits at the sides. She could be humble or forceful. Duke liked that. She could be expressive at times when he wanted to be but couldn't, because of who he was. She knew people all around the world and was a great ambassador for him.

Duke said, "She makes sure I eat all right, and that's enough for me to give her whatever she wants." They shared the basic law of survival. She needed Duke as much as he needed her.

When they arrived at an airport—he with his incredible poise and regal bearing, she with her fur coats and blond hair and sunglasses—they looked like a royal couple on the road. She looked as though she should be sunning herself on a yacht in the Greek Islands with her friend Aristotle Onassis, but she said, "I love to follow Dukie, because I just love Dukie." She accompanied Duke on every European trip and to Japan and the Far East. They journeyed through France, Italy, Germany, England, Austria, Sweden and Denmark.

She knew how to be grand and gracious, but when necessary, she was blue jeans and ham and cheese and "Let's make sure Dukie is comfortable. I'm fine." She would even clean his dressing rooms, saying, "This is too dirty for Duke."

On the trips in England they traveled in a big Rolls, and Duke, who favored doggie bags, was pleased because Fernanda always ordered enough at the Dorchester to keep the ride comfortable, just in case by the time they arrived in the next town, the restaurants were closed and Duke couldn't get to a double cheeseburger on toast, which isn't too hard to prepare around the world. She had enough ingredients in the car to keep him going: crackers, cheese, champagne, wine, steaks and fruit. She found grapes in places where you couldn't find grapes. She found everything Duke liked.

Everybody knew her wherever they went. She was greeted by name. "*Bon jour*, Countess," "*Buon giorno*, Fernanda." Duke often said, "She knows every maitre d' in the world."

Still, she refused to enter certain countries, preferring to wait at the border for Duke's return. To add to the mystery, she turned her face away from the cameras and stepped quietly into the background whenever they were confronted by the press.

In Milan she told Duke that she took an overdose of sleeping pills. Duke, practicing his eternal avoidism, called Toney Watkins and said, "Get somebody and come on up here. Fernanda has just taken some pills and I don't want her to go to sleep. So get up here and take her out." She was probably just trying to keep Duke anxious, because she and Toney then visited the bar of every chic hotel in Milan and wound up dancing in a very New Yorkish disco where everyone knew her.

At the casinos in Biarritz and Monte Carlo, Duke and the Countess were welcomed with open arms, deep bows and deeper curtsies. "Oh! Monsieur le Duke and Madame Countess."

With her manner and appearance, she could have come from any exotic background. She was a great bargainer. One morning in Ceylon she stepped off the elevator, her hair done up, looking like she belonged on the cover of *Vogue*, resplendent in a great bejeweled and sequined caftan, ready for the world at 10 A.M. in her bare feet. Everyone else was recovering from the embassy party the night before. She floated into the jewelry shop in the lobby of the hotel, picked out a ring that had a two-thousand-dollar price tag and dickered the proprietor down to seven hundred dollars. She asked Toney Watkins, "Do you think I did all right?"

He replied, "You deserve an Academy Award for that performance."

She tossed her head. "Now we have to convince Duke that he has to pay for this."

In Mexico, upon hearing someone speak disparagingly of Fernanda, Duke defended her, saying, "She is the reason I eat comfortably. She speaks all of these languages and she orders the food. And that's what I'm worried about . . . my stomach. She can rant and rave and spend as much as she wants, but she looks out for my stomach."

They ordered breakfast in the hotel in Acapulco, and it didn't come back correctly. Fernanda got on the phone to room service and laid them out. They brought it up a second time, and she sent it back again. Duke said, "I've learned when you make the people in the kitchen mad, they pee in your food. I don't send anything back. I keep whatever they send and order something else, but never send something back. I've worked in enough kitchens to see what the waiters do."

Fernanda was easy to like. One reason we all liked her so much was because she was on Duke's side. She was one of us. We all like to hold onto things that are dear to us, but she didn't seem to mind sharing Duke, and that was another reason for her being there, to make sure he was happy and healthy enough to be shared.

Usually for interviews but even when other ladies came, she would go to the dressing room of the female vocalist and talk about something concerning the tour, even though she realized Duke might be making love to some other lady. She sensed it because she knew Duke. But she had the savoir faire to see and yet not to see. Duke always used to say, "We have to be clever enough to say it without saying it. You go to the barber and say, 'I want a haircut, but I don't want it to look like I got a haircut.' "

Some people wondered what he needed her for. But they weren't in Duke's room those days in Mexico when Fernanda was ordering food and getting things together, or when she had gotten him up and packed for him. It is easy to see the public figure at the airport and at the theater and concert hall, but the road is a lonely place, and when Duke was in his private world, when he needed someone to love, he needed someone like Fernanda—a woman who was voluptuous, international, gorgeous. They were a respected couple. People saw them together and said, "Yes, that's the Duke and that's the Countess, and who's going to challenge that kind of loyalty?"

All in all, she was a trooper. With all the jewels and the furs and the languages, when it came to being up at three or four o'clock in the morning to get to that airport, not only was she up with her bags packed in the lobby, but there were Duke's bags and he was up, too. Fernanda was like Duke's personal manager. "What time is the car coming?" or "What time is the plane leaving? I'll take it from there." Many times she said to call her instead of Duke. "Let Dukie sleep up to the last minute. I'll take care of everything. All he has to do is get dressed. Everything will be packed."

144

There were so many nights when Duke needed her. Wherever she is, ten stars—ten big, beautiful, lovely, gold stars—to Fernanda for being there when he needed her.

Rubberlegs

RUBBERLEGS WAS AN ITINERANT SONG-AND-DANCE MAN WHO HAD BEEN A friend of Duke's for many years, ever since they met at the clubs that Duke and Sweetpea frequented where Rubberlegs worked. He earned his nickname because of his unique dancing ability, although he was also a talented vocalist who recorded with Charlie Parker and Trummy Young on National Records, singing mostly blues. His big, always requested song was "A Hundred Years from Today," which became a national hit.

He was over six feet tall and presented a rugged appearance, which was enhanced by his deep voice.

He was the gayest of the gay, but like Sweetpea, he kept his place and bothered no one. Everyone liked him, and he came around to visit often.

Duke had always accepted him for what he was and trusted him implicitly as the guardian eunuch in any and all circumstances in which he wanted one of his ladies protected (from guys like himself) until his return from a gig or a press appearance or a visit to his barber to have his hair conked.

Duke had been booked into Philadelphia, the City of Brotherly Love, for a week. The very first night in the club he saw a lady who was so beautiful she took his breath away. He tried all his ploys—the halo on the ceiling, the reclining crescent moon, everything he could think of, all the romantic maneuvers that had never failed before—but nothing seemed to work. Duke, for a change, was the ardent pursuer instead of enjoying his usual casting as the casual pursued. He dedicated a performance of "Satin Doll" to her, but she ignored it. He sent champagne to her table, but she didn't drink it. He asked the management who she was, but no one knew. They had never seen her before. Duke couldn't get to first base with her, yet she appeared every night, sitting alone at the same table, listening to the band, watching him.

On his closing night, just as he was about to give up the

chase, she stopped him on his way to the bandstand and asked him which hotel he was staying at, saying she would meet him there later. Duke took no chance of losing the lady at this stage of the game. Calling Rubberlegs over, he gave him the keys to his hotel room, saying "Rub, take this lady to my hotel. No, don't worry, I'll get duplicate keys at the desk. And Rub, order some champagne and caviar and anything else the lady wants. Just sign my name, and keep her company till I get there." He was acting like a schoolboy. "We're going to play a short show tonight."

When the gig was over Duke rushed back to his hotel without taking time to change into his street clothes. When he got to the door of his room, he heard loud noises. Turning the key in the lock, he hurried inside.

There were Rubberlegs and the lady of Duke's illusions, making mad, passionate love. The champagne bottle was empty, the caviar was gone. Dismayed, Duke looked at Rubberlegs and exclaimed, "My God, and all these years I've respected you as a woman. Why, you're nothing but a counterfeit."

The Private Man

YOU CAN'T BE AS STRONG AN INDIVIDUALIST AS DUKE WAS ALL HIS LIFE without having unusual confidence in yourself, a feeling that you're going to be your own man and do your own thing. He was a style setter rather than a follower. He was an innovator and a first in every direction. He gave creative thought to pleasing his audience. Once he was onstage it was a house party to him. Whether it was in the White House or a saloon, it was always the same kind of fun.

It was not so much that he wanted to be a crowd pleaser, but more that he was dedicated to his music, and he was also compulsive. He could no more stop writing than he could stop breathing. He had manuscript paper in his room wherever he was, and a little keyboard piano. He always heard melodies, felt things that had to be put down. When you're as creative as Duke, you're never able to stop writing as long as your mind is functioning. In the thousands of nights I spent with Duke, I can't remember one night when he didn't write something. It was as necessary to his way of life as breathing in and out.

Each one of us has some kind of dedication. Duke Ellington was certainly not your average human being; but even the average human being can't consider life without doing the thing he loves most or is dedicated to doing. And Duke had his two things: the music and the women. And the women and the music. And the ice cream. At times I felt that he felt he had to prove his masculinity. Over and over again. He tasted everything in life, but having so very many women may have only been to prove to himself that he was really a man, because he may not have been convinced of it himself. It was the Don Juan syndrome. At times it seemed like a contest between Duke and approximately one hundred million American males to bed all the females of America. Still, his performance must have remained more than adequate, according to the charming lady who confided, "I love him so much, I douche with Lavoris."

He would have been very much at home in the era of the French court. He adored pomp and ceremony and phoniness and affectations and costumes; the whole fanfare. He liked to parade like a peacock. Everything about him was for show and appearance and theatrics; always theatrics. Life was one great big stage and living was a big fairy story and he was Prince Charming throughout the whole thing. There were so many contradictions to Duke. At one time he'd be one character, and then he'd change to a totally different character. He assumed all kinds of roles. The most genuine role he ever played in his entire life was that of a son.

Just to perform the various roles of the average person, just to go through the ordinary steps of living requires responsibility and dedication in great degree. But Duke was so involved in himself and what he had to do that other people and other things were like side dishes. They were just there. He took them for granted. When someone needed help, he'd have somebody who was around make a call or do whatever was necessary to salvage the situation, but he'd never personally get involved. He was always on the outskirts, on the fringes. He would never permit himself any kind of attachment that would demand something of him he didn't want to deliver. He didn't want a role that would give him permanency in anyone's life. He didn't want anyone to have permanency in his life. He felt that when you became deeply involved with someone, you became involved with responsibility and troubles.

He would enter wholeheartedly into what was happening at the moment if it was something that pleased him. A person of importance like Duke, a person who can communicate to a crowd, contributes something to an era. Let's say we're talking about a ball player. He's a crowd pleaser, he's a communicator with the crowd. If we're baseball enthusiasts or football enthusiasts, we have our heroes. We as Americans have very strong characteristics. And we've infected other parts of the world with them. We worship our heroes and heroines. There's no country in the world that gives accolades to politicians or sports figures or rock stars or musicians like we do. We go all out. We're true hero worshippers. When someone has gotten recognition and becomes a hero or a heroine in the eyes of the public, his life becomes inspirational.

The inspiration and dedication of Duke were demonstrated not only in his music but in the teamwork of the musicians in his band. America understands this because we are the only country in the world that gets as crazy as we do about our World Series. When Duke's compositions were performed by his own band, it was like having a National League pennant winner or an American League pennant winner go to bat for him. These men were stationed at their positions, and they played with the same kind of teamwork that a ball player has to use in a World Series. It was an everyday occurrence, but they knew their craft. It was this kind of dedication and ability to inspire other musicians to work well together that created the excitement for Duke as a performing artist.

He inspired a togetherness that was, and still is, unique in the history of jazz.

The man the people all know and talk about doesn't have anything to do with the kind of private man that Duke really was. He was not only very private but was quite fanatic about it. Like a lot of people, he talked a lot, was glib and eloquent and free with opinions, but that really was his way of protecting all the things he didn't want to talk about; and he didn't want to talk about an awful lot; so he never did. It was amazing how he hid himself. You can find Ellington quotes all over the place, including in his book, and if you knew him well, you realize it was a marvelous screen for protecting what he didn't want to say and didn't want people to know.

He was very vain. He was very concerned with his health. He wasn't a true hypochondriac but he was always fussing about it, traveling around with boxes and bags of pills and calling his doctor every day. Vanity always interfered. His eyesight was terrible, but he wouldn't think of wearing glasses, so he poured drops into his eyes in order to try to see the page in front of him.

He had unusual fetishes about clothes. He loved having a huge wardrobe but wouldn't wear any binding things: He never wore a wristwatch or a belt or shoelaces. He hated ties, and when he had to wear one he wore a big, high-collared, soft shirt so he wouldn't feel them.

He had strange conflicts about blacks and his commitment and association with black problems. He was always fascinated with high society and royalty. He loved their company, and yet he didn't want to turn his back on his own people. Essentially Duke had an absolute phobia about involvement of any kind. Every town he went to he checked into a hotel where the band couldn't find him too easily.

His advice was, "Never talk on the telephone unless you're flat on your back." He was almost always in bed when he talked on the phone. The reason was that he hated annoyances and arguments and trouble of any kind, and he wanted to be as relaxed as he could be if he had to face any of it, and he faced very little. He ducked any kind of argument, even with the band. He would sit at the piano and noodle in the dark on nights when he couldn't collect the band all at once to go on the stand at the correct time. He would do it as a cover until they all got up on the bandstand; then he would hit a chord and they would all come on in unison. He never fired anybody in his life, because he just couldn't face it. He wouldn't let anybody annoy him no matter what happened, and all kinds of things did happen. He made the best of any situation. If Gonsalves was too drunk to play, or Hodges didn't show up, or somebody walked off with the first trumpet part, nothing would faze him; he just wouldn't allow it. He was a fanatic about noninvolvement and not letting anybody or anything upset him.

149

Familial matters were terribly important to him. He was a family fanatic. He did a lot of messing around with a lot of women, but he disapproved highly of anybody else doing it. He would be horrified if he knew that someone close to him was unfaithful to his wife; at the same time he himself would be swinging away with some chick in a hotel room.

He hated gossip, and he hated talk about his own family life. Any publicity about his private life disturbed him. He wanted to keep his life away from everybody. And he did. Very few people really knew much about Duke. He seldom talked to critics, because they might print something he said. His conversation was superficial and filled with all kinds of clichés to avoid anybody penetrating the wall. People who talked about Duke in print and thought they knew him because they were around so much didn't realize he was on edge and on guard all the time with them.

He never read anything about himself. He always said, "If you never read anything about yourself, then you'll never read anything bad." He ignored it all, good or bad.

Duke would stand up in front of an audience and talk and talk and talk. So people got the impression they really knew Duke, but that was the biggest smoke screen and the most effective one of all, because the more he talked, the less he said. People don't think about what you're hiding if you talk. Only if you keep quiet. That was one of Duke's tricks, and it worked beautifully.

Besides Billy Strayhorn and Arthur Logan and perhaps one or two other people, no one knew him behind that screen. He has friends all over the world. He had close friends in every city he went to. But he kept everybody in different circles. One circle contained the fellows in the band. They knew things about Duke that people in other circles didn't know. But the fellows in the band never knew many of the things that I knew, or Arthur Logan knew, or Billy Strayhorn knew. Another circle was his family. People who were related to him were in a very special place in his life, but that didn't mean they knew most about him or were closest to him. He kept everybody separate.

He was amoral, not immoral. He belonged to anyone who approached him that he responded to.

Warm Valley

ONE CHRISTMAS DUKE'S PRESENT TO LADIES OF HIS CHOICE WAS A BOTTLE of cologne with a printed label on the front that read:

> Eau de cologne,
> Warm Valley,*
> Expressly blended for............

Then the printed name of the recipient.

Geoffrey Holder

AMONG DUKE'S GREATEST ADMIRERS IS GEOFFREY HOLDER, THE GREAT ACtor, dancer, choreographer, director and painter. I dropped by to see him one day at the charming house he owns on Lexington Avenue in New York City, and after coffee the conversation quite naturally turned to Duke.

"I first met Duke at Roosevelt Raceway," said Holder. "We were doing a benefit. Lena was there and Duke was there. Carmen [de Lavallade, Holder's wife] and I were there with Alvin Ailey. It was raining that night, and it was the weekend before Carmen and I got married. I was in awe of Mr. Ellington, because very few stars had that extra thing. Josephine Baker had it. Bette Davis had it. People of a certain era were born aristocrats. Aristocracy has nothing to do with breeding. And Duke was one of those. He was a Duke. You felt that. It had to do with the aura he gave.

"Being brought up in the Caribbean, in Trinidad, which was the British West Indies, where you have the whole protocol, the comedy of manners, I was always standoffish until I was introduced properly. I am not somebody who slaps somebody on the back and says, 'Hi, I'm a fan of yours.' I don't do that. When I'm with my wife, I have to be introduced quite formally, which I was with Duke. We invited him to our wedding the following weekend. I remember him saying, 'I thought you were married. I thought you guys were married already, on top

*The connotation was obvious.

151

of a mountain, with the blood and the thunder and the mambo jambo.' He was so down-to-earth, like an aristocrat is. The true aristocrats are very earthy, with all their honors and all of their grandioso. They know how to mix with the common man, with dukes and kings and queens. When you rarely meet the true aristocrat, he's like that. And that was Duke.

"Duke was like a lovely strawberry. My description of Duke is that he was like a big, lovely, juicy, luscious strawberry.

"He was a poet and an impressionist. To me his music is very much like Debussy's. An example of that is found in his 'Prellude to a Kiss.' It is so much like the waves of the sea. It takes you all over. It wanders. I never knew that he was a painter, which must have been very natural for him. One thing leads into the other. He is consistent. When you hear him speak or do one of his little poems, it's all a part of the whole. He is consistent in his poetry and his lines and his music, and obviously his painting, which I have not seen. He is so supercool that he allows you to float.

"He called me at four o'clock one morning and asked me to dance at one of his sacred concerts. I was working with a group of young dancers. They were all men. I put them in different colored togas (red and green) and choreographed the dance to go down the aisle of St. John the Divine, where the concert was being held. I had heard the music. It was a very long piece where we started when we heard the choir sing the words, 'Praise God and Dance.' It worked successfully, because these men just took over, dancing down the aisle in their long togas. They were all black and moved to the tempo of the jazz. When I dance, I improvise. When I choreograph, that's all set. Because my body becomes a musical instrument and works in syncopation against whatever is played. I never know what I'm doing until the music starts. It was a great challenge for me, as though I were a saint who should not have been there. It was a marvelous feeling, dancing in a church, because religion started with music and dance. People danced before they sat.

"I'm not talking about paganism. You knew there was a higher form, but you didn't know its name. You didn't know what it was. The only way you could express it was with your body. It was true with every religious group; the Indians, the Africans. You give thanks with your body because you are physical. Your body knows because it feels the air, the sun, the heat, the cold. You react when the sun comes up in the morning. You open, you release. You contract at night when the sun goes down. The flowers do that."

I couldn't resist. There was no way I could stop myself from saying, "Everybody did that except Duke. Duke opened in the evening and contracted in the morning."

Holder replied, "Well, there are some night flowers. Orchids bloom at night, and night-blooming jasmine." He continued, "What do you say to a man like Duke? It's like opening a Bible. Where do you start? Where do you begin? I didn't talk to him about his music because the music speaks for itself. I loved to observe his presence, and his manner and his attitude with people. He was one of the great men of his era. His upbringing, his courtesy, the way he was with his public; that's why he was a giant. I compare Duke with the great French performer Josephine Baker, who is one of my favorite people, because they are of the same mold. There is a similarity in the great people of that era. The most beautiful experience I had working with Josephine Baker was to see her stay onstage until the orchestra was through playing her theme song, although the curtain was closed. She would not leave the stage until she went to the orchestra conductor and apologized for being off-key in the first part. Now, that's a *grande dame*. People like Duke and Baker have spoiled me. When I work with anyone else, I look for that greatness, but it is so seldom there. Everybody's trying to be a star. [Gesturing] You don't try to be a star. You are or you are not.

"There was very little contact between Duke and myself. Only a smile and an admiration and a quietness. A silence that meant more than anything else. We respected each other. His presence was always majestic."

Paris Blues

IN 1960 SAM SHAW, THE EMINENT FILM PRODUCER AND CINEMATOGRAPHER, contacted Duke about composing the background score for a film he was planning called *Paris Blues*. When Duke heard the story line, he became very excited about the project.

The story involved two jazz musicians in Paris, one white,

one black. The white musician, played by Paul Newman, was deeply involved in the exploration of new jazz music and new musical sounds. The black musician, played by Sidney Poitier, was happy to be living in France, away from the racial conflicts troubling the United States. In France Poitier was recognized as a complete man, an artist, and not a hyphenated man. The two musicians proceed to become romantically involved with two schoolteachers from the States, played by Joanne Woodward and Diahann Carroll.

What excited Duke was the possibility of the exploration of both new jazz music and the theme of the black-white struggle in America.

After Duke's acceptance, Shaw went on the road with him. Their first stop was Chicago, where Shaw visited striptease joints, concert halls and nightclubs while Duke was playing at the Blue Note. When Duke got through playing the final set at 3 A.M., he went in and washed up in the dressing room; then the band boy brought in three or four quarts of different flavors of ice cream, which Duke finished before taking Shaw with him to the all-night State Street movies to watch, as Duke called them, the shoot-em-ups, either gangster or cowboy. He loved those corny pictures. They'd watch the Rocky Lane pictures and laugh like hell. When Lane would be thrown in jail, the prop jail was made of cardboard which rattled and shook, and Duke got his kicks out of that. He also loved *The Untouchables* and would stay up all night to watch that type of program on television, keeping up a steady stream of encouragement to the people on the screen.

The band went from town to town on one-night stands. In a small town in Delaware at a Saturday-night dance for the Elks, Duke and the band were really swinging. The dancing of the young people predated rock and disco and made one realize how white-oriented our mass culture is. Duke wrote "Rock City" before the white musicians made rock the international anthem, and the young black people in that little Delaware town, and others like them, were part of the beginnings of the new music.

Back in New York, Shaw had an appointment to pick up Duke at the Hotel Warwick, where the Countess was staying. (Shaw's wife and Evie were in another part of town.) They

154

were walking past the Chemist shop on Fifty-fourth Street and Sixth Avenue when Shaw asked Duke, "How do you juggle two women at one time? After all, we're working on the picture, and you have a play date tonight with the band."

Duke replied, "Sam, not two women—four. I love it. It keeps my juices flowing, and that's where I get all my ideas for the music I write."

One of the most beautiful moments in Duke's life occurred in Manhattan at the synagogue on Lexington Avenue in the fifties, where he performed one of his sacred-music concerts. He was a man floating, an artist reaching the point in life that was worth all the trouble he went through to reach that moment of fulfillment. That night the sacred music had a special, deep significance. The sound of the saxes, the drums and his piano spanned time; it was jazz without apologies that came out of ballrooms, Harlem ghettos, rural Southern backwoods, honky-tonks, cafés, jukeboxes, bordellos. One could hear the rumble of the Lexington Avenue subway outside and below the ground—the sounds of Africa—and the desert of Jerusalem with Abraham and Isaac and all the people in the Bible. The full statement of this sacred concert eventually rocked its way into the Cathedral of St. John the Divine.

On location in Paris, whenever Duke and Shaw went out to eat, it seemed as though Duke himself turned out to be the appetizer. Whichever restaurant they went to—Maxim's or any of the chic Left Bank restaurants—the maitre d' would always come to the table, followed by a steady stream of waiters, presenting Duke with calling cards and telephone numbers from the most beautiful women in the place.

One woman Duke completely flipped for was Oriana Fallaci, the great Italian journalist. When she showed up to get an interview, he really slicked up with his blue silk dressing gown, ascot tie and long cigarette holder. He rather resembled a golden tan version of a roadshow Noel Coward.

For the picture Duke created an entirely new kind of music; avant-garde jazz. He wrote some marvelously original tunes, including one of the first rock tunes. He wanted to use "Satin Doll" as one of the main themes, because he felt that it had

155

inspired Dizzy Gillespie, Charlie Parker and all the other musical explorers in a new form of jazz. United Artists stepped in because they were financing the picture, and they owned a record company and wanted a classic album of Ellington standards. They didn't want "Satin Doll," they didn't want "Rock City," they didn't want any of the new music. They wanted all the old-time things from the forties, which disappointed Duke tremendously, because to him it was music of the past. He didn't sound off with United Artists but took it with a sort of calm resentment.

A Belgian television crew arrived to do a documentary about Duke making the picture in Paris. All of a sudden he exploded and ran off the set, ran down the street. Shaw was amazed. He had never seen him display temper, because he was always calm and sweet, and here he was—talk about temperament in an artist—a man climbing walls. He had been insulted because all the Belgian people wanted was Duke's music of the forties. He was finally coaxed back by Shaw, who realized the entire episode had been triggered by the attitude of the United Artists people.

Duke did have his way without doing the standards in the dramatic, emotional scenes of the film, where the score lies beneath and enhances the drama. The power and the scope of his creative underscoring were tremendous. The music has since been more than casually emulated. Many current films and TV shows have purloined entire passages from Duke's score for *Paris Blues*. Musical scholars and film buffs study that film, particularly scenes like the one in which Sidney Poitier and Diahann Carroll are on the bridge in Paris and she asks him to come home, and he says that he doesn't want to sit at a counter and be thrown out. Carroll pleads with him that he must go back and face these things for their people. The music under that scene was ahead of its time not only with respect to the scoring being done then but even of anything being written today. It is an emotional explanation of everything that is happening, and in musical terms it is absolutely breathtaking.

Duke didn't get story credit on *Paris Blues*, despite the fact that much of the authenticity of the story came out of his inspiration, his personal knowledge of that life.

During the filming Shaw was asked to omit scenes showing the prejudice against blacks that existed in America, such as restrictions at lunch counters, streetcars and other places, which embodied their day-to-day revolutionary struggle. This he refused to do, and *Paris Blues* became the first picture of its kind to be released. *Paris Blues* was nominated for an Academy Award. According to Shaw, "That was without any campaign by the production company, which is highly unusual. United Artists was campaigning for *West Side Story*, where they had a heavy financial involvement." He shook his head. "Well, that's all water under the bridge. It's a bigger and more important film now than when it was first released, and most of that is due to Duke's musical score."

Frank Sinatra

ONE NIGHT SAM SHAW AND I WERE DISCUSSING DUKE. TO QUOTE SHAW, "He is the most beautiful man I ever met. I love his face lines—the depths, the bags beneath his eyes. His charm is true at all times. When he says 'I love you madly' on first meeting anyone—especially women—he means it. Of all the great men of our time, men with high moral standards, in a world of corruption, men of compassion, Duke is the most sophisticated and the most eloquent. He can say and communicate what is within his soul. I compare him with Frank Sinatra. He and Frank are the smoothest, most sophisticated individuals and the coolest. Possessing all the emotion and warmth in the world, these men have a knowledge of culture that the public doesn't know about. Frank Sinatra, like Duke, is one of the best-read individuals I have ever met. He told me he can't sleep at night. He reads books on mathematics."

I interrupted, "Really?"

Shaw continued, "Philosophy . . ."

I interrupted again, "Philosophy, yes, but mathematics?"

Shaw replied, "He's an engineer, a scientist. He knows higher mathematics."

I asked, "What kind of engineer?"

Shaw said, "A sound engineer."

I reflected. "I thought those great records came instinctively from him."

Shaw shook his head. "It's more than that. Frank knows sound, he knows the sound room. He knows baffle boards and the technical higher mathematics. People think he's just a nightclub performer and a guy that does an incredible job of singing lyrics, but he's profound as hell."

I said. "Duke loves Frank. He loves him as a singer, but even more as a person. He talks about Frank often. He told me that in the beginning, when Frank first made it big at the Paramount Theatre as a single, he went around to the different public schools in New York City talking up civil rights to the kids, a political position which was extremely unpopular at the time. At one school he even got into a fist fight protecting a black kid.

"I remember whenever Duke was booked to appear at Basin Street East, they would get a call from Ava Gardner or Frank's buddy Jilly, saying they were coming in. They'd come through the back entrance on Forty-ninth Street, through the kitchen and sit at a little table in the corner. Gardner loved to hear Johnny Hodges play 'Passion Flower' and 'Lush Life.' Every time Frank was in town he'd come to hear Duke.

"I remember Frank coming to the Rainbow Grill. They got a call from one of the people associated with Frank saying that he was coming up. Would they have a secluded spot for him? He said to tell Duke that 'The Detective' was coming." Shaw looked puzzled. "That must have been the film he was making."

I agreed. "He never identified himself any other way except as 'The Detective.' He came up frequently to see Duke. There was always a marvelous rapport between them."

Shaw smiled. "Don, those guys knew each other well. They really cared for each other."

I continued, "Once when Frank was married to Mia Farrow, he called Duke and gave him the title 'Baby, You're Too Much' and asked him to write a song that he could dedicate to Mia. We wrote the song [see lyrics at end of section], but Duke is the greatest procrastinator of all time, and before he got the song to Frank, he and Mia had split."

I paused. "One thing has always puzzled me, Sam. The media always rap Frank when he does something impulsive, but seldom if ever praise him for the many wonderful things he

158

does. When Sammy Davis, Jr., had that terrible automobile accident in California where he lost his eye and was so badly injured that he wanted to die, Frank stayed at the hospital with him until he was able to be moved, then took him to his home in Palm Springs and practically single-handedly nursed him back into wanting to live again.

"When Judy Garland was tapped out and in the hospital trying to kick some bad habits, Frank quietly picked up the tab. On numerous occasions when people were in trouble, the anonymous benefactor has been Frank, with no fuss and no fanfare. Duke is the same way, always extending an unseen helping hand. Let's face it, Sam, these men helped create Americana. They are as American as apple pie and hot dogs, and they recognize that quality in each other. I've been with Duke at one, two o'clock in the morning, when a phone call went either way, when Frank was at the Fontainbleu in Miami, and he said to Duke, 'Catch the next plane down. I'll spend the next day and a half with you, except when I'm doing my shows.' "

Shaw agreed. "There's no doubt about it. They like to hang out."

I nodded my head. "They sure do love hanging out with each other."

BABY, YOU'RE TOO MUCH

Like a purple thrill from scarlet lips.
Like the friendly lights of passing ships.
Like a moonbeam that escaped eclipse.—
BABY, YOU'RE TOO MUCH!

Like an orchid wrapped in cellophane.
Like a sunbeam dancing in the rain.
Like a pleasure that begins with pain.—
BABY, YOU'RE TOO MUCH!

Each time I gaze in—
your love dipped eyes,—
Baby, I jaywalk through paradise.—

Like the grass that grows across the way.
Like a second golden wedding day.

Ev'ry time we love I have to say—
BABY, YOU'RE TOO MUCH!
You're the real Valhalla.
You're more than divine.—
And praise be to Allah you're mine.

Taipei

IN 1963, AFTER A CONCERT IN TOKYO, THE BAND FLEW TO TAIPEI, WHERE THEY arrived very early in the morning. Despite the time the twenty-four-hour bar at the airport was jumping with GIs who were outnumbered by "ladies of the morning" at least two to one. The Seeburg jukebox in the corner, anticipating Duke's arrival, was loaded with Ellington records, at the moment playing "Take the A Train." While waiting for their transportation to the hotel, the band soon discovered that there was plenty of rice wine, beer and vodka manufactured in Taipei, but there was no whiskey to be had for love or money. Making the best of things, most of them were soon drinking combinations of what was available, with varied results.

After checking in at their hotel, they set out to do some shopping, realizing that what cost twelve dollars at Macy's could be purchased for ninety cents in Taipei because of the cheap labor.

To the astonishment and delight of the local citizenry, some of the more exuberant band members changed places with the native men pulling the rickshaws.

After dinner, when things had calmed down somewhat, the band adjourned to the hall where they were booked to give a concert. Seated in the orchestra were the American ambassador and his wife, and Mrs. Chiang Kai-shek, owner of half of Fifth Avenue in New York City, and her son, representing the respective governments of the United States and Taipei. The place was packed, with the cream of Taipei society and GIs jammed shoulder-to-shoulder.

The band was set up and the concert was about to begin when there was a commotion at the rear and the military came in and unceremoniously emptied the hall, hurriedly escorting everyone to the street outside and reentering with a group of trained, bomb-sniffing dogs. After the hall was thoroughly searched, the bomb scare turned out to be a false alarm and the audience returned to their seats to enjoy the concert. The program proceeded splendidly until the third number.

Paul Gonsalves, who had spent the entire afternoon in the hotel bar, was playing "The Lonely Ones" when he slowly sagged to the floor of the stage and played the whole thing on his back. Duke went over and put the microphone way down. It had to look as though it was in the show. Gonsalves just couldn't stand up. His knees gave way and he went right down to the floor; but he kept playing, and Duke just stood there holding the microphone.

When it was over and they were in the dressing room, Duke was furious. He sat there with his head in his hands and spat out the words to the band manager. "Put him on a ship. No, wait. Put him on a plane. Unh, unh. Put the bastard on a fucking freighter. I don't care if he ever gets back home, but get him out of my sight. Goddamn it," he yelled, "get rid of him."

Ten minutes later it was all forgotten after somebody reminded Duke, "Hey, man, remember who saved your ass in Newport in 1956."

In the reviews the next day, there were glowing accounts of this new gimmick in Duke's act, with Gonsalves laying on his back, playing in a very unique fashion, giving added spice to the entire joyous occasion.

Lizards

IN THE HOTEL IN RANGOON DUKE MADE SURE THERE WERE LIZARDS IN HIS room. He explained, "You see, there have to be lizards in your room, because the lizards eat the bugs that eat you."

The Nuns of St. Croix

FOR MANY YEARS THE ONLY MUSICAL SOUND THAT COULD BE HEARD IN THE Virgin Islands, Barbados, St. Thomas, St. Croix; in the entire Caribbean, and Puerto Rico, was the sound of tin drums and steel drums played by grinning, gaudily dressed natives wearing wide-brimmed straw hats with gaily colored bandannas adorning their necks. The music was mainly reggae and calypso, particularly the kind that Harry Belafonte helped popular-

161

ize back home in the States. There was no American popular music and no jazz.

As much as the American tourists loved the islands, they wanted to hear some of their own music. The management of the Hotel on the Cay in St. Croix (affectionately known by the tourists as the Hotel on the Rocks) and the Holland-America Cruise Lines combined to call Duke's manager to ask if it was possible for Duke to come down to St. Croix to play a concert. Duke loved the idea. It was winter and cold, and he wanted to get into the warm. It took about two minutes for him to make up his mind. He got the band together, and we all cruised down on one of the great Carnival ships. The weather was beautiful. The food was gourmet, which pleased Duke, and the ladies aboard were attractive and generous.

Coming in for the landing at St. Croix, the water was so clear we could count the fish. White coral sands stretched as far as the eye could see. Hibiscus, bougainvillea and other exotic flowers and plants wound around the lush tropical trees, forming a palette of red, purple, gold, blue and white living rainbows. Beyond the dock, low limestone buildings made of concrete blocks, with pastel-colored pink and blue and green tin roofs, sat smiling in the sun, waiting to put their arms around us. (I had tears in my eyes. This was really something for a ghetto kid like me, who was brought up in Hell's Kitchen in New York City. We had no bathtub and the john was in the hall. We often couldn't use the john at night, when the local ladies of the evening were hustling guys there at twenty-five cents a shot. On Saturday mornings we went to the YMCA on Tenth Avenue for a shower, which cost five cents and included soap and a towel.)

Once we were on shore we were profusely welcomed by the governor of the island and his bowing entourage. The entire Main Street was only three blocks long, but with due pomp and circumstance we were provided with a motorcycle escort to the hotel.

It had originally been planned to hold the concert on the terrace of the hotel, but the news had spread all over the Caribbean that Duke was in the area, and with it being February, the peak of the season, the islands were filled with thousands of tourists seeking diversion. On the day of the concert, there

162

was a stampede in the direction of St. Croix. Yachts were pulling in from all over the islands, people were flying in from as far off as Bermuda in chartered planes; the tourists and townspeople of St. Croix and Christiansted, the capital city, all lovers of Duke's music, jammed the area so completely that the concert had to be moved to the public ball field at the Catholic school, the only place on the island large enough to hold the tremendous crowd.

The nuns were very excited about Duke coming out to the school. They wheeled an old upright piano from the gym and managed to struggle it out onto the field. There was no piano stool, just a rickety old chair, and no one really knew if the piano was in tune. Duke had intended to wear a red linen jacket with his tuxedo trousers, but when he heard what the nuns had done, he said, "I'd better wear something suitable to honor the ladies," and changed into a white full dress suit, just like the one he wore at the Royal Albert Hall. The nuns were so smitten with Duke that they had taken the trouble to learn one song, "When the Saints Go Marching In."

Duke had the band and the nuns line up behind him and led them onto the field, the band playing and the nuns singing "When the Saints Go Marching In," spurred on by the roar of the crowd. When he sat down to play, he flung those white tails behind that rickety chair just as though he were performing for the Queen of England. He was enchanting. He absolutely enthralled them all. He was no longer a jazz musician. That day he came close to being what the nuns called him. Saint Ellington.

On the Road

IN HIS WAY, WITH HIS CREATIVE MIND, DUKE MOVED BACK AND FORTH ON the calendar. He could be forty years old today, twelve years old yesterday and seventy tomorrow. He set his own time. Sometimes he was as playful as a kitten. Other times he could be as sober as the Pope. One never knew. We had to swing with him, because that's the kind of man he was. No matter how well you knew him, you were in for all kinds of surprises. He was a many-sided, multifaceted man who showed different sides of himself to different people. He could get along with kids, he could get along with adults. He was buddies with presidents and with guys pushing junk on Lenox Avenue. There was so much to him that there was something for everybody.

The side of him that touched me deeply was the little-boy side, the childish, almost shy side of his personality that was capable of being awed by people as diverse as Queen Elizabeth and Raymond Burr. It was charming that Duke, the adored, the admired, the idolized, reverted to the little boy idolizing his childhood heroes like Perry Mason. And so it was a great thrill when, one night in Cincinnati, Raymond Burr, who was on a national tour promoting a commercial product, came backstage to see Duke at the Living Room, the popular club where the band was playing. Everybody from miles around had come to hear the band. People who wouldn't normally speak to each other came in and jammed to "Satin Doll" and "I'm Beginning to See the Light." When Raymond Burr arrived, Duke dedicated the entire set to him. He told everybody how he went to bed by Raymond Burr in Vegas.

"When Perry Mason signs off," he said, "I can go to sleep. We've solved the murder." Duke was completely overwhelmed. He told Burr, "I've read all of Perry Mason. After you, I'm the world's greatest detective." They took pictures together, and before Burr left, Duke asked him for his autograph. In Vegas the band was hired to play at Frank Sinatra's birthday party. Duke insisted that all the band members show up in uniform prepared to jam. He was very definite. "Frank's having his birthday party, and he's the boss."

It started about two in the morning, after everyone's show had finished, at Caesars Palace where Sinatra was appearing. All of the young Hollywood starlets were there, and a few other ladies with various other desires on their minds. The famous restaurant owner, Jilly, a good friend of Sinatra's, had flown out from New York for the occasion. Sammy Davis, Jr., performed, singing "Happy Birthday" and "What Kind of Fool Am I." There were seven birthday cakes, all three or four tiers high, looking like wedding cakes. Lola Falana stopped in, the Mills Brothers were there, with Lainie Kazan and Ellington and his entourage. It was a carefree occasion with a great deal of drinking. About 6 A.M., as they were carrying Paul Gonsalves out, Frank agreed with Duke, "This is the biggest party we ever had for Gonsalves."

Duke had a way of comfortably getting out of situations without offending anyone, but still doing what had to be done. We were in New Mexico. Duke had been invited to judge a teenage beauty pageant. There were twelve girls in the semifinals, and they eventually broke it down to six for the finals.

The girls were standing in a row. Duke looked at me and said, "My God, Don, they're all so pretty. How can I send any of these girls home crying?" A list of questions had been prepared. The most important one seemed to be: If you're out on a date at that special prom and you're supposed to be home at midnight, and the car ran out of gas, and you really did have a flat tire, and that's why you're out there at three o'clock in the morning, your parents are probably thinking something else. How do you cope with this? Duke visibly brightened when one of the girls said, "I trust my parents and I trust that they trust me, which means that I'll be truthful. What else can I do?"

It was strange that one person should be given the responsibility of picking the winner, but they had put all the weight on Duke. They obviously thought: Who needs a panel of judges when you can have Duke Ellington? He can certainly speak for ten people when it comes to judging beauty and talent and personality and charm.

He did pick a winner. He picked the girl who answered the 3 A.M. question so well. He got the envelope and the girl's name and he said, "Well, ladies and gentlemen, I've seen them all and I've interviewed them all and the judges tell me that so and so is the winner." When we left, everybody in the room was still looking around for the judges.

Duke and the band were booked into the Fairmont Hotel in Dallas. Lainie Kazan was appearing in the Burgundy Room, and Duke's band was playing in one of the ballrooms for a local organization that was having a hundred-dollar-a-plate dinner.

Before the engagement the management of the hotel had laid down a number of rules:

The band is not permitted to mingle with the guests.
The band must remain in the ballroom.
The band is not to drink at the bar.

Some of the fellows resented the rules because they knew so many of the guests from previous engagements in Dallas, but Duke told them to be cool, as there were six or seven portable bars set up in the ballroom, and they could probably slide around a bit.

Joan Crawford was in another of the ballrooms, presiding over a Pepsi-Cola benefit-award dinner. She had been invited up to the ballroom where Duke and the band were playing to present some of the door prizes, which were well above the average, including a trip to Hawaii, a new car and two weeks in Vegas. Duke introduced Crawford and started to hand her the microphone. She may have been a bit tipsy, or the lights may have been too hot (the room was air-conditioned), but she fainted dead away and fell back into the saxophone section. between Johnny Hodges and Harold Ashby. Not wanting to violate the rule "No mingling with the guests," they moved their chairs slightly and calmly let her lie there, until eventually one of the hotel people came and picked her up.

Duke was asked, "Why didn't you pick up Joan Crawford?"

He held up his hands, palms out, shaking his head, and took a step backward, saying, "Not me. I wouldn't lay my hands on a white woman in Texas."

Duke always liked Chinese food. In Reno, while he was writing a sacred concert, it was his diet after each show. At four o'clock in the morning the man from the local Chinese emporium would pad in, carrying every kind of oriental goody imaginable. One early morning was spent by Duke and his granddaughter Gaye, going over lyrics for the sacred concert, while eating kumquats and snow peas and sweet and sour pork. Duke, infinitely more far-sighted than our State Department and agreeing completely with Nostradamus, had kept announcing since the early 1950s that the whole world was eventually going oriental.

Everywhere the band played, Duke had the band boy and the band manager canvass the audience to find out who should be mentioned from the stage. Duke jotted the names down and put the list on the piano. After different numbers he would get up and announce, "This evening, ladies and gentlemen, we're happy to have so and so, and so and so here," which blew the minds of the people in the audience, because they wondered, "My God, these people really know Duke Ellington."

It surprised the people themselves for Duke to acknowledge the local jazzman who had a band that played around town. Someone asked Duke, "Why do you do that?"

He replied, "It always makes us look good. It makes the other guy look ten feet tall, but it really makes us look good. That's where the ambassador part of the gig comes in."

Tony Bennett, Duke and Jackie Leonard were on tour. Although Tony was top billed, he always relinquished the star's dressing room to Duke, especially when they got to certain posh locations where there might be champagne and flowers and sofaed dressing rooms. Tony always arrived at the concert at intermission, already dressed, which meant that he would sit out in the limo until it was time to go on or just come in and shoot the breeze for a bit. Tony knew that with his schedule, which was just a matter of flying in to do a particular concert and then joining up with the band about a week later, Duke would be here tonight and God knows where tomorrow, and if he could halfway contribute to Duke's comfort, he gave him the big room.

The band played two weeks at the Shamrock Hilton Hotel in Houston, then went out for a week of uneventful one-nighters throughout Texas, and then returned to Houston to play for the Governors' Conference. After the first set Governor Rockefeller and Happy made their way through the crowd of governors to Duke, whom they had met previously at a concert in Harlem at the Mother Zion Church. Rockefeller asked Duke to play "Time's A-Wastin'," a song he had heard and liked back at the church, and then announced over the loudspeaker system, "Yes, I am Duke Ellington's personal governor. We both represent the State of New York."

Back in Vegas it was a kick going around with Duke, who managed to make it to every show that was appearing on the strip in the big rooms. His theory was, "Not only do we go and make those other people look good, but all of their audiences find out where we're playing." Invariably the announcement came. "Ladies and gentlemen, there's a man in the audience tonight. He and his entire aggregation are appearing at the Sahara. Won't you say hello to America's foremost composer, the mighty Duke Ellington." Debbie Reynolds announced him, Wayne Newton acknowledged him, as did Ann-Margaret and Diana Ross at her farewell performance with the Supremes. They always saved Duke for last. He was the dessert. Duke would stand up and throw kisses, and the spotlights would shine on him and the people would just go crazy.

Gas Station, St. Louis

WHEN PEOPLE SAW DUKE WALKING AT AN AIRPORT OR GETTING INTO OR out of a cab, they knew it was one of the big three: Ellington, Count Basie or Louis Armstrong.

It was in St. Louis at a gasoline station that two local cats were staring at Duke in his white coat and porkpie hat. "Hey, man, that's Duke."

"Unh, unh, that's Count. I know Count."

"No, man, you're wrong. That's Duke."

One of them walked up to Duke and asked, "Hey, man, ain't you Duke?"

Duke said, "I'm whoever you want me to be, baby."

Woody Herman

DUKE HAD PROMISED WOODY HERMAN THAT HE'D DROP BY FOR A HALF-hour. And so late one afternoon we drove up Kings Road to Woody's house on Hollywood Boulevard, high above the Sunset Strip. The house was built on four levels on the side of a hill, with the garage and the dining room and the kitchen on the top level, which was where we entered. In the orchid john, one level down, was an oblong bathtub at least five feet deep, which looked like a miniature swimming pool. Charlotte, Woody's lovely wife (to whom I had given a kitten once, which wound up licking her toes in the middle of the night while she was sleeping and Woody was out of town, causing a great deal of consternation), was an animal lover, and there were cats, dogs, birds, a lamb and a goat wandering around, constantly pursued by Woody's young daughter, Ingrid.

Woody had just finished a tour of one-nighters with Chicago his last stop, and was glad to be home. After he showed us around, we settled down in the den to talk and to listen to some of his latest records. Particularly outstanding were the cuts of "Lady McGowan's Dream" and "Lazy Lullabye," both with arrangements by Ralph Burns.

Duke and Woody were deeply involved in a discussion about the old days in Chicago, when Woody was unknown and Duke came to the basement of the Sherman Hotel every night to attract attention to Woody's band, which was playing there.

During their reminiscences the phone rang, and the maid came in, saying, "Excuse me, Mr. Herman, there's a long distance call for you."

Woody picked up the extension. "Hello . . . oh, hello, Mom, sure I have time . . . Duke Ellington and Don George." Woody grinned at me and spoke into the phone. "What's that? You've heard of Duke Ellington, but you never heard of Don George? . . . He writes songs with Duke." Woody listened some more, then hung up the phone, doubling over with laughter.

When he calmed down, Duke asked him, "What in the world was that all about?"

Still gasping for breath, Woody said, "You know my bass player? That was his mother calling from Chicago." He mimicked the old Jewish lady. "She said, 'Woody, be a good boy and be sure to tell my son the stash is inside the bass'."

Philharmonic

EVERYTHING HAS TO HAVE A BEGINNING. YOU HAVE YOUR FORERUNNERS, you have your founders. Talk about anything that's happened—art, science; anything that's happened in the development of anything in the world. There are those who have founded it, developed it. Michelangelo, da Vinci, Pasteur, Einstein . . . Duke was a founder. Duke was the beginning. Duke was a developer of all the things that have been laid down in American music. Almost everything that people are doing is a takeoff from him.

We got our original inspiration for melody from the classics. From England. From Europe. From all the masters. The jazz artists who just did primitive jazz music played a combination of African chants and something spiritual, because people were into their gods and whatever their native folk songs happened to be. Duke was the next plateau after that. He was the beginner and the forerunner of refining jazz; he didn't just do something improvisational or interpretive; he treated his music with a seriousness and composure that made it very special. He was a founder, he was a developer, he was a stylist in every way. He made strong personal contributions to the liberal arts and to the music of America and to spreading musical inspiration throughout the world with his unique, original style of music.

He wrote things for the people who could interpret them best—his musicians. His band was like a family. His band was almost like his piano. Each instrument was like a single note. All together it made for one instrument: his orchestra.

Duke's voice was his orchestra. There's a difference between the Beatles and Manilow and other people who wrote and performed their own material and Duke, who did the very same thing. He was the originator. He wrote the song, arranged the song and performed the song. Only he used fourteen men to do it. And they weren't strangers. They really were a family. Duke was the Beatles and Manilow and the Bee Gees and Kenny Rogers and Bob Dylan all wrapped up in one. He started the whole damn thing. He was both the teacher and the student. He had the ability to do anything he wanted to do, but he really excelled musically in one area. He could, if he wished to put his mind to it, write for any kind of musical group. But what pleased him most, and what he did best, was the music that he was most known for, his popular music.

170

In recognition of his important stature as a composer and conductor, Duke was booked for an evening conducting the New York Philharmonic Orchestra in one of his own compositions, "The Golden Broom and Green Apple," in an evening that included Van Cliburn, the pianist, as a featured performer. The sell-out event took place in Avery Fisher Hall at Lincoln Center in New York City and was equally well attended by both jazz buffs and the haut monde.

At the rehearsal on the day preceding the concert, the only members of Duke's band onstage were Louis Bellson, the great drummer who is married to Pearl Bailey, and John Lamb, the bassist. They were placed right up near the podium where Duke was going to conduct. Bellson, who had flown in from the Coast for the engagement had never seen the music before and had expected some kind of drum part, but there was nothing at all. Duke, seeing the worried look on Bellson's face, leaned down just before he started conducting the rehearsal and said, "Hey, Lou, don't worry about a thing, the first part's in three-four."

Lou replied, "Thanks a lot, Maestro."

The orchestra rehearsed for about an hour and a half. Bellson kept watching Duke because he was accustomed to him and all his signals and could anticipate what was coming. But the way Duke worked was quite different from the usual style of symphonic people. He was really very casual in contrast to their strict discipline. He did things in a different vein, and at first they didn't quite understand his unusual technique. It took a long time for the orchestra to really hone in on Duke.

Van Cliburn was standing backstage waiting to rehearse, and he was getting nervous. He didn't know what was going on. Duke was conducting from the piano, and it took a while for the musicians to pick up their various cues, because they were accustomed to someone up on the podium, waving a baton.

Bellson, taking no chances, borrowed the score from Luther Henderson, the arranger, and wrote himself a drum part. After the final rehearsal on the next day, Duke said to Bellson, "Boy, you played the hell out of that. See, you didn't need a drum part."

Bellson replied, "I hope you don't mind, Maestro, but I got the score from Luther and I made a drum part for you, because if I'm not around, maybe sometime you'll need it."

Duke went to the same hokum I've heard him pull hundreds of times; but it always worked even when you knew it was coming. "You see, Louis Bellson, that's why I didn't write a drum part; because I knew you would do one, and who could write a drum part better than Louis Bellson?"

Before the performance anybody who didn't know Duke thought:Wow, what's happening? This is going to be a catastrophe. Everybody was nervous except Duke. When people finally became accustomed to the way he was conducting the rehearsal, and after they had had a chance to run through it, they realized he was giving them the right cues. By the time the performance was over, everybody was saying, "Hey, man, I don't know what we were so worried about in the beginning. It all came together."

Van Cliburn performed first, to his usually very receptive audience. Then the entire New York Philharmonic played "The Golden Broom and Green Apple" in three movements, conducted by Duke, mostly from the podium, but occasionally he wandered over to the piano to noodle around a bit and give some cues from there. At the end of the performance, Duke and Bellson and Lamb (the bassist) took over downstage by themselves and just plain jammed. I have never heard drumming like that in my life. The drum inspired the piano and the piano inspired the bass. It was an incredible performance. Before it was over the people in the audience were standing and screaming. They were so carried away by what they couldn't believe they were hearing. Duke was playing from way back in the early days; from the two-bit gigs; from the rent parties. He was striding, striding, striding on the piano. Bellson and Lamb were roaring along with him. One hundred of the greatest musicians in the world, the entire Philharmonic Orchestra, were stamping their feet, applauding and screaming along with the audience. The crescendo built and built and built until the walls actually shook. When it was finally over, the three men stood, hand in hand, grinning, pouring sweat and completely exhausted, taking innumerable bows.

The savoir faire disappeared somewhere on the steps leading up to his dressing room. Duke had worked hard. He looked old and tired and worn. We went out and had something to eat and we just sat and talked about the concert. In about an hour you could see him relax and twenty years come off his face. He looked beautiful. There was a glow about him because he realized how good he had been. I knew Brother Edward was back to normal when he looked around, then leaned toward me and said, "Don, dig that pretty waitress serving the other tables."

Tony Bennett

DUKE HAD A WAY OF MAKING YOU FEEL IMPORTANT. EVEN WHEN YOU knew you were already an important person, Duke's way of giving you his total attention convinced you that he really cared about you and was fascinated by what you had to say. Coming from the great Duke Ellington, this was high flattery. Duke played a lot of games with people, but this was not one of them. He meant it. It was part of the charm that attracted women to him in droves and brought him friendships with men that lasted a lifetime. He usually told parting visitors, "Love you madly." He meant it, and they believed him.

One person who was a recipient of Duke's affection for many years was Tony Bennett. Duke and Tony loved each other as friends and as artists. They made records together. When they appeared in the same city, they made a point of catching each other's show when it was possible, and they would get together after their gigs and talk all night. In New York Tony often dropped by at Duke's apartment on West End Avenue or at the house on Riverside Drive when Duke stayed there. It was the same around Hollywood, no matter where Duke was staying. Their meetings were instant harmony regardless of when they had seen each other last.

Once it happened that unknown to each other, both Duke and Tony had to be at LaGuardia Airport early in the morning to catch flights upstate. Tony had a gig in Syracuse and Duke was going to Rochester. Coincidentally, they were booked on the same plane. After the takeoff somebody told Duke that Tony was on the plane. Duke got up and went quickly up the aisle. When Tony saw him he stood, and the two of them hugged each other.

But let Tony tell the story.

"It was a nice sunny crisp morning in New York on the way to Syracuse and Rochester, and Duke just got me in front of the whole group. He just grabbed my hand and said, 'Come to the back of the airplane,' and I didn't know what was happening. He took me to a little girl that was blind and was playing a mouth accordion, and he said, 'You know Tony Bennett.'

"She said, 'No, I'm sorry, I don't.'

"He said, 'You know the boy who sang "I Left My Heart in San Francisco."?' And oh she jumped and was so joyous over meeting me. He told her to play and that I would sing it, and before I knew it I was halfway through the song, before I realized I wasn't getting paid for it. Before I knew it the whole audience gave us a standing ovation in the airplane, at nine in the morning. These incongruities were the things that Duke knew about more than I think even Sartre of France. The fact that he knew the joys of life were not the things that you plan, but the great things that just happen. He made those his miracles in life, right until the day he died."

It was Christmas Day, 1964, and Tony Bennett was sitting in his room at the Gotham Hotel in New York, brooding through the winter of his discontent. He was very much alone, very much by himself. Alone, away from his family because of personal reasons, and very confused, very mixed up, one of those who-can-I-turn-to moments in life. He wasn't working, and here it was Christmas without his wife and kids.

He had locked himself away from the world, too down to contact any of his friends, not even Duke. He didn't answer his phone or his door. He just sat there, suffering in silence.

At the time Duke was rehearsing his band and a choir for a concert of his sacred music at the Cathedral of St. John the Divine, up on Amsterdam Avenue in lower Harlem.

Somehow he found out about Tony. Later that evening Tony was sitting in the dark silence of his room at the Gotham, not even caring to look out the window. Suddenly he heard music. He checked the radio; it was off. The TV set was off. But he still heard the music. He went to the door and opened it.

There, crowded into the narrow corridor, was the entire choir from St. John's, men and women of every race, color and creed. Standing in front of them was Duke Ellington, conducting the singers in an arrangement of "On a Clear Day You Can See Forever."

Tony told me later, "You have no idea what that did to lift my spirits. Duke Ellington, a great star and a busy man, took all that trouble to bring the choir to the hotel to serenade me. It changed my whole attitude. I came back to the human race."

Religion

ONE DAY I WAS SITTING WITH DUKE WHILE HE WAS COMPOSING SOME sacred music. He smiled at me and said, "Don, this is one way I pray."

Religion was a very real thing to Duke. That he played in Lutheran churches, in Episcopal cathedrals, in Jewish temples and synagogues and in Roman Catholic churches indicates how much at home he was in all religions. He called himself God's messenger boy, although he was not so much involved with the ritual or the liturgical aspect or the formalities. The structure itself was not as important to him as the essence.

He was ecumenical about religion the same way he was about his music. "Don, if it's good music it's good. If it speaks about love and brotherhood, it's all right with me." He wasn't Lutheran or Roman Catholic. He was everything. He had the same universal spirit in his religion and his music. His sacred concerts were quite informal. They were concerts and not worship services. He called them sacred concerts because they permitted him to feel completely free to do what he wanted to do within his own integrity, without being hampered by the thought that now I have to turn to the right or genuflect here and do this sort of thing, which are all very important to most religious observance and worship.

For Duke that was not the essential. It was the message that he brought, in both the words and the music. He had read the Bible completely more than four times. He had rabbis and priests and pastors and people of the cloth of all shapes and sizes as his friends.

One of his closest earthly contacts with the Lord was Pastor John Gensel, who conducted the jazz vespers every Sunday afternoon at St. Peter's Lutheran Church in New York City.

175

Pastor Gensel was a warm personal friend whom Duke turned to whenever he felt the need for spiritual guidance. Duke composed a gospel number called "Shepherd of the Night Flock," which he dedicated to Gensel.

Another heavenly bulwark was Father Jerry Pocock of St. Mary's Roman Catholic Hospital in Montreal, Canada, who occasionally toured with Duke and who was Duke's guest at the sacred concert in Westminster Abbey in London.

Whenever I spoke to Father Pocock about Duke, he was very guarded in what he had to say. He said, "I'm a priest, and although Duke was not a Catholic, he confided in me a great deal, which I will never reveal except for this . . . Duke was a kind man. As far as I know, he never willfully hurt anybody."

Duke did not follow the strict Western Christian interpretation of sin. He was not legalistic. He was extremely tolerant of others. In spite of the fact that he himself did not indulge in drugs, if someone else did, he was not the kind of person who went around slapping the wrists of either the men in his band or anyone else for doing something wrong, whether it was a peccadillo or some greater form of sin. He was a person who said, "You lead your life, I'll lead my life."

His concept of sin involved a much deeper idea of God's relationship to man. To him the great sins were man's inhumanity to man; if a man did not accept another man as his brother or another woman as his sister, these would be the greater sins against God; not the sins of the flesh but the sins of spirit and attitude. He was very loyal. There were many people in his pocket. He'd been ripped off from time to time, and rather than put the culprit in jail or bring suit against him, he would say something to the effect of "Well, maybe he needed it more than I did."

He did not feel that if he involved himself in the pleasures of one woman while he was married to another he was committing a sin, because his many-faceted relationships were necessary for the creativity which was the very core of his existence. He didn't flaunt his actions. He enjoyed his personal pleasures, though he would have felt badly if he had hurt some other person or hurt someone else who also may have been involved with the lady. That to him was a sin.

176

Duke played in St. Peter's Church twice in one year, once at Christmas and once at a sacred concert. As a result, the congregation of St. Peter's, in building their new church at Fifty-fourth Street and Lexington Avenue, suggested that as a token of the importance of the Jazz Ministry which was founded and headed by Pastor Gensel, there should be a jazz rehearsal room for musicians, to be called the Duke Ellington Music Center. The fifth tallest building in New York City has been built above and slightly behind the church, leading to Pastor Gensel's jocular comment, "St. Peter's is the only church that can hold up a bank and get away with it."

As the musicians rehearse in the Center, they realize that it is because of the way Duke thought about music and his fantastic contribution to music in our country and throughout the entire world that this room is theirs.

Duke touched so many areas of life; the church, the world of music, politics and government. He was literally the most honored musician the world has ever known. He received seventeen honorary doctorates, including ones from Harvard and Yale. Each time I visit the trophy room at 333 Riverside Drive, where all Duke's awards are kept, I am repeatedly amazed. They run into the hundreds, and deservedly so. Duke gave so much of his life to the love and entertainment of others, but above all, particularly in his final years, he devoted his heart, his soul and his hope of the hereafter to the church, to sacred music and to God.

Strayhorn's Death

SWEETPEA WAS ILL. BADLY ILL. TERRIBLY ILL. AT THE HOSPITAL FOR JOINT Diseases uptown on Madison Avenue, the staff and the consultants diagnosed it as cancer of the esophagus. A tracheotomy was performed, and they inserted a plastic tube to replace the esophagus, which meant that the only way he could eat was through a straw, after the food had been thoroughly pulverized in a blender. After a while he was permitted to go home and return to the hospital as an outpatient for chemotherapy treatments.

I visited him at his home a number of times, and Duke was up there every day when he was in town. Duke couldn't visit all that often because of bookings he had to take care of. Sweet-pea had a cook living with him, helping take care of his wants. I finally asked him why he needed a cook to put together all the great meals that he couldn't eat. Billy smilingly responded, "I can smell it, can't I?" (Billy knew he was terminal, but he, being Billy, wasn't about to bug anybody.)

And there was Lena, always Lena, the great, wonderful, glorious Lena, taking care of her little buddy Sweetpea when he couldn't fend for himself; being friend, nurse, mother, everything to Billy (who, as John Wayne would phrase it, was on his way back to the barn), taking him to her home in California for one last time in the sun; coming back to stay near him when he returned to the hospital; making sure he had the latest *TV Guide*, for he could still work the remote-control device to bring in the soap operas all day long that he loved so much. When Billy died it was between three and four o'clock in the morning. He died in Lena's arms, Lena, who had stayed with him and comforted him right to the very end.

Duke was absolutely inconsolable. There was no way to describe his incredible depression. He was a very emotional man in his love for the people he cared about. And he cared tremendously about Sweetpea.

The service was held at St. Peter's Church at Fifty-fourth Street and Lexington Avenue, where Sweetpea's pals had come for a final adieu. Jackie Robinson, Billy Taylor, Otto Preminger, John Hammond, Lena Horne, Mrs. Gail Lumet (Lena's daughter), Carmen McRae, Dr. Arthur Logan (his and Duke's physician and buddy for many years) and so many, many others. Pastor John Gensel read a tribute to Billy that Duke had written in Reno, where the band was playing on the night Billy died. It was a tribute to Billy's courage; to his majestic, artistic stature; to the grandeur of his talent; to his magnificent grace and sensitivity.

The Billy Taylor Trio played a medley of Billy's songs: "Lush Life," "Passion Flower," "Chelsea Bridge." When Ray Nance played Billy's "Take the A Train" in slow, New Orleans street-funeral-march tempo, there wasn't a dry eye in the church.

Duke was sitting by himself, frozen, immobile, staring straight ahead, not seeing, hearing or recognizing anything or anybody. This was the greatest loss of his life; his brother, his right arm, at least half of himself, was lying there in that coffin, being eulogized by Pastor Gensel. All through the services I stayed close to Duke, in the event that he might need a fast shoulder.

After the service we all went over to the Hickory House on Fifty-second Street. Duke and John Popkin, who owned the Hickory House, had been great friends for years. The steaks were superb, and Duke would have no other when he was in New York. We comprised a fairly cosmopolitan table—among others, Lena Horne, Gail Lumet, Pastor Gensel, Duke and myself. Lena still possessed her sense of humor. I was speaking with Gensel and addressed him as baby, which is sort of an endearing term that slips out occasionally. Lena corrected me. She said, "Don't call him baby, Don, call him preacher baby."

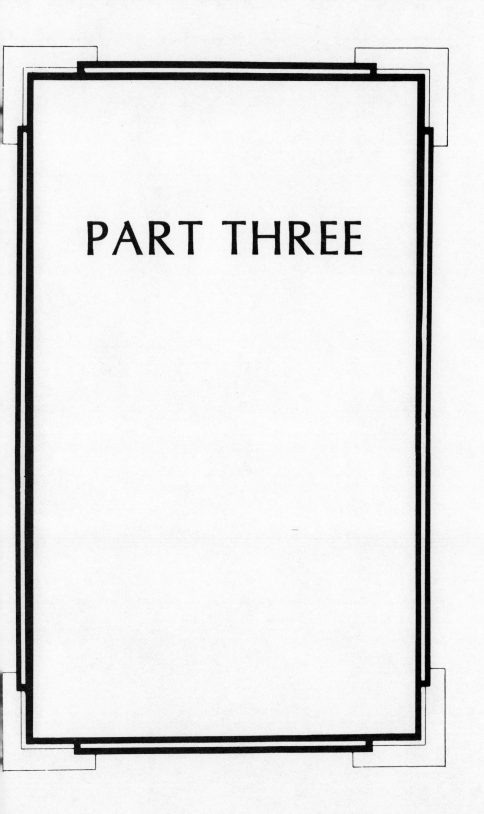

PART THREE

Duke's Seventieth Birthday, 1969, The White House

Early in 1969 Leonard Garment, clarinet player, attorney, good friend of President Nixon and member of the administration, had the idea that it would be good for Nixon's image to have Duke's seventieth birthday celebrated at the White House. He put the wheels in motion, and on the added premise that both Duke and Nixon were piano players, he elicited an enthusiastic response from the President.

Duke was asked to submit a list of fifty people he would like to have as his guests. The White House, in an extremely charming gesture, submitted their list of suggested guests for Duke's approval, all but a few of whom Duke eventually approved.

Security was very tight. Upon entering the big gate people were escorted through a little guardhouse, where everyone was more than casually patted down by the marines waitng there for that purpose. There was no open sesame to the White House.

The next plateau was the reception room, where Mr. Nixon was the first person on the receiving line, followed by Pat. The contrast between Duke's warmth and Mr. and Mrs. America, Pat and Richard Nixon, was incredible. They were more than square. They were cold, really cold. Nixon's eyes weren't sincere. His gestures reminded one of all the jokes about him as a used-car salesman. He and Mrs. Nixon, fluttering, wearing her pasted-on mannequin smile, were a tremendous contrast to Duke's gladsome greeting of people; "Hey, baby. What are you doing here?"

Standing around the fireplace in the small white room next to the reception room were Willie "the Lion" Smith, Arthur Wetzel, Freddie Guy and most of the original band that Duke had come to New York with. Over to one side Vice-President Agnew was playing Duke's "In a Sentimental Mood" in conversation style on a small upright piano.

There was nectar and ambrosia in the guise of wondrous food and drink all over the place. There were bars at every turn and Marine guards in red uniforms standing in as ushers, guides and assistant hosts, and a Marine accordion band self-consciously rendering "Hail to the Chief." In a smaller, more

183

intimate room, Richard Rodgers, Billy Eckstine, Harry Carney and Dylan Ripley (head of the Smithsonian) were engaged in animated conversation with Leonard Feather.

The concert and the presentation to Duke were to take place in the East Room, where the long gold and white expanse had been laced with chairs facing the stage at the far end. The festivities eventually began with a concert of Duke's songs played by a band employing such contemporary greats as Clark Terry, Bill Berry, Gerry Mulligan and Joe Benjamin.

President Nixon approached the microphone. "Now it is my privilege to introduce the man who is going to receive the Civilian Medal of Freedom tonight, the highest award granted to civilians. It is my privilege to introduce Edward Kennedy—" and he stopped. Everyone there knew of his ill-concealed dislike for Ted Kennedy; people looked around in surprise, disbelieving. "What?" "Is he here?" Having achieved the desired dramatic effect, Nixon then said, "Ellington," completing his enunciation of Duke's full name. Everyone laughed in relief. He continued, "Even though I'm just a half amateur, I'd like to render something in tribute to my friend, Duke. Right now I'd like to play 'Happy Birthday' in the key of G."

He sat down and played (in Sunday School fashion) two full choruses and got a big hand. He rose and presented Duke with the medal. Duke, as was his custom, kissed Nixon four times, alternating twice on each cheek. Nixon was uptight. He really froze. He didn't know how to react, particularly when Duke explained that the four kisses were meant one for each cheek. You could almost feel Nixon's cloaca constrict as the lines around his mouth tightened. He just hung there, kind of suspended in space for a brief moment. He didn't know whether to fish or cut bait or jump out the window.

Duke picked up the microphone and said, "I am reminded of the four freedoms Billy Strayhorn created for our sacred concerts—the four major moral freedoms by which he lived, and I use those four major moral freedoms by which Strayhorn lived as a measure of what we ourselves should live up to.

Freedom from hate. Unconditionally.
Freedom from self-pity.

184

Freedom from the fear of possibly doing something that would benefit someone else.

And freedom for the fear of being better than one's brother."

There was tumultuous applause. The place went into an uproar. He really knocked them dead. He crossed and sat down at the piano.

Duke, being a consummate politician himself, had written a beautiful piano piece in the key of B major (a key he very rarely played in), a beautiful, beautiful, wistful thing, a truly beautiful little ballad. When he finished playing, he said, "Yes, that was something lovely, something lovely," and he paused, then continued, "like Pat*," and he looked through the crowd and spotted Mrs. Nixon and said, "Ah, this is her." And they ate it up.

The chairs disappeared. Earl "Fatha" Hines played a solo, "Perdido." Sweating, red-faced Gerry Mulligan and Paul Desmond blew a wild "Perdido" after Fatha Hines. Anyone who wanted to play, played. The place was jamming and jumping. The atmosphere was great.

About two in the morning Nixon made an announcement. "Pat and I are going to bed now." He dismissed himself. The juice was flowing, everybody was jumping, folks were dancing. Duke was there playing stride piano with Willie "the Lion," Duke played the top, Willie played the bottom. They went through half a dozen tunes and had everyone riveted. It was the nicest time of the whole affair, the band swinging, the cats blowing, everybody with their heads on, all those so-called stuffed shirts throwing their heads all the way back.

Black Is Beautiful

DIANA VREELAND, THE EDITOR IN CHIEF OF *VOGUE* MAGAZINE, CONVINCED the Metropolitan Museum of Art, when Thomas Hoving was director there, that fashion truly was part of the art of

---

*Pat at times wore an almost wistful look. She seemed to possess a depth and warmth, well hidden, completely subjugated to the whims and foibles of her bedmate, the President. She was well programmed.

185

America. If that is true, what about music, our American music? What about jazz, whether it be Aaron Copland or Jerome Kern or Duke Ellington. The music set the mood and the lyrics told the story. Somewhat like the old town criers of England, our musicians were the unified town criers.

When we sang "Yes, We Have No Bananas," we envisioned the fruit peddlers and the orchards and the vast farmlands that blanketed our country at that time. "Brother, Can You Spare a Dime" brought home the realities of the Depression. There were songs like "Alice Blue Gown" about the crinoline days and what our society was like when everything was feminine and romantic and make believe, and we preferred everything light and gay. There were the spirituals like "Deep River" and "Sometimes I Feel Like a Motherless Child," which reflected our feelings about faith and our social classes; and the sorrowing slavery songs. The pictures on old sheet music are illustrations of what our songs had to say about the times. Consider the artwork on an old copy of "My Blue Heaven" or what a girl looked like on a copy of "Miss Annabelle Lee" or the man on the cover of "Alexander's Ragtime Band." "Yankee Doodle Dandy" and "It's a Grand Old Flag," written by George M. Cohan, were necessarily military and patriotic.

Songs by Bob Dylan, like "The Times They Are A-Changin," or by Stephen Sondheim, like "America," describe more contemporary social injustices. Leonard Bernstein's *West Side Story* is a modern adaptation of Shakespeare's *Romeo and Juliet*, with the social events incorporated into musical-comedy form, to reflect musically what was actually happening as a result of the influx of Puerto Ricans into a completely new way of life.

Jazz is a peculiarly American art form. When people heard "Alexander's Ragtime Band," some called it jazz, some called it ragtime. It depends on how close you're going to cut it. Duke's "Satin Doll" is a beautiful melodic pop song. It's also pure jazz. Where do you begin and where do you stop? What we have in the way of our music tells more about the development of the social changes in our life-style than clothes do, because the lyric tells a story, whether it be about a president or a riverboat or a steam engine or an automobile. Whether it comes under the heading of popular music or what is called jazz, it's all part of American culture.

186

Duke is a great part of the American scene. His theme song, "Take the A Train," was about a time when the Independent subway line was built in New York and the A Train journeyed through Manhattan on its way uptown to Harlem. Duke wrote "Caravan" and "Mood Indigo" during the days of Rudolph Valentino and the romantic Hollywood era and ballroom dancing. The music and the lyrics enhanced the way we were dancing. Touch dancing.

Duke was a powerful voice in the history of his time, starting with his very first song, "Soda Fountain Rag," which he wrote while working behind a soda fountain. "Satin Doll" is typical of the way men felt about women and their sensuousness. You can almost visualize Diana Vreeland employing whatever the style was then, with women in their satin dresses, with their boyish hairdos and high-heeled shoes, which is all pictured in the song "Saturday Night Is the Loneliest Night of the Week," written during the Second World War when most of the fellows were away, and it was hell for a lady to be alone. Saturday was a big night for dance halls and movies. Near the end of the war, the song Duke and I had written, "I'm Beginning to See the Light," became popular just as the blackout was lifted. The song was interpreted in many ways, including that in dreams or at the end of the road, there is sunlight and the brightness of the future.

The language of Duke's songs, the tempo, the melody, the importance of the melody against the beat, continually illustrate the temper of the times. In his own way he was a historian. His voice was a strong voice because, in the form of entertainment, it illustrated a very serious development in our world, in our country, in our life-style.

Duke was doing more than just writing songs or creating cantatas. He was originating new musical forms. He was painting musical murals mainly featuring the word *black*. There is no question that Duke's creations had an emotional impact on our language. They certainly helped tremendously in bringing the phrase *black is beautiful* into being.

In 1927 Duke wrote "Black and Tan Fantasy."

In 1934 he wrote "Symphony in Black."

In 1936 he wrote "Black Butterfly."

In 1938 he wrote "Black Beauty."

In 1943 he wrote "Black, Brown and Beige."

Duke was tremendously well versed in black history. He told me about the invasion of Africa by Portugal, shortly after Columbus discovered the New World, when the Portuguese set up the slave system as we knew it. He told me about Crispus Attucks, a black who was the first casualty of the Boston Massacre; about the underground railroad that smuggled slaves to the North during the Civil War; about Harriet Beecher Stowe. He made me aware of Marcus Garvey and George Washington Carver.

Duke did more than just discuss black history. He musicalized it. In the three movements of "Black, Brown and Beige" (written in 1943), he starts with a work song sung by the chained blacks laboring on the Southern docks and in the cotton fields. The theme of the second movement features a blues describing the process leading up to the eventual emancipation. The final movement is about blacks and whites as a mixed people.

On the night that "Black, Brown and Beige" was introduced at Carnegie Hall, the United States was still at war. After the music Duke ended his performance by announcing, "Our country is in trouble. Now they need us, and we're responding. The 'Black, Brown and Beige' is all set to fight for the red, white and blue."

Satin Doll

THE HICKORY HOUSE STOOD FOR MANY YEARS ON WEST FIFTY-SECOND Street in Manhattan as a tribute to great steaks and good jazz. Duke came in often and always preceded his tussle with the T-bones by absorbing a huge amount of ice cream, every flavor they had. The owner, John Popkin, was a big fan of Duke's. He just loved him. He made a big deal of it every time Duke arrived and always sat with him, explaining why the horses he bet on preferred being followers instead of leaders.

Whenever Duke came in, Billy Taylor, who was playing piano on the raised bandstand that was surrounded by the huge circular bar, dug back into his mental file of Ellingtonia and tried to play something obscure or one of the older things that Duke might not remember. One night Taylor played "Satin

Doll." (Duke had written it with Johnny Mercer and Billy Strayhorn and recorded it, but he didn't have it in the book. The band wasn't playing it. Taylor had liked the song and recorded it and kept on playing it.)

Duke called him over and said, "Hey, man, that's a nice little arrangement."

Billy replied, "Thanks, Duke. I'm glad you like it. We get a lot of requests for it."

Duke nodded. "I'll have to put that back in the book. You've got it sounding very good."

Sure enough, the next time Taylor went to hear the band, they were playing "Satin Doll." From that time on Duke stayed with the song, playing it wherever he went, until other bands and singers picked it up, laying on it until it became a jazz standard.

Duke's usual introduction to "Satin Doll": "The next song is dedicated to the most beautiful lady here. We will not point her out because we do not want her to feel conspicuous. We will just let her sit there and continue to feel guilty."

Miss USA

DUKE DIDN'T PARTICULARLY CARE FOR MAKEUP WHEN HE WAS DOING HIS TV appearances, although when he got in the chair, he enjoyed the fuss that people made over him. He did the *Today Show* once when Miss USA was on, and she was seated in the chair next to him. Of course, his first line to her was, "And whose pretty little girl are you?"

They were introduced, and Duke looked in the mirror, and looked at Miss USA, and looked around and said, "Isn't it nice to have two of the country's prettiest people in the same room at the same time?"

Jazzmobile

ONCE WHILE DUKE WAS PLAYING AT THE RAINBOW GRILL, BILLY TAYLOR came by to hear the band and told Duke that he'd really like him to play the Jazzmobile.

Duke said, "Sure, Billy. Anything for you."

The Jazzmobile is a program that was originated by Billy

189

Taylor, the great piano player, occasional producer, member of the Board of Directors of the American Society of Composers, Authors and Publishers (ASCAP), and close friend of both of us. It was created for the purpose of bringing musicians closer to the people. Too many people living in New York City couldn't afford to hear Duke Ellington, couldn't afford to hear Count Basie or any of the other major musical stars. In the old days people could afford to go to places like the Savoy Ballroom or the Apollo Theatre. But those places just don't exist anymore. The ones that do exist, like the Village Gate or Michael's Pub and similar places, are far too expensive for the ghetto purse. When the top musicians come to town, they play Carnegie Hall or Lincoln Center, as they should, because they are great artists. However, they are inaccessible to poor people. Jazzmobile filled that void by taking a mobile bandstand through the streets of Harlem, Bedford-Stuyvesant and the South Bronx and similar areas. They'd always have some great artist like Duke or Clark Terry or Cannonball Adderley, whom the people wouldn't normally get to see. They also featured young musicians like Chick Corea and Herbie Hancock, who would lead their own groups. The Jazzmobile served many purposes, but its major importance lay in bringing somebody like Ellington to the people.

The Jazzmobile was booked to play in Harlem on 129th Street, between Lenox and Fifth avenues, which was a street Duke had lived on way back in the early days. Billy Taylor didn't know this when he asked Duke to play there. Jazzmobile worked with the block associations in and around the city, and one of the people in the 129th Street Block Association said, "Well, you know, Duke Ellington used to live in this house."

Taylor didn't know what to believe. "Yeah, yeah, that's fine. That's lovely."

Sure enough, when Duke showed up he said yes, he used to live in that area, in fact he had lived in that very house. It was a hot August afternoon and they had an air-conditioned limousine just relaxing in the street for him, but he said, "No, no. I'll go inside."

He went in and sat down, and he was so very gracious that he charmed the lady who lived there right off her feet. The

190

lady made some lemonade and served some soul food that she had prepared on the off chance that Duke Ellington was really going to show up. There had been quite a bit of tension and doubt. A number of people had said, "Yeah, we know you guys had Cannonball Adderley and all that stuff, but Duke isn't going to show up. He's too big."

There were signs all around the street saying, ON SUNDAY, SPE-CIAL CONCERT BY DUKE ELLINGTON.

Some people said, "That's nice." Other people mocked. "Come on, man, you kidding? Duke Ellington on this street?"

There was a Steinway right in the middle of the street. The Jazzmobile itself wasn't big enough to hold all of Duke's band, so another mobile platform had been added to it, with the piano front and center on the platform.

Duke came on and did his regular concert set. He played for about an hour and a half out in the hot August sun. Even in those days he wasn't in such great shape that he could do that a lot. But he always rose to the occasion. Besides, it was something he wanted to do. He knew when he agreed to do it what it was going to be like, and he knew he'd be comfortable with the people. I really think he originally figured that he'd let the band play a few tunes, then make an appearance, play something, feature a singer and get the hell out of there.

When he came on the scene in his white ice cream suit and went into the lady's house, there was pandemonium. Word spread like wildfire. There were wall-to-wall people on the block. People came from everywhere: Washington Heights, the Bronx, Newark, Brooklyn. After the band played an opening number, Duke came out and played and talked with the folks. It was really a delightful afternoon, a tremendous outpouring of respect and love. The people had seen Duke in the movies and on television, they had heard him on the jukeboxes and on the radio, but they never had seen him in person. It was an exciting adventure for them to be that close to him. You could feel the warmth. It just knocked Duke out.

The vibes were so strong you could almost taste them. It was just beautiful. The people didn't want him to go. They wanted him to stay all afternoon. He got on the mike and said, "Yes, I used to live here," and he reminisced about what used to hap-

191

pen, about the after-hours joints, and how much fun it was in the old days of Harlem and how nice it was to be back home.

It was the only street event of its kind Duke ever did. While Duke was playing his signoff song, "Time's A-Wastin'," he noticed a lady dancing on a fire escape and had the band play a couple of extra choruses so that she could keep on dancing.

After Duke left, the old women were still sitting in the open windows, resting their elbows on pillows to keep them from the hard stone sills. Some of them had been sitting there for years, staring out at nothing. Now they finally had something to look at, someone to see. One of their own had made it and had come home to momentarily enchant their eyes.

The young people were standing up straighter, exuding pride. You could almost hear them saying to themselves, "Hey, man, he's black and he made it. Maybe we can too."

TIME'S A-WASTIN'

Listen, baby, the TIME'S A-WASTIN',
And I'm tellin' ya it's disgracin'
Missin' kisses we should be tastin',
Sugar child,—now I'm beggin' your lips to hasten.
I need 'em so,
'Cause I got a feelin' I gotta glow.

While there's a moon up
Can't our song be more than just a tune up?
Lately, darling, I have learned a lesson,
More than just my dreams desire caressin'.
So, hasten now
'Cause, baby, the TIME IS A-WASTIN' now.

Alvin Ailey

DUKE CONCEIVED THE IDEA OF WRITING THE MUSIC FOR A BALLET TO BE performed by two separate dance companies, on two separate stage levels, one above and one below, with the orchestra playing on a platform sandwiched in between. In his words, "One company will do the bass line and the other will do the filigree."

He recruited the assistance of Alvin Ailey, a friendly, handsome, tall and powerfully built man who much more resembled the football player and gymnast he had once been than the internationally known dancer and choreographer he had become. The first rehearsal was rather a mess. Duke was directing and coordinating and attempting to handle the choreography himself. Ailey became aware of what was going on and started staging the action. Duke liked what Ailey was doing, and right there they sort of fell in love with each other.

Ailey was somewhat surprised at the inseparability of Duke and the Countess. To quote him, "She was very much there. I mean, under his armpits. He couldn't walk out onstage and direct the orchestra without her being next to him. William saw her going into the bathroom with him once. The dancers nearly fell over. He said, 'You know, that woman went into the john with Duke.' "

Duke was on the National Endowment Board with Lucia Chase, who was director of the Ballet Theatre. She suggested to Duke that he write a ballet for them. At the same time she asked Ailey to choreograph a ballet. Ailey agreed to work with Duke, who was in Vancouver, British Columbia, at the time. The Ballet Theatre flew Ailey to Vancouver. He arrived at the club where Duke was playing at about two in the morning, between the first and second shows.

Duke was stretched out on a couch in a blue bathrobe in his dressing room when Ailey walked in. He yawned and said, "Hi, Alvin. We're supposed to have a meeting about this ballet."

Ailey agreed. "Yes, we are. But if you're tired, we won't do it."

Duke remonstrated, "No, no. We'll do it after the second show."

Ailey replied, "After the second show! That'll be four in the morning."

Duke smiled, "That's a good time to work."

They got to the hotel at about four thirty and went up to the Presidential Suite, where Duke was staying. There was a piano at the end of the bed and sheets of music scattered about. Ailey started talking about an idea he had for a romantic ballet.

Duke had just been honored at the White House on his seventieth birthday by Nixon. He grumbled, "If that guy hadn't given me that birthday party, nobody would know how old I am." He was concerned about that.

He poured Ailey some Scotch from one of the little airline bottles and had a Coca-Cola with four spoons of sugar in it. After they drank, Duke said, "There's a piece I've wanted to do for a long time. It's called *The River*. It's a life cycle about a young man who grows from childhood through the phases of water into maturity, finally emerging as a glorious, full human being. There are a number of sections in it. The opening section is called 'The Spring.' You can almost picture where it starts bubbling in the mountain. The next section, which is a little slower, is called 'Meander.' " As he continued his voice acquired an edge of excitement. "There's a 'Vortex,' there's a 'Falls,' there's a 'Giggling Rapids,' there's 'The Sea'—"

Ailey interrupted, saying, "That sounds fantastic."

Duke sat down and played a gorgeous melody with a Latin beat, which turned out to be "The Lake," which formed the center of the ballet. Then he played something sort of Middle Eastern, which was the first piece, "The Spring."

Ailey was ecstatic. "That sounds absolutely wonderful. It sounds like something I can really get my teeth into."

Duke played little sketches of things. Of "Giggling Rapids," of "Meander." He played a complete section of "Her Majesty the Sea," all the while asking Ailey, "Do you really like it?"

Ailey responded, "I do. I do. I love every bit of it."

They carried on until about eight in the morning, when Duke hurried to catch a 9 A.M. plane to his next gig in Los Angeles, and Ailey headed back to New York with both his head and his heart full of *The River*.

They didn't meet again for six or seven months, when Duke called Ailey from the Royal York Hotel in Toronto, saying, "Come on up here, man. We'll work every day for a week and put the thing together. You can live down the hall from me."

Ailey caught the next plane to Toronto and got into the lifestyle of the band. Duke called him constantly. Ailey watched Duke's nine o'clock show, came back upstairs to Duke's room, watched him socialize with dozens of ladies who were massag-

194

ing his feet (he was so proud of his feet) and his ears while he was lying there in his bathrobe, then caught the last show, which ended about three in the morning.

About four thirty or five, when Ailey was dead asleep, Duke called him, saying, "Hi there, Alvin. This is Duke. You ready to work? Come on, man. I have something I want you to hear."

In preparing for *The River*, Duke had gathered around him all the scores and recordings of the world's greatest water music. He had Debussy's *La Mer*. He had Handel's *Water Music*. He had Britten's *Peter Grimes*. Duke started each session by listening to a few things. He particularly liked *La Mer*. He played it for Ailey and said, "Do you like this?"

Ailey replied, "Oh, yes. I like the rhythm."

Duke again had the small piano at the foot of the bed, the small portable piano that went wherever he did. *The River* was becoming solidified into thirteen sections, each one a different tempo, much of it reminiscent of the history of jazz.

Ailey spent the week completely inundated by Duke's personality and amazed by his energy; playing two shows a night, conducting a band rehearsal every afternoon, creating *The River* and structuring the arrangements with young Ron Collier. One afternoon Ailey said to me, "Don, he is marvelous. He's a real genius. Things just flow out of him. He is so much different than I thought he would be. I saw this flashily dressed man on the bandstand and thought that people like him were superficial; just entertainers. To find out that he is really a studied, caring, compassionate man is what blows me away. He's become a model for me: a man who can lead his kind of organization, with their background and history, and still go on and do the performances and find time in his life for new creative projects."

Three days before rehearsals were due to start, Ailey still hadn't received the written music. He had occasionally received bits and pieces in the mail, a few bars now and then that didn't quite seem to match up. One day he got a tape with four pieces, and he was trying to choreograph those. He finally threw up his hands. All the Ballet Theatre people were in the rehearsal studio and Ailey was all hot to go, but he was completely frustrated because he didn't have the music. He flipped. He went clean out of his mind. He hurled the whole

195

thing—notebooks, tapes and all—up against the mirror and yelled, "Fuck it, I can't work like this."

At that precise moment the door opened and in walked Duke in his white cashmere coat, surrounded by his entourage. The whole room stopped. In fact, it fell to its knees. Ailey told me later that what he wanted to scream was, "Motherfucker, where's the music?" Instead they went outside and sat and talked. Ailey told Duke he couldn't work without the whole score.

Duke said to Alvin, "Listen, if you'd stop worrying about this music and do more choreography, we'd be a whole lot better off."

Ron Collier came in to arrange the music. It was all there. Under Duke's guidance, Collier started getting it down on paper.

The orchestrations were finally finished, and the ballet completed. It turned out to be a truly beautiful work and a smashing success. The Caracas Ballet in Venezuela and the Opera Ballet in Budapest performed it. It landed in the repertoire of a big company in Israel, and excerpts from *The River* were used by skaters in competition. The Ballet Theatre, which originally stimulated its creation, has been performing it since its inception, but Duke unfortunately never got to see it. When *The River* was performed in Venezuela, he was with the band in Russia. When it was done in Budapest, he was in Africa. When the Ballet Theatre staged it in New York, he was in San Francisco.

Typically, Duke, who preferred never to sign anything, had no contract with the Ballet Theatre people or any other source involving payment for performances of the work.

Painting

IT WAS PLEASANT IN DUKE'S APARTMENT ON WEST END AVENUE, LISTENING to one of Duke's albums on the stereo, with the rain splashing on the terrace just outside the window. It promised to be an interesting evening. We had just surrounded a couple of John Popkin's friendliest T-bones, and Duke had retired to the blue room to adjust his coiffure before our departure to join the carriage trade on Fifty-seventh Street, where Duke was to grace the opening of a one-man show of his paintings at the Center Art Gallery, a stone's throw from Milgrim's and Jay Thorpe and across the street from the Sherwood Studios, home of Chagall and Mane-Katz.

The buzzing of the intercom interrupted my thoughts. Duke's voice came floating in. "Would you get that, Don."

"Sure thing," I called back, heading for the kitchen.

A moment later Duke came into the room. "Anything important?" he asked.

I replied, "Just the doorman calling to tell us the limo is waiting. I told him we'd be down in a few minutes."

Riding down in the elevator with us was a distraught young couple. The size of the girl's belly provided a visual clue to the reason for their nervousness. Duke spoke to her soothingly, lovingly. "Don't worry. Everything will be all right."

The husband was beside himself. "We called down for a cab. I hope the doorman got a cab. We have to get to the hospital in a hurry." In the lobby the doorman was apologetic. Because of the rain he had been unable to get a taxi. Duke came to the rescue. "I've got a car here. Come in my car . . . No, it's no trouble."

We took the couple to the hospital. On the way Duke asked, "How soon is it?"

The girl replied, "Any minute now. The pains are very close."

We reached the hospital in the nick of time. The baby arrived just as we got there. It was a boy.* After calming the new father, we proceeded to our original destination, the Center Art Gallery.

As we entered the gallery, an avalanche of affection descended upon Duke. A tremendous outpouring of the greats of the entertainment world had been waiting to greet him. They were much relieved at his appearance, late though it was, as some of them had given up hope of his showing at all. There was much embracing, backslapping, handshaking and kissing. Among the giants present putting a dent in the caviar and champagne were old friends Jack Benny, Peggy Lee, Nat Cole, Ella Logan, Xavier Cugat, Leonard Bernstein, Tony Bennett,

*We found out later that they named the baby Edward Ellington.

197

George Burns, Irving Mansfield with Jackie Susann and so many others too numerous to mention.

Walking around the gallery looking at the pictures, some of which I had not seen before, and occasionally stopping to chat with friends, I noticed tiny red paper stars pasted on the lower righthand corner of every visible frame. The show was a sellout. Evelyn Marks, the beaming proprietress of the gallery, told me that every picture had been sold long before Duke's arrival.

Watching him standing there in the center of the crowd, a smiling target for all the attitudes and platitudes being verbally hurled at him, I was amazed at where and how he had found the time and the concentration necessary to complete enough pictures for a one-man show, what with his playing one-nighters, composing, arranging, romantic interludes, ice-cream eating and 4 A.M. telephone calling.

After a while, without being obvious he shook loose and joined Peggy Lee and Tony Bennett in a quiet corner of the room.

Seeing Duke and Peggy and Tony talking and laughing together reminded me of a night back when Duke was playing at Basin Street East and Phoebe Jacobs, the gracious lady who handled the entertainment both there and at the Rainbow Grill, received a telephone call from Tony Bennett from Detroit. Tony said, "I just finished my last show. I'm at the airport. What time does the Maestro go on?"

Phoebe told him the last show started at 1:30 A.M. Duke was so popular, they had three shows a night with lines around the block.

Tony said, "I'm on my way in. I should be there before the show ends."

When Duke was told Tony was flying in, he said, "Fine, we'll just make the show a little bit longer." He started the show on time, and when Tony arrived, Duke announced, "I'm going to do the show all over again for a guy who just flew in from Detroit to catch it. There will be no additional music charge. This one is on the house." He introduced Tony and replayed the entire show.

Peggy Lee was living in Suite 41H in the Waldorf Towers at the time. She was the first entertainer who had been able to break their rule barring performers from occupying space there. She had subleased the suite from Henry Kaiser, a great fan of hers, whom she had met through Edgar Bronfman when she did a Damon Runyon Cancer Fund benefit for him. Peggy was opening at Basin Street after Duke closed. She had come in a couple of days early to take care of her gowns and for rehearsals. After having a late dinner in Jimmy's La Grange, which was right across the street from the club, she came in to catch Duke's last show and for the first time met Tony Bennett, who had always been very much in awe of her.

Duke and Peggy and Tony and some of the regulars hung out together after the show. Duke wanted everybody to go to Reuben's, but Peggy had an interview early the next morning at her place and said, "Come on up to my apartment in the Towers." She had some of the pictures there that she was painting, which she did for therapy to help her relax. She and Tony got along splendidly and mostly talked about painting till well after five in the morning, long after Duke had taken the rest of the gang to Reuben's.

I ran into Tony on the street one day maybe half a block away from where I live. We had been close friends for years, ever since he first came around and started to hang out in the Brill Building. After our usual embrace, I noticed how depressed he seemed. I asked him, "What's the problem, Tony?"

He said "You know, Sandy* and I have broken up, and it's lonesome out on the road. I'm doing all these one-nighters and split weeks without my family, and it's damn lonely out there. Before I work and after I work, I have nothing to do."

I said, "Tony, have you got a few minutes?" He nodded. I took his arm, "Come on up to the apartment. I want to show you something."

When we got to my place, he looked around the walls, where there were thirty-five or forty paintings hanging, looked at the signatures and exclaimed, "Wow, these are all your paintings."

I told him, "I had a one-man show."

He nodded. "I know. I read about it in the papers. It was in all the columns."

I said, "When Duke found out I was having a one-man show,

*His first wife.

he wrote letters to all the columnists and to the trades." I shook my head in wonderment. "That man is really something else."

I paused a minute, then said, "Tony, I'll tell you what I think you ought to do. You were always very good with pen-and-ink drawings. How are you coming with that?"

He shrugged. "I haven't done any for a long time."

I repeated, "That's what you should do, Tony; you've got to do that. Remember how you used to draw bridges and cars and people and different theater things?" I leaned on him a little bit. "Tony, in this world, nobody does it for you. You've got to get out there and shake your ass. Why not? Your pen-and-ink drawings were wonderful. They were just great. I know artists who work with pen and ink, and I've never seen any that are better than you. What you should do when you're out there and you get lonesome and you feel dragged, just pen and ink it, man. Draw whatever you see. Draw a taxi, draw a building, draw a person, draw the desk. There's always something to draw."

He looked slowly around the walls again, then said, "Jesus Christ, Don, if you can do this, I certainly can do the drawings."

I visited him some time later in an apartment where he was living with his second wife (also named Sandy) on East Sixty-eighth Street. He had graduated from pen and ink and was painting with oil. I looked out the window at a building under construction across the street that he was painting. The wet canvas was still on the easel. He showed me other paintings that he had done. His work was good enough for me to realize he was on his way to becoming an important and successful painter. He had signed the canvases with one name, his real name, Benedetto.

The Franklin Mint threw a big opening party at the Four Seasons Restaurant for a book they were publishing containing one painting apiece from important people in the performing arts. Duke and Tony Bennett and Peggy Lee were each well represented with important works, which were later shown at an exhibit at Lincoln Center.

I've often wondered, if Tony and I hadn't run into each other on the street that day, if he ever would have painted.

Peggy Lee

PEGGY LEE WAS A FANTASTIC HOSTESS WHO ENTERTAINED LAVISHLY IN HER charming home on Kim Ridge Road in Beverly Hills. Frank Sinatra came to one of her parties and flipped for the house and the location. He asked Peggy as a good friend to check out the neighborhood and see if there was anything available in the immediate area. Peggy was successful, and Frank became a neighbor.

The same thing happened in the same way with Benny Carter, the great arranger, musician and composer.

Not long afterward Peggy invited her neighbors to a Christmas party. Benny and Marge Carter came, and Sinatra came, and the milkman came and the cleaner. At a party people ask, "Who are you? What do you do? What do you work at?" She had invited her butcher and her grocer and all her neighbors. That was her Christmas party. That was Peggy, warm and wonderful.

Peggy had written the lyric for Duke's theme melody for the film *Anatomy of a Murder*. She called it "Gone Fishin'," and the success of the song created the occasion for a dinner party she gave in Duke's honor. Charlie Barnet was there with his sixth (or seventh?) wife, and Frank Sinatra showed up with Juliet Prowse. Peggy had just bought a Jaguar, and Cary Grant came by to take her for a test drive. Everybody loved the way Peggy had decorated her house. The seats of the chairs around the table in the dining room were each a different color velvet: orange, yellow, green, blue, brown, white. She teased Duke, "You're the guest of honor: you take the white seat. That is, if you're not prejudiced."

Cary Grant loved to sing. After dinner he asked Duke to play for him. They all gathered around the piano while Cary sang song after song. After a while Duke turned to Peggy and said, "Come on, Peggy, let's sing some songs with the man." (Cary Grant later recorded a song that Peggy wrote for him and dedicated it to his daughter.)

Duke and Peggy had always been strongly attracted to each other. After the dinner party their friendship deepened into a warm and lasting relationship. Peggy was very similar to Duke. When she spoke, you saw pictures. In addition to being an excellent lyricist, she was a great housekeeper, a fantastic hostess and an accomplished painter; she had magnificent taste in music—all qualities that Duke respected and appreciated.

Through the years they kept running into each other (as Peggy phrased it, "On the road to Mandalay"). They worked together on *The Ed Sullivan Show*. They met in Vegas when Duke was starting to write his sacred concerts. Peggy had just returned from a Command Performance for the Queen of England when she told me, "I had such tremendous respect and awe for that man. He had a fantastic charisma. It was exciting just to have him around. It was also nice to talk to him in quieter moments. There was something so awesome about him and at the same time so very loving and affectionate. He had a grandeur that made you want to hang onto every word he was saying. He usually said something highly complimentary. He called Leonard Feather's wife the Golden Feather and he called me the Queen."

I remembered the first time Duke had called Peggy the Queen. One of the more important ladies from the National Association for the Advancement of Colored People (NAACP) had appeared on the scene, saying that they were planning to hold an all-black salute to Duke.

They had engaged Madison Square Garden well in advance for the occasion. When Duke was told there was to be an all-black salute in his honor, he became slightly hysterical. He said, "Oh, no. An all-black salute! For me? I'm not showing up."

When Peggy heard about it she said, "You can count on me to be there."

The NAACP lady was asked, "What can we say to Peggy Lee? She heard about the tribute to Duke and she wants to fly in." The lady was pleasantly startled. "Oh, dear, can we print that? Can we publish that she's going to be there?" She was advised to drop Peggy a note saying that she'd heard Peggy planned to help honor Mr. Ellington, and might they use her name to help gather other attractions.

At the Garden on the night of the event, Peggy not only flew in but she had organized a band headed by Quincy Jones to play her salute to Duke. The Garden was jammed. People were hanging from the rafters.

Peggy was spotlighted on the stage, singing to the house, when Duke, who was standing in the wings with Louis Armstrong, turned to him and said, "Louie, now we really have royalty on that stage. She's the Queen."

Another time, at Basin Street East, Nat "King" Cole, who had come in to hear his buddy Duke, got up and sang a couple of songs with the band. Peggy, who was opening a couple of days later, had come in to catch Duke's last show. She sang "Sometimes I Feel Like a Motherless Child" while Duke accompanied her on piano. Nat came into Ralph Watkins's office and started to cry. He said Peggy sounded so much like Billie Holiday (Nat had been Billie's accompanist in the old days). They started reminiscing. Duke told a Holiday story, and Watkins told the story of how Billie didn't show up and Nat took her place vocally. As Peggy walked into the room, Duke took her by the hand and in a voice filled with respect and affection said, "Children, here's the Queen."

They had so much in common. They were both out of Sartre, both existentialists. They shared the same fanasies, the same make believing. Occasionally they went on walks together and like two little children, talked to the clouds and the butterflies.

Otto Preminger

OTTO PREMINGER HAD ESCORTED ME ON A TOUR OF HIS LOVELY TOWN house in New York City, where paintings and sculptures by Picasso, Miro, Modigliani, Henry Moore, Giacometti and additional beauty ad infinitum lined the walls, then sat in his combination office and projection room on the top floor of the mostly white house, designed by the great man himself. Preminger was extremely alert, very charming and more than a bit devilish, despite his seventy-odd years.

I asked him about the film *Anatomy of a Murder*, for which Duke wrote the music in 1959.

"How did you fellows get together?"

Preminger replied, "I knew him socially when I used to live

in California, and we became very friendly. He was an ideal man for a director to work with. Usually with musicians, more than with other parts of a picture, you find when you ask for something, they say, 'Possibly.' Duke never did that. Whatever I suggested, he did very professionally. If I asked him for something at night, he had it ready in the morning. This was the only time that I used a musician who was already well known in any of my independent pictures, because what I usually do, I take a young composer and he's with me from the very beginning; when I'm working on the script, when I'm rehearsing, so that he becomes part of the picture. You can only do it with very young, inexpensive musicians, because they usually have to spend close to a year on the project.

"Duke was different. He was such a great composer and so completely professional about everything he did that for the first time, I made an exception. I was right. Both the picture and the music were very successful."

I asked, "Did you have any problem with Duke?"

Preminger shook his head. "On the contrary, I had no difficulty at all. Duke worked right along with me. I gave him a part in the picture, playing a pianist in a roadhouse, and he really enjoyed himself."

Preminger chuckled, remembering, then continued, "Ten years later, in 1969, I was in my office, opening the morning mail. The first letter was a note from Senator Hubert Humphrey, thanking me for supporting him in his unsuccessful try for the presidency. The second letter contained an invitation for dinner from the President and Mrs. Nixon. I called my wife and said, 'Darling, somebody's playing a strange joke on us. Why should Nixon invite us for dinner? He knows we supported Humphrey and didn't vote for him. We knew Lyndon Johnson for years before he invited us for dinner, and Nixon invites us to the White House after he's in only about eight weeks.'

" 'Well,' my wife answered, 'maybe he's desperate for guests.' " We learned later it was a party to celebrate Duke's seventieth birthday. Duke's grandfather had been a servant at the White House. Duke had put our names on the guest list and arranged it so that my wife sat at Nixon's table and I sat with Mrs. Nixon. We had a very pleasant evening."

The Dance Concert on Mt. Tamalpais

THERE IS AN OUTDOOR STONE THEATER ON TOP OF MT. TAMALPAIS IN MARin County, California. Modeled after a classic Greek amphitheater, it seats five thousand people, which makes it greater than the Hollywood Bowl or any similar structure. There is no electricity, so all the events take place in the daytime by natural light, with any necessary power supplied by generators that are hauled up the mountain. The shell has perfect acoustics, so there is no need for miking or amplifying an orchestra. It is truly an exciting place to have a concert or dance recital. To reach it one crosses the Golden Gate Bridge to Marin County, to the first Mill Valley exit, then chooses the winding road to the left to the top of the mountain. At the peak, where the theater majestically waits, you are a million miles from nowhere and centuries back in time.

It was here that Duke held a combined concert and dance recital that had been conceived when we were at a reception held in his honor at the Sausalito houseboat of Alan Watts, the noted Zen philosopher and writer. It was a rather formal party, with the music being supplied by a harpist. Among those present was Shela Xoregos, the dance director for the Atheneum Arts Foundation of Marin County, who was talking to Duke about doing a concert at the theater on top of Mt. Tamalpais.

When Duke heard that Xoregos was a dancer, he said, "I'd love to see you dance. Won't you dance for us?"

Xoregos replied, "I can't. I don't have my leotards and tights."

One of the ladies who graced the household said, "I've got some tights and leotards in my cabin."

"Well, there's too much furniture. There's no room."

Duke said, "We'll move the furniture."

"Oh, but there's a rug."

Duke said, "We'll take the rug up."

"I have no music."

Duke said, "That's all right. I'll play for you."

I made a gesture of interrogation in Duke's direction. He pretended to ignore it.

While she changed her clothes, they moved the furniture and rolled up the rug. After the dance Duke came over to her

205

and said, "I'm going to write a piece for you. Would you dance it with my orchestra if I write it?"

She didn't take him seriously. "Why, certainly I will. Just give me a call when you have it finished."

A couple of months later he telephoned her from Bangkok and said he'd been trying to reach her. "Well, I've written that piece for you. Are we going to do it on the mountain?'"

She almost fainted when she realized he was serious, that he had actually written a piece called "Psychedelic Suite" just for her. In the ensuing few months Duke phoned her from various places around the world, never telling her where he was. Xoregos would always ask him for the music, and he'd say, "I'm working on it."

She asked him to hum it over the telephone. "Don't worry, you'll get it."

She couldn't pin him down. She wanted to rehearse because she wanted the concert to be great, but Duke obviously thought she should improvise, the way she had that evening at the party on the houseboat.

Duke checked into the Fairmont Hotel a few days before the concert. The Countess was there with her chauffeured limousine, bringing him vitamins and minerals and pills and yeast powder. She was a health nut and brought him all the things she felt would keep him healthy. She was always concerned that he was up late, that he wasn't getting his rest, that he wasn't eating right. "Be sure you take the pills, Dukie. You'll need your strength when we go to the Bahamas." Dukie took the pills.

During the next few days Duke spent a good deal of time with his buddy S. I. Hayakawa, the internationally renowned writer and psychologist, who was then president of San Francisco State College. They felt a lot alike about many areas. They ran around together; they went to parties together. They were really good friends, two brilliant men, each of whom understood and respected the earthiness of the other.

Because of his scholastic responsibilities Hayakawa was unable to keep the same hours as Duke, so Duke had time on his hands. He took to hanging out in the Fillmore district, the black area of San Francisco. He'd get his hair cut there, he'd get his shoes shined there, he'd talk to people there. Starting at two or three A.M., after he got through writing music in his room, he'd stand on street corners, jiving with the local prostitutes, killing time till daybreak, when he'd be able to go to sleep.

"Hi, Duke. Back so soon?"

"I missed you, baby. You sure make the street look pretty."

One evening Duke was recruited to emcee the Fol-de-rol, the annual benefit for the San Francisco Opera Company. It is a very famous event that is held in the Civic Auditorium, which is so huge that people can sit in the bleachers for a dollar or two.

After the event he hosted a late supper for a group of people in his suite at the Fairmont, at which time he unveiled his latest airline stewardess. What happened afterward I don't feel privileged to say.

Except for their telephone conversations, Xoregos had had no contact with Duke since the night of the party on Alan Watts's houseboat, until he phoned her the day before the scheduled recital, asking her to meet him at a television station to help publicize the event. He still hadn't given Xoregos any music or any idea what the music might be like.

At the theater on the mountain the next day, there were no showers or hot water and only very primitive dressing areas. Duke was in a talkative mood. He told us that he and the Countess had just had dinner at Hayakawa's home, who then drove them up to the concert.

He said, "You know, I had a rough time last night. I had to go to a reception over in Orange County, then I played a concert, then I had to walk through a livestock exhibition with all those boring people. What a night."

He perked up as the time for the recital drew closer. He stood near the door of the dressing room and handed the musicians their parts. It didn't look as though there were very many notes. Four of the leading section men came to the dressing room right before the concert to get the music. He had written the melody line for some of the instruments and the harmony for some of the other instruments.

He explained, "We'll run this down a couple of times, and we'll put a little coda on there, then we'll go back to the beginning. Watch me, I'll let you know when we'll take it on out."

Xoregos was on the spot. She had still never heard the music, never rehearsed. She had no idea what was going to happen.

When Duke made his entrance after the band played their theme, "Take the A Train," it was something to see five thousand people come off their backsides onto their feet, applauding and yelling. The audience went mad from that point on. When Duke said, "I love you madly," they yelled, "I love you madly" right back at him.

Picture five thousand people with their backs to the hot sun, with the sun most of the day pouring down on the stage like a giant follow spot, a huge illumination blazing into the eyes of the performers. The band was out in the open, with Duke sheltered under an oversize beach umbrella that was aimed to throw a shadow over him, to keep him and the piano in the shade.

The audience was made up mainly of a great number of ladies wearing kooky summer straw hats and other weird head coverings they had improvised to shield themselves from the sun. Seeing the plight of the band, the women started coming down out of the audience, bringing them their hats. Soon the entire band was sitting there playing their instruments, wearing the weird straw hats. Duke and the band loved it. They were far away from the smoke-filled nightclubs, on top of a mountain, with a jeweled crown known as San Francisco shimmering below them in the distance.

Xoregos danced onstage, improvising in a fashion in which she could change the choreography when she heard the music change. Duke was watching her and cueing the band, who knew Duke so well that with the movement of his head or his hand or his arm, they changed mood, tempo, everything.

The dance came off beautifully. It couldn't have been done better if they had rehearsed for weeks. Xoregos reached the climactic moment of the dance just as the music peaked. They were an absolute smash. It was an eerie, awesome feeling being one of more than five thousand people cheering and applauding the superb performance we had just witnessed in that stone cathedral high above the world.

At the reception afterward people approached the director,

Lyle Leverich, and asked, "How in the world did you get Duke Ellington to play on the mountain for you? How did you do it?"

Leverich smilingly replied, "We just asked him, and he said, 'Of course I'll do it. I've always wanted to play on top of a mountain.'"

Xoregos offered to drive Duke to the airport.

Duke said, "Fine."

She had a beat-up old Volkswagen that was a total wreck. No muffler. Just a mess of a car. He was shocked, but he got in. They got on the freeway and people were staring at him and you could almost see their lips forming the question: Is that Duke Ellington? Then they'd look at the car and shake their heads. It couldn't be.

Every time he came to town after that, if anyone would say, "I'll drive you here or I'll drive you there," he'd always ask, "What kind of car do you have?"

Pepsi-Cola

IN THE SUMMER OF 1971 DUKE WAS MADE THE HOST OF THE CITY OF New York, with Gloria Swanson as hostess. They were selected by the New York Convention and Business Bureau to launch the New York Is a Summer Festival season, to lure additional tourism to the city. They made a charming and sophisticated couple. Duke was a fantastic salesman. He was subtle and suave and smooth. He was New York. He was everything about New York. Lowdown, highbrow, anything they wanted him to be. Needing someone to match his elegance, they chose Swanson. Duke was very proud of having her on his arm, even though they parted company at mealtimes, when Gloria headed for her health food and Duke made a beeline for his steaks.

They were officially launched as host and hostess at a cocktail reception on the roof of the Empire State Building. Duke ordered a Coca-Cola with four spoons of sugar, to the horror of Swanson, who never touched the stuff.

They made all the rounds. They opened the first day at Belmont; they threw out the first ball at Yankee Stadium. They were guests at a big bash thrown by the Fifth Avenue Association, aided and abetted by Larry Tish and Lew Rubin, the big real estate moguls, and NBC. Duke, who was a great wordsman and a fantastic creator of phrases, kept calling New York a slambanger.

Duke was sitting and doodling on the piano in the Rainbow Grill one afternoon, waiting for Willis Conover, who was representing the *Voice of America*, and his staff to come up and do a videotape interview. Before they arrived, Duke looked out the huge glass window and saw the city at his feet. He started writing a song called "New York, New York," about his great love for the city. He played a few chords and then created the melody. He hummed it for a bit and then proceeded to write his own lyric. It was instantaneous. That night, after they were through working at the Grill, he took the band to a recording studio on Fifty-seventh Street and recorded the song, doing a head arrangement (telling each musician individually what to play) and teaching Toney Watkins, his vocalist, the lyric. After Toney got through singing it, Duke cut a side doing the vocal himself.

He sang it like a love song.

At the Grill, Duke consumed a tremendous amount of Coca-Cola, so much that it seemed like a good idea for him to become a spokesman for the company. Phoebe Jacobs, the lady in charge of entertainment at the Rainbow Grill and an ardent devotee of Duke's, placed a call to the advertising agency in New York that handled the account. They passed the buck to the office of the president, which was located in Atlanta, Georgia. The president was informed how avid a Coca-Cola drinker Duke was, how identifiable and articulate he was and how he would make a marvelous figure for a commercial. The president said he would contact Duke's agent, which he never did.

Some time later a group of influential Russians came to the Grill to hear the band and to meet Duke. They negotiated a deal for Duke to play in Russia. The president of Coca-Cola was phoned again to ask if he would arrange for a supply of Coca-Cola to be sent to Russia for Duke, as there was none there, and that it would be paid for in this country. After many phone conversations and letters and wires, they said they were sorry but no. It was decided to flimflam Duke, who was told that he had inadvertently been drinking Pepsi-Cola because the Grill had temporarily run out of Coke and had substituted Pepsi. (By the time he got through putting the four teaspoons of sugar in the drink, which he always did, he couldn't tell the difference anyway.)

He said, "You're kidding. I love it."

He was told, "Okay, that's what you're going to drink in Russia."

Shortly after he returned to the States, Pepsi-Cola was the first American beverage to be shipped to Russia. Duke was responsible. He kept offering a taste to all the people he met, who became so enamored of it, they proceeded to import it in great quantities.

When Duke came back to the Rainbow Grill, Joan Crawford, who was married to the chairman of the board of Pepsi-Cola and who was an old friend of Duke's, showed up with Marlene Dietrich to thank him.

Duke was never told that he had been drinking only Coca-Cola at the Grill and that he had never really tasted Pepsi-Cola until he drank it in Russia.

Russia

WHEN DUKE AND THE BAND TOOK THEIR TRIP TO RUSSIA FOR THE STATE Department, I was unable to go, but Duke phoned me often, and when he returned, we spent many hours talking about the tour.

Upon landing in Moscow Duke and the band were taken straight from the airport to the ballet, where the senior company of the Bolshoi was performing *Swan Lake* that evening. Everyone was dead tired, trying to keep their eyes open and trying to recover from all the Scotch consumed on the plane. No one had had dinner; they all had been hustled through customs right to the ballet.

After the performance they all checked into the Russia Hotel, the largest in the country, with its six thousand rooms and four identical lobbies. The upstairs was so crisscrossed by myriad endless hallways that you wondered on leaving your room whether you'd ever be able to find it again.

Duke told me, "I warned the heavy drinkers against getting bombed and maybe floating around the hotel forever like the legendary Flying Dutchman."

Moscow turned out to be depressing. The fellows lost weight because they couldn't eat the food, and there really wasn't any decent booze.

GUM was the only department store on Red Square. It was constantly filled with Russians looking at jackets and coats and things evidently too expensive for them to buy. There was nothing that Duke or the band wanted that they couldn't find better at home.

They rode the "hard train" from Moscow to Leningrad. The compartments were the same as in all European trains, but the seats, which were also used to sleep on, were very hard, and the mattresses were very thin. The fellows sat up all night drinking cherry juice and eating black bread, which was the only immediate means of sustenance to be found on the train.

In Leningrad Duke was presented with a brochure by a Russian artist that contained biographies of Ella Fitzgerald, Sarah Vaughan and Count Basie, with a picture of Duke on the cover. There was a full-page picture of Duke inside. The artist had taken about twenty copies of Duke's picture and superimposed them on a sheet that opened up to about two feet long and folded them in such a way that it was like looking through a series of mirrors. It was beautiful. Duke loved it. The artist came to present it personally in Duke's dressing room at the concert hall. Just then the Russian secret police dashed in, grabbed the artist and threw him against the wall outside of the dressing room, and all hell broke loose.

I said to Duke, "I guess there wasn't very much you could do about it?"

Duke replied, "I didn't care who those guys were. Even if they were Stalin. I turned to them and I said, 'Listen, you bastards,' and I told them, 'This man is an artist. He is a creator. He is beyond category. How dare you offend him by throwing

212

him out of my room when he comes to present a gift such as this?' I was really mad, Don. I yelled, 'You people are crazy!' "

(I wondered what the State Department would have done if the Russians had sent Duke to Siberia for that outburst.)

Toney Watkins, the vocalist in the band and one of Duke's favorite people, who was in the room at the time, told me much later that he still trembled when he thought about it. He said, "I could see the bus pulling up ready to take Duke and all the rest of us to wherever the cold is."

However, cooler heads prevailed. Orders came to the Russians from higher up to forget the entire affair.

Duke was ecstatic about the subway in Leningrad. "Don, the subway is literally like a museum. The gold, the silver, the brass, the paintings, the crystal chandeliers are simply unbelievable. Remember the subway stop at Fifty-third Street and Lexington Avenue, one block from Benton and Bowles, that stop that goes all the way down? Well, the subway here has to be at least three flights deeper. You just never think you're going to come up again. There are marble floors and statues and paintings all around, and every ten or twelve feet you see these royal blue doors. Royal blue, my favorite color . . . they must have built this subway with me in mind. Where's the train? Oh, it's coming. You hear a little buzz and the doors open and the trains stop right at the doors. In other words it's impossible to jump into the tracks, fall into the tracks or be pushed into the tracks. If Strayhorn had ridden this line instead of the Eighth Avenue subway, he never would have written 'Take the A Train.' "

"As to the ladies," said Duke, "that was a big drag. They gave us a briefing before we went over. They said, 'Guys, control yourselves for the five weeks that you're going to be there.' I was never with any ladies there except the two interpreters, and they always left me in the lobby of the hotel; and man, they have those big ladies on each floor as you get off the elevator, and they keep your room key. There's no way you can avoid them. They're in every hotel, every shift. I asked this one lady, 'Don't you ever go home?' "

The band usually played four nights a week, which left plenty of time for the sightseeing trips that had been planned for them. Wonder of wonders, Duke, who never ever went sightseeing, really enjoyed them. Above all, Duke, being a painter himself, enjoyed the Hermitage, the museum that contained so much of Russia's greatest art.

He was the world's worst sightseer, but he managed to get up. "The bus leaves at ten in the morning, Mr. Ellington." Or, "The car will be here at ten." And he was up and ready.

In Rostov a variety group alternated with the band in the concert hall. It was a Vegas-Broadway-type production, with Vegas-type girls and singers. They were staying at the same hotel as the band. But there was no way Duke could get near them, despite the fact that a bar of soap and a bottle of perfume went a long way.

The food was hardly any better, although it was the only place where they saw fresh eggs for breakfast.

"Don, there was just no way of getting past those big ladies on each floor."

In Kiev, where my father was born and where he barely escaped a pogrom, the band stayed at a hotel that had over a hundred steps leading up to the entrance. You could either walk up the steps or drive up a little driveway if you had transportation. One night Duke actually managed to hang out in a club around the corner in another hotel. Duke showed up with the two interpreters and the head man of the Russian Arts Council, and they stayed about an hour and went back to the hotel. The Russians had a place in each city called the Friendship House, where they welcomed composers, writers and dancers from different countries when they came to Russia. Duke said it was the only place where he could mingle with their top artists.

Each concert had been sold out for months. Duke pulled a big surprise on the audiences by having Paul Gonsalves, the great jazz saxophonist who had broken it up at the Newport Jazz Festival some years before, feature the famous Russian waltz "Ochy Chornia" as an encore, and they loved it.

214

There were many nights when Harry Carney, Cootie Williams and some of the other band members told Toney Watkins, "Look backstage and see what kind of a mood Duke's in," in the hope that he was tired, because many times they had seen Duke kind of drag into the dressing room, then hit the stage, do a full two-and-a-half-hour concert and then respond to the audience screaming, "Duke, Duke, Duke" and do a whole additional concert for the encore.

Watkins chided him once, "Duke, man, you played something like seven encores."

Duke replied, "Well, frankly, I wasn't ready to go to bed yet, and besides I can't get all of those people back into my hotel room. As much time as we spend with them, I'm getting off, and the band has noplace else to go. They don't know anybody here."

Meals had been planned by the Russian state department. At each hotel the band was seated at the same table and ate mostly at what would be considered off-hours. Many times only the Ellington band was in the dining room. Duke thought it might be for political reasons, to keep the people away from the band. The menu seemed to be the same in every restaurant in Russia: food of indeterminate parentage, surrounded by the inescapable aroma of cabbage and fish oil.

In one of his phone calls, Duke told me of a completely mystifying occurrence. The band was off one day, and Duke received a phone call from someone he didn't know. A female voice came on and said, "Hello, may I speak to Duke Ellington?"

Duke said, "This is Duke Ellington."

The voice said, "Do you like Aretha Franklin?"

Duke said, "Yes." And then the caller hung up.

About fifteen minutes later the phone rang again.

"May I speak to Duke Ellington?"

"This is Duke Ellington."

"Do you like soul singer Aretha Franklin?"

Duke yelled, "Yeah, I love her."

The girl played about five minutes of an Aretha Franklin record and then hung up again. And that was it. Duke never heard from her again.

215

The band started looking around in all their rooms for hidden bugs and tape recorders because of all the rumors they had heard.

Duke said, "When you're in Russia you believe everything you've ever heard about it. It's as simple as that. The basic colors are dingy gray and brown. You don't see too many bright colors or the fashions that we're accustomed to seeing back home."

Duke believed in no intermissions or very short intermissions; a lot of places they played, the band had stamina enough to play for ninety minutes straight.

"Oh, but Mr. Ellington, we have to have an intermission. We have to have an intermission."

Duke replied, "The person who tells you that you must have an intermission is the man who has the concession stand. He's the guy who has the key for the curtain. When he's sold out all his stuff he gives the key back to the man backstage and says, 'Now you can raise the curtain and start the second half.' It's the same here in Russia as it is back home. Now, frankly, I don't mind an intermission, but tell me, how can three thousand people go pee in fifteen minutes?"

The last week of the tour, the band played in Moscow. All over Russia they had played in huge theaters and concert halls, but in Moscow they were booked into a hall that held only about 1200 people. Duke thought it a political move to not permit the people who lived in the capital to see the band. The Ellington fans in Moscow and other nearby cities were so upset at the thought of not hearing Ellington and the band that the Russian government, preferring not to create an incident that might become international in scope (and with the assistance of a pianissimo push from our State Department), wisely decided to book two additional concerts in the huge Sports Palace that seated 12,500 people. All 25,000 seats were sold in less than seven hours, and the cry "Duke, Duke, Duke" reverberated throughout the streets of Moscow for days.

It was with light hearts that the band left Russia and continued the rest of their tour. At the airport in Copenhagen there was a four-hour wait for the plane connection to Sweden. That was when everybody got a chance to see Duke Ellington the shopper in action. He was like a little kid in a toy store. Those

216

big eyes opened wide and he said, "Evie would like this," and "I'll get this for Fernanda." And he continued buying gifts and loading up Jim Lowe, the band boy, and Toney Watkins.

Looking around, he returned the smile of one beautiful lady, then another. When last seen he was heading off with both of them. He was a free man once more.

Spain

THEY WENT CRAZY ABOUT DUKE IN SPAIN. DUKE AND ELLA FITZGERALD were booked to work in a theater, but they sold so many tickets the promoters moved the show to a bullfighting arena.

After the show the people picked Duke up and carried him off the stage on their shoulders. Ella was close by on some other shoulders. Everybody was screaming *"Olê, olê,"* and Duke kept smiling and yelling, "Yeah, man, go, go, go."

Odyssey House

AS LONG AS I KNEW DUKE, AS WELL AS I KNEW HIM, AS MUCH TIME AS WE spent together, I never knew him to touch drugs. I never knew him to drink. He grew up in the world of music, so he grew up in a world where drugs were prevalent. He knew there were men in the band who were hooked. He knew about the trumpet player who lived on a diet of heroin and whiskey, who turned on a sax man who became famous for blowing sixty-eight frantic choruses at a jazz festival. They both combined to turn on the drummer.

Though he didn't condone their habit, when he knew that one of them was in a desperate emotional, physical dilemma and needed a fix, he would discreetly leave two hundred dollars on the music stand in the fellow's score.

Duke would tell people he knew were using drugs, "It ruins your music. It doesn't make it better. If you want to get high, get high on the sound. Don't get high on drugs. Don't get high on martinis. Get high on music." He became very angry if anyone told him he did better on drugs. He felt that drugs were an inhibiting rather than a creative force.

Duke wanted so much to help people get off drugs that he

217

agreed to do a benefit concert for Odyssey House, a New York organization that helped kids with drug problems. I learned about this from Dr. Judianne Densen-Gerber, the founder and head of Odyssey House.

The concert took place in the now-defunct Fillmore East, a popular rock theater in the East Village. After the concert there was a buffet and dance at the Electric Circus. Duke asked Dr. Densen-Gerber's seventy-eight-year-old mother to dance. The lady, who had been a hundred-thousand-dollar-a-year-plus corporation attorney and as Old Greenwich as it is possible to get, had never been that close to a black man before. After the dance she came back to the table beaming and said, "Why, he's charming! He dances better than a white man."

The Odyssey mother house was on East Sixth Street, between First and Second avenues. After the party at the Electric Circus, we limousined over and met with the residents. Duke shook hands with all of them and wound up on the piano bench playing "Chopsticks" with a fourteen-year-old white boy who had been living in the streets for six months prior to coming to Odyssey, sleeping over the subway gratings in order to keep warm. He had been abused and had run away from his home in New Jersey to New York, where he landed in Times Square. A prostitute picked him up and brought him home to be her baby-sitter while she went out and worked the streets. She paid him off in heroin and got him addicted when he was thirteen. He ran away when he was fourteen and was picked up by the truant runaway squad, who brought him to Odyssey. He was obviously musically gifted. He asked Duke, "Would you come on our board?"

From that moment on Duke was totally involved. He became a member of the board of directors and devoted as much of his time as possible to helping the kids who were in trouble.

One Sunday night Duke and I were watching the David Susskind television show about Odyssey House when one of the five formerly addicted teenagers in treatment at Odyssey who was on the show casually referred to the fact that the kids were buying drugs from their high-school teachers and other school employees. Duke was shocked and furious. He muttered under his breath, "Son of a bitch," then more fiercely, "Those motherfuckers ought to be strung up by their balls.

218

Fucking up those kids that way." For the only time in his career, Susskind made an on-the-air appeal for funds and succeeded in raising $45,000 for Odyssey House.

Duke became vice-president of the Odyssey board. Shortly thereafter (and perhaps not too coincidentally), Governor Rockefeller fortuitously discovered $65 million lying around unused beneath his pillow one night and apportioned it for the treatment of adolescent drug users in New York State.

Odyssey was given some property on Tiffany Street in the South Bronx, which is in the heart of Fort Apache, one of the most turbulent areas in the entire world. It wasn't safe to walk down Tiffany Street even in the daytime. Police officers refused to go on foot patrol there. Several schools had no teachers because they were afraid of the students. Some kids overdosed and died right in the classrooms. Most of the stores in the neighborhood stocked stolen goods, and 80 percent of the adult population were either alcoholics or heroin addicts.

Duke had the idea that he and Odyssey House could help change the environment, as well as people's attitudes toward halfway houses at the same time, by creating a center for young people, particularly those interested in music. He confided in me that he wanted to make the buildings a memorial to Billy Strayhorn, but this dream was not destined to come true because, much to Duke's disappointment, the buildings he planned to use were leveled by the city.

Occasionally, when Duke played at Topsfield, Massachusetts, a summer concert area something like Tanglewood, or at the state fair in Danvers, Massachusetts, Dr. Densen-Gerber would come by and pick up our piano-playing insomniac friend at twelve or one o'clock in the morning and take him for an hour's drive to the Odyssey House facility in Hampton, New Hampshire. The residents there were kids ranging in age from twelve to seventeen who were in trouble with the law.

One time when she came for him Duke was tired, very tired.

He asked Dr. Densen-Gerber, "How important is it to the kids?" She told him how very important it was, so he crawled into the car and exhaustedly fell into a deep sleep while she drove.

At the facility he played and the kids sang along with him,

and he told stories about kissing Nixon four times on the cheek and they all had a big laugh. Duke played an hour or so for the kids, joked with them, and then the doctor drove him back.

Dr. Densen-Gerber would reprimand Duke for all the sugar he used, particularly the four spoonful in each Coca-Cola. She teased him about the satchel full of pills and vitamins he always carried.

"How can you come to Odyssey carrying all those pills?"

He would smilingly reply, "I'm an old man, and I need all the help I can get."

As far back as the 1950s, Duke was tremendously disturbed by the amount of heroin coming into the United States, with minority people as its basic victims. Like the rest of us, he knew that a great deal of it was coming through Cuba into Florida, and since the Russian sponsors of Cuba were engaged in a cold war with the United States, he believed the heroin epidemic to be part of an attempt on their part to weaken our national strength.

Iran, Afghanistan and Pakistan are sending the United States twenty times more heroin than they did in 1970. And it is much purer and stronger—so strong that there are 500 percent more addicts ODing now than just a few short years ago. Dr. Densen-Gerber told me that she was informed by H. Carl McCall, US Ambassador to the United Nations, that drugs are becoming a national defense problem; that there's so much heroin now coming into America that it's actually affecting our ability to defend ourselves.

Duke very often discussed the drug situation at the board meetings of Odyssey House. He also talked to the kids about it. "How can you throw your lives away when there's so much you can do with yourself and for yourself?" He knew that the residents he met at Odyssey House were former addicts; a lot of them had long criminal histories, and it disturbed him a great deal. He wanted to do anything he could to uplift them, to inspire them, to show them there was something different, something they could be dignified and proud about. He accomplished that just by doing what he was doing, just by being Duke Ellington. He was a role model for millions of people, the kind of person whom you want to pattern yourself after. Black, white or Puerto Rican—it made no difference. When we were there, all the residents would say to me, "I want to be like Duke Ellington."

I explained, "There can only be one. But that kind of dream is good."

Duke's being black and having the stature that he did had a tremendous impact on the residents, many of whom were black. Having a man whose name was a household word, like the name of a president, coming into the house and sitting down and sharing his gifts in a very natural way was an inspiration to the patients and the greatest gift he could give. "Here I am. I'm well known. I've made it big, but still I love my people." He was very proud of being black. His compositions showed a deep appreciation of the black roots of music. If anyone made jazz a respectable, classical music, it was Duke. He turned it from honky-tonk into a major symphonic art form. He brought that sort of dignity to Odyssey, along with his charisma and his smile and his warmth. When he visited, the residents literally felt that they had been touched by the master.

One evening Dr. Densen-Gerber told the residents that Duke would be coming by to do a concert at about midnight. Some of the residents who had attended Duke's previous concerts passed the word that it was usual for him to be about an hour and a half late, so everybody assembled at about one o'clock in anticipation, sitting around talking and joking.

An hour passed, then an hour and a half, and still no Duke. Some people started to grumble, saying they wanted to go to bed. At about a quarter of two, somebody yelled, "He's here."

He came in wearing a flowered shirt and brightly colored slacks, and apologized for being late. He introduced himself and the singer he had brought with him. "This is the lovely, darling Anita Moore. She sings with my band." He had all the residents and the staff introduce themselves.

Duke sat down at the piano and played "Satin Doll," "A Train," "Night in Tunisia" and some other of his well-known songs, with Anita Moore singing an occasional vocal. He encouraged those who knew the lyrics to sing along. "If you want to dance, go ahead and dance." Pretty soon everyone was doing something to the music, whether they had a musical ear or not. They were tapping their feet; clapping in tempo; they

221

were singing, dancing. Someone picked up a bongo drum, someone else picked up a tambourine, and Duke suddenly had his own little rhythm section from among the residents. He was just making music and smiling, despite the fact that the piano was out of tune. It was so funny to see a man who played all over the world, who wherever he went invariably had a Steinway grand in front of him, playing on an out-of-tune piano with four keys that didn't work. He didn't care; he played on it anyway and made it sound like a fifteen-thousand-dollar grand.

The residents were mesmerized by his presence. They were all being treated to a command performance of the great Duke Ellington. The atmosphere was so intimate, Duke could see almost everybody in the room. It was like playing to an audience of friends. When he rose to leave, it was nearly four A.M., and he received a standing ovation. He stood in the center of the stage, surveying all he possessed with an air of royalty, and orated in his best Chaucerian manner his traditional "I love you madly" in six different languages.

That somebody as celebrated and world renowned as Duke would take time out to perform at a time when obviously he could have been doing something else was a great emotional boost to the residents. There were a number of musicians in the program at the time who were so greatly encouraged by his presence they eventually became professionals.

I don't know how to measure that sort of thing, but without a doubt he inspired some of the people in that room just by being there and asking what their names were. He performed more like he was playing for royalty than for people down on their luck. And he wasn't doing them a favor. He wanted to be there.

Black Brain

DR. JUDIANNE DENSEN-GERBER OF ODYSSEY HOUSE STOPPED BY TO VISIT just as Duke's Swedish girl friend was giving him a massage. He was sitting in his b.v.d.'s and drinking his Coke filled with sugar. It was a bit crowed in the tiny blue dressing room at the Rainbow Grill, so Dr. Densen-Gerber and I adjourned to one of the cocktail banquettes outside the main room and enjoyed the view through the floor-to-ceiling windows on top of the RCA Building until Duke joined us.

The conversation veered in many directions until Duke asked, "How about this for a movie idea?"

The doctor was curious. "What's the plot, Duke?"

He leaned back, knuckle-rubbing his eyes. "It's about a black man who is in an automobile accident and his brain is removed and transplanted into a white man's body . . . a white man who has had a brain tumor, so they make a quick switch not to waste the brain."

I was skeptical. "Come on, man. How in the world are they going to do that?"

Duke dismissed the question with an imperious wave of his hand. "We'll figure that out later." He paused, "Just think about it for a minute. The white man is an executive who has been living a corporate life in Connecticut, and the black brain finds it difficult to adjust to being in this particular social set, where acceptance is given immediately. Just walking into a room and becoming part of the group is a phenomenon that takes many months for the black brain to understand."

I interjected, "Maybe he can't figure out why the people don't put him down or start to show him where the kitchen is. That Greenwich crowd is a little bigoted."

Dr. Densen-Gerber, who is a psychiatrist as well as an M.D., said, "I can understand that, because when I walk into a board meeting or a business conference, I have a hard time, as a woman, adjusting to a room full of men."

Duke squinted his eyes, gazed off into space and continued. "It's a shock being instantly accepted wherever he goes, getting the best tables. 'Are you sure this will do, sir?' Joining the best country clubs. 'Just sign here, sir, we'll send you the bill'; and getting a shot at any job he's able to do. The white man is unable to deal with the black man's sexual drive. The black brain has retained its constant sexual thoughts, but the white body can't function as well. In their previous, separate existences the black man relaxed and appreciated all the pretty ladies, while the white man was a busy-all-the-time, once-a-week, after-golf-on-Sunday lovemaker."

The doctor laughed ruefully and said, "Edward, cut it out. It's too true. The men who make movies would never let you get away with it."

Duke looked up into his head for a minute, then continued. "He has difficulty adjusting because their worlds have been so

223

separate and far apart. The white man is unable to deal with the musical soul of the black man, particularly in the area of sacred music. He can't understand where these feelings are coming from."

Duke was obviously projecting, thinking about how nice it would be to start again as a young, vigorous, tremendously potent man who had another time around. Thinking, with a twinkle in his eye, how much fun it would be for a white man to have to cope with a black man's brain.

(Duke was a great believer in reincarnation and perhaps was fantasizing about himself and his next visit to this earth. But what, I wondered, if he returned as a member of the animal kingdom? With his tremendous interest in food and females, he might return as a golden retriever whose psychology was, if you can't masticate it or fornicate it, urinate on it.)

Duke looked at each of us in turn, searchingly. "Well, children, what do you think of the story? Will it make a good movie? Do you think I ought to write the score?"

Before we had a chance to reply, Bigi, the maitre d', came rushing breathlessly out of the Grill and over to Duke. "Duke, the band is playing the fourth number. You'd better hurry."

Duke rose, gave us the kisses, said, "We'll finish this later," and disappeared.

We never spoke about it again. To this day we don't know whether he was fantasizing or spoofing or whether there actually was a film, and perhaps he did write a score, which may be lost or hidden or just drifting around somewhere.

Brooks Kerr

ONE EVENING I RECEIVED A PHONE CALL FROM BROOKS KERR, THE BLIND piano player and entertainer, inviting me to his opening at Michael Phillips, one of the more posh East Side spots in New York City. It was with a happy heart that I set forth, looking forward to a pleasant evening with my good friend. Stepping out of the taxi, I circumnavigated a bag lady who had taken up residence on the sidewalk outside the restaurant and entered a large room with a long bar on one side and an upright piano on a raised area at the far end. Every table was occupied and every seat was taken, but after crossing the maitre d's palm with a modicum of silver, room was made for me by placing a chair right next to the piano where Brooks was playing. Out of the clear blue sky, he announced that I was in the room and played and sang a number of songs that Duke and I had written together, among them, "I'm Beginning to See the Light," "The Wonder of You," "Every Hour on the Hour," "Tulip or Turnip," and "I'm Afraid," opening wide a floodgate of memories.

I first met Brooks Kerr when his mother brought him to the front of the bandstand at the Yale Bowl in New Haven at the end of one of Duke's concerts. Brooks, who was about eight years old at the time, started asking Duke questions about the music. Duke smiled down at the strange-eyed little boy, who was almost completely blind, and patted him on the head. Duke was astonished when Brooks told him that the band had played one number in a different key from the record he had at home.

The next time we met was at another concert in Connecticut, when Brooks was about ten or eleven. Duke recognized him immediately and introduced him to the band, speaking to him about solos and improvisations as though he were an adult.

When Brooks was fourteen he was led up the bandstand in the Riverboat, the huge club that used to be in the Empire State Building, where Duke was playing. Duke made room for him on the piano bench, saying, "You just stay right here with me. You belong here."

After the set Duke led Brooks back to the table where Brooks's parents were. He sat with them awhile and said, "You know, this fellow is a real musician." He shook his head in amazement. "He knows everything I've ever written. He knows more about my music than I do myself."

From that moment on he was Duke's protégé. Wherever Duke played, if it was at all possible, there was Brooks, listening, learning, remembering.

With the little bit of sight he possessed, Brooks was unable to read or to identify objects, and lead sheets remained a forever closed door to him, but he was able to differentiate colors. I remember when he first told us that in his mind's eye every musical note was a different color and that the scale resembled a rainbow. He fingered a C on the piano, explaining, "This

225

note is red." He hit a D. "This one is dark blue." He hit an F. "This is yellow." His finger wandered to a G. "This one is light blue . . ."

Duke, who was an accomplished painter and constantly thought in terms of color, could hardly believe it, saying, "Music strikes me the same way, Brooks. I hear a note by one of the fellows in the band and it's one color. I hear the same note played by someone else and it's a different color. When I hear sustained musical tones, I see just about the same colors that you do, but I see them in textures. If Harry Carney is playing, D is dark blue burlap. If Johnny Hodges is playing, G becomes light blue satin."

Duke turned toward me. "Let's take your initials, Don." He studied me a moment, then spoke my name very distinctly. "Don George. *D.G.* Dark blue and light blue. Hmm, G is one sharp. D is two sharps. That's virgin territory, good for violins, violas and cellos. Both D and G denote the sky. D is dark blue. That's the evening sky, bringing serenity and tranquillity. It's very peaceful. G is the afternoon sky; earlier in the day, between noon and five P.M. A lighter shade with more sun. G is a faster tempo. The animals are out and a lot of noise is being made. D is quiet and cool. D is blue cellophane, just after the afterglow, as the day is winding down. A gas flame is blue. Blue flame, as any chemist will tell you, is hotter than yellow or orange flame. It's a higher temperature." Duke smiled at me affectionately. "Everything about D.G. is blue. It's the best of pairings. It's very harmonious."

When Brooks was eighteen years old, Duke took him on a European trip with the band. They went to France, Italy, Germany, Belgium, Denmark, Holland and just about every other European country. Duke had Brooks come to his room every night after the concerts and play for him till five or six in the morning. Then he tried out his new compositions on Brooks. "Hey, Brooks, how do you like this?" "What do you think of this one?"

In Brooks, Duke had found someone who was almost a complete continuation of himself, not alone because of Brooks's knowledge of his music and his talent as a piano player, but also because of the love they shared for the same kind of music

226

and the same pianists, particularly Willie "the Lion" Smith, the great stride pianist who had been Duke's mentor when he first came to New York. (Willie gave Duke his first lesson in a taxi-cab riding around Central Park, practicing chords with their voices. Willie was as elegant as usual, with his derby hat, big cigar, spats, cane and striped trousers, spouting interjections of Hebrew, which he spoke fluently.) Occasionally when Duke played the Rainbow Grill, he would have Brooks sit in at the piano for him while he roamed the room in his constant quest for interesting conversation and devastating females.

On one such occasion, when Willie the Lion was in the room, Duke was teasing Brooks, trying to stump him by asking him to play "Portrait of the Lion," a piece he had written and dedicated to Willie.

Brooks asked, "Which one, Duke? The one you wrote in 1939 or the one you wrote in 1955?"

Duke had forgotten that he wrote two "Portraits." Willie stood there grinning as Brooks played both of them.

Their association occasionally prompted random remarks like, "Say, who's the blind ofay kid with Duke's band?" To which Duke would replay, "That kid can see very little, but he can hear and remember everything. Anything you want to know about my music, ask Brooks Kerr. He's our encyclopedia."

When Duke was writing his book, *Music Is My Mistress*, there were times when memory didn't serve as well as it might have; occasions and people from the long-ago beginnings seemed imbedded in an impenetrable haze. During those moments Duke turned to Brooks, telephoning him from all over the world, knowing that somehow, the Good Lord only knew how, Brooks would have the answers about events that had occurred long before he was born. (No matter what time zone Duke was in, the calls always came at about 4 A.M. New York time.)

Duke called from Japan. "Brooks, what was the name of the fellow who sponsored me when I first came to New York—the one who staked me to room and board?"

"That was a fellow named Forney, Duke. Forney Brooks."

Duke called from Prague. "I can't seem to remember the name of the fellow who wrote the words to the first tune I ever

227

had published. He owned a rehearsal studio on Forty-ninth and Broadway."

"No problem, Duke. The song was named 'Choo-Choo'; in parenthesis—'Gotta Hurry Home.' Dave Ringle wrote the words and it was published by Fred Fisher."

Duke called from Paris. After the usual greetings came the inevitable question. "What was that little riff tune that Willie 'the Lion' used to play at the Capitol Palace uptown on 138th and Lenox that I liked so much?"

"It was called 'The Sneakaway' . . . "

One night after a concert the three of us—Duke, Brooks and I—were in Duke's dressing room. Duke looked like a ghost. He had undergone a rugged week and was really exhausted. He kept calling for his valet, who was nowhere to be found. Brooks said, "If you need something why don't you ask me? I'm right here. You know I'll get you your coat. I'll do anything for you."

Duke quieted down. "I'm sorry, Brooks, I should have asked you." He took Brooks's hand. "You would do it for love. The others do it for money."

The Three Black Kings, or Les Trois Noir Roi, or Soul, Silk, Stone

THE FIRST WORK SESSION BETWEEN DUKE AND LUTHER HENDERSON, HIS ARranger, took place in a hotel room in Chicago. Duke was seated at the small portable piano that traveled everywhere with him, and Henderson was at the writing desk.

Duke started by intoning majestically in tempo with the chords he was striking on the piano, *"Les Trois Noir Roi?* Hey, man, that's good. We'll call it 'Les Trois Noir Roi.' "

Henderson shook his head. "The only problem is . . . I think you ought to call them "The Three Black Kings," instead of "Les Trois Noir Roi"."

Duke disagreed. "No, because you have to go to Africa, and nobody in Africa speaks English." He laughed. "Shit, I almost starved my ass off in Dakar. Big nigger. I went downstairs and ordered a steak and some rice and lettuce. I looked up; there was another waiter. Ten of them walked away on me. So I finally started speaking French. I said, *'S'il vous plait, l'eau chaude, et cravatte, le petit foie, et le fromage.'* And everything was great."

Henderson interrupted. "You know what you should do if you're going to use French? I think you should call it 'Les Trois 'Roi Noir' instead of 'Les Trois Noir Roi.'"

Duke asked, "Is that proper? I think I'd better call up Fernanda."

HENDERSON: I think you're supposed to say the noun before the adjective.

DUKE: Well, I really shouldn't be beastly with the Troi Roi anyway, because I wrote it in that hotel in Africa called The Three Kings. They have a little piano in the bar, and it was late at night, and I was writing in there. [Smiling in memory.] It was a wonderful atmosphere.

HENDERSON: You say one king is Silk and one is Soul. What's the third king?

DUKE: He could either be Solid or Stone.

HENDERSON [rolling it around on his tongue]: Soul, Silk, Stone. It's got a good sound.

DUKE: The way I started thinking about this thing, I was thinking about three movements in three different degrees. Remember I was speaking to you about the West Indies? I was thinking about the music. The music came across the ocean to the Caribbean, and from there it branched up. As far as we're concerned we've been in the Sugar Hill penthouse, and here we are suddenly talking about soul. That's the trouble—no matter how high you get up into the penthouse, you always roll back into the soul.

HENDERSON [nodding]: True. You say one would be the Caribbean influence?

DUKE: Yes, and the other would be the West Indian influence. I've got a little West Indian number. It's called 'Tago.' [Looking at Luther.] How does it go?

HENDERSON [perplexed]: How *does* it go?

DUKE: Damn, we haven't played it in so long. How does the thing go? [Shaking his head.] Oh, well, all my West Indian things sound the same anyway. [Duke played eight bars and shrugged.] I can't think of it. [Changing the subject.] Do you know my friend John Raleigh? He lives in Wilmington and he's mixed up with all that money. He owns Montego Bay. We played down there one day. It's the goddamnedest thing you've ever seen in your life. I'm a real fool that I just don't move down there. This man stood on the southern shore of Montego Bay and pointed way across. He said, "You see that mountain over there?" I said, "Yes." "Well," he said, "I own the next seven miles." He owns the property where the White Witch of Rose Hall, a white woman, lives; a beautiful bitch who was raised in Haiti by a Negro woman who was a real voodoo priestess. She rules the goddamn island. That whole Jamaica island. That end of it, anyway, with the voodoo.

HENDERSON: That voodoo lady—is she Soul or Stone?

DUKE: She's Stone. She's a dark lady. She tells the White Witch how to rule.

[Duke was warmed up now. His mental decks were cleared and he was ready to compose. He started playing a theme on the piano.]

HENDERSON: That sounds like Stone.

[Duke played some more.]

HENDERSON: If she's a Stone lady, maybe it ought to be one of those drum things.

DUKE [considering]: Instead of having three movements, we might have two movements. One of them could be Satin to Soul, and the other might be Africa to the West Indies. We could start off with all this bang, bang, bang, bang and wind up in the West Indies with a melody. But we've got to wind up with soul. We're back to "Tago." I remember it now. [He played sixteen bars of a lovely melody, humming along with his piano playing, then repeated it and doubled the tempo as he went into an exciting counterphrase and back to the opening sixteen, then into a third theme.] We'll use this other theme with the African. [Duke emitted animal growls and bird calls as he played, increasing the tempo until both he and Luther were pounding away and perspiring. Duke slowed the tempo.] We can take it straight down now. We can punctuate now and then with nothing but beats, and let it finally evolve to where we do that thing on the D flat major seventh. [Duke paused.] Then we'll think of something. We don't want the blues. We don't want no old funky blues.

HENDERSON: Play me the funky blues.

DUKE: Oh, no. This is West Indian.

HENDERSON: This whole thing needs heavy rhythm and bass.

DUKE: A drum choir, they call it.

HENDERSON: You know the African piano? It would go great with the West Indian thing you do. It's got bars on it and you hit it with your thumb. Also, for a piece of dance music, they'll get their jollies when they hear that drum choir. You can build it into whatever your rhythm pattern is going to be for the calypso.

DUKE: We'd have to change it from the African to the West Indian.

HENDERSON: I like the idea of Silk featuring good jazz soloists. Don't you?

DUKE: Yes. It's consistent with the title.

HENDERSON: That piano sounds soft.

DUKE: When I work at night like this, I just don't turn it up. I can play it as softly as this. [Duke illustrates, lowering the volume way down.] Even with that, the son of a bitch who lives under me in New York City tells me his wife swears she hears instruments. She damn near had a hemorrhage. That son of a bitch wrote the politest goddamn letter. Evie got the letter. There was just Evie and Davy at home. You know who Davy is, don't you?

HENDERSON [shaking his head]: No.

DUKE: He's the little black poodle who owns the place. He's the king. [Duke stood up, stretched, walked around the room and returned to the piano.] Let's get with this thing now. [Playing.] This one is Silk. The first one is Soul.

HENDERSON: Right. Let's put the other one down.

DUKE: All right, here we go. [He plays a few bars, stops, waiting.] You got it?

HENDERSON: Okay. Now I need the three-quarter part.

DUKE [plays some more]: Write that down for me.

HENDERSON: Got any more manuscript paper? The routine is . . .

DUKE [waving his hand]: Oh, you know the routine. I'm not concerned about that. [He continues playing.]

HENDERSON: Is that twice or just once?

231

DUKE: Once, unless you see an opportunity.

HENDERSON [holds up his hand, counting] One, two, three, four, five, six, seven bars of this. Then come back and eight of this.

DUKE: Repeat these eight bars. [He plays the eight.] Then we go here. [He stops, puzzled.] What's this? Oh, I remember. We go back to the top. [Duke sings.] Di-be, di-be, di-be, di-be, di.

HENDERSON: Oh.

DUKE: When you go back to the top, do it the same way you did the first time, then come back to this theme, di-be, di-be, di-be, di-be, di.

DUKE [has had enough for this session. He begins to stroke Luther.]: You're brilliant, man, brilliant. You look at a piece of paper and it stands up and thanks you. Ever see a piece of music stand up and thank Luther? A piece of blank paper. All you have to do is look at it and the paper says, "Ahhh!"

HENDERSON: What's the name of this? [He plays a theme.]

DUKE [puzzled]: What? The name of that? . . .

HENDERSON [plays the theme again]: We have to compose the libretto from your titles.

DUKE: Naturally, of course. That is . . . that has to do with our relative positions as animals in the universe . . . Like me; I'm a primitive illiterate.

HENDERSON: I know. You told me that.

DUKE: When I walk I see a tree. One side of the tree is a tree. The other side is a bear. I don't know whether I'm going to have tree salad or bear pot pie, but I may as well have the bear pot pie because then I can have a nice fur coat for the winter.

HENDERSON: Yes, yes . . .

DUKE [laughing]: And so I mean, you know, I'm a primitive illiterate.

HENDERSON: You still didn't tell me . . .

DUKE [pointing]: I don't have to. It's all written there on the paper. [He is suddenly silent.]

HENDERSON: Why are you sitting there like that? Why don't you say something?

DUKE [laughs, puts his arm around Luther's shoulder]: Let's get something to eat, man. We'll pick up on this again later.

232

Teresa Brewer

BOB THIELE, WHO OWNED THE FLYING DUTCHMAN RECORD LABEL, DESPER-ately wanted his wife, Teresa Brewer, the well-known country-pop singer, to cut an album with Duke. He called me every day, sometimes two or three times a day, saying, "Please, Don, nobody can get Duke to do it except you."

Duke was at the Rainbow Grill. Finally I started thinking the thing out, and I said to myself, "Wait a minute. That may not be such a bad idea after all. She's had a number of hits. Maybe it can happen again."

In the meanwhile Thiele kept calling me and calling me and calling me. Eventually I went toe-to-toe with Duke on it. It was one of the very few times in thirty years that we stood face-to-face and yelled at each other.

I shouted, "Duke, come on, for Christ's sake, and listen to me. I'm so much in favor of this for only one reason—"

Duke interrupted me, saying, "Don, if we make this album, the musicians will get paid, the engineer will get paid, the electricians will get paid, the security people will get paid, but who knows if we'll ever get a dime from the record sale?"

I explained, "The reason that I'm so involved is because Brewer is a contemporary singer, and we'll pick the songs. We'll pick five or six songs that we wrote together, and all the others will be yours and off we'll go."

I went up, down and sideways with Duke. Meanwhile Thiele kept calling me, and I called Duke in Atlantic City and everywhere else he went.

Finally he was back in town again at the Rainbow Grill, and I cornered him in Rockefeller Plaza late one night after the band closed. Harry Carney was standing by with a station wagon, waiting to drive him up to Boston for a gig, and Duke finally said okay. My position was that with Brewer as vocalist, there was an outside chance that one of our songs might step out. If it created an important copyright for us, it was worth the whole mess. Since all the rock 'n' roll going on was getting all the action, we had to take whatever shot we could.

The album was cut on three successive afternoons. The press

and the TV people were there, snapping pictures of Duke and various celebrities and shooting the action, with their wires underfoot all over the place. The diminutive, bouncy Teresa Brewer made a glamorous entrance, dressed in a sequined leather outfit, looking and acting every inch the star.

She was running down one of the songs when she was interrupted by a rude noise. Ray Nance had come staggering in, so drunk he didn't make sense. He tripped on his own feet, knocked over a couple of music stands and sat there belching, with a silly grin on his face. Paul Gonsalves was drunk as usual.

Duke remained patient and dignified. It was a show in itself, the way he handled the men that day. Bob Thiele was cold, almost silent through the session. The only time he nearly came to life was when he fired Ray Nance, who was completely unable to work, but who hung around anyway, generally disrupting the proceedings. The rest of the musicians, obviously having experienced similar circumstances before, went right on in the most magnificent way, as though nothing were wrong. Duke maintained his dignity; he didn't reprimand Nance or Gonsalves. Finally he hit a two-handed chord on the piano, and in the ensuing silence he said to the men, "All right, we've had it. Now let's go." Just that one short sentence and the band straightened up—alert, ready for action.

It was as though Duke had waved a magic wand. Except for a couple of tentative forays by Nance that were quickly smothered, and with the press being constantly underfoot, from that moment on the recording went like clockwork.

The band played superbly and on cue: Brewer sang with authority; and the smiling Duke, adding an aura of intrigue to the occasion, kept throwing kisses to a beautiful blond lady sitting off to one side as everyone, especially the reporters, tried to find out who she was.

Eventually everything turned out exactly as Duke had predicted. As always, his instincts were superb. We never did get paid one dollar in royalties from the sale of the album.

Black Belt

MANY OF THE LADIES FELL IN LOVE WITH THE MUSIC FIRST, THEN WHEN they saw the man and all that charismatic power, they couldn't help but give him anything he wanted. He told one lady named Pat, "You know, I think you should become a black belt so you can protect me from all the wolves."

She said, "Okay."

Duke went away and came back about five or six months later. After their first reunion Duke said, "My God. Do you know that silly bitch went out and got herself a black belt? Now I'm scared to have her around. She may turn on me and kick my ass."

Music Is My Mistress

SAM VAUGHAN, NOW THE PUBLISHER AT DOUBLEDAY, WAS JUST A WORKING editor at the time he obeyed his impulse to get Duke Ellington to write a book about himself. Vaughan contacted some people who knew Duke well—people like John Wilson and John Hammond and others. They all told him the same thing. Duke would never want to write a book; Duke would never write a book.

(At one time Strayhorn and Duke's doctor, Arthur Logan, with the help of Duke's family and friends, had gotten together as complete a collection of Duke's manuscripts as they could find and had them leather-bound. Duke looked at it, put it away and never looked at it again. It was a great idea because it contained so many invaluable compositions that had been scattered around in various forms and really deserved to be preserved. The thing that disturbed Duke was the finality of it. He wanted nothing in his life ever to be that complete and final. He felt the same way about writing a book. He said to me, "Don, people shouldn't be written about until after they're gone. How do we know what a guy is going to do tomorrow?")

Vaughan got permission to offer Duke an advance against royalties and started to chase him. He went to concerts and went backstage whenever he could manage it. Marian and Arthur Logan took him to a rehearsal up at the Rainbow Grill, and Vaughan even showed up in Duke's dressing room when he was changing. "Man," said Duke, "you really pick the wrong time and place to chase a guy about a book."

Occasionally Vaughan became discouraged and thought: The hell with it, the guy doesn't want to write a book and I can't talk him into it. Then he'd hear the music, and that would start him up again. Duke was always speaking to Vaughan through the music, even though he was straight-arming him in person. In any event, Vaughan didn't have a lot of money to offer.

Time passed, and Vaughan was blowing hot and cold. Then one day Nelson Doubleday, the big boss, came into Vaughan's office. He had met Duke the night before at a concert and quickly and impulsively had said to him, "Listen, Duke, write a book for us and I'll give you X dollars for it."

Duke went for it. The X was about five times what Vaughan had been able to offer. Vaughan was both chagrined and elated. His boss had been able to get a book that he couldn't get, but he had done it with a big stick. They had an Ellington contract, but now the question arose. Was there going to be a book?

In the process of putting the manuscript together, Vaughan had many meetings with Duke and was charmed and thrilled and impressed. The manuscript was beginning to take shape. By that time Vaughan had been promoted and wasn't able to do the editing himself. He assigned the book to a young woman editor, and although at first her relationship with Duke seemed to be working well, at some point Duke began to get cantankerous. He telephoned Vaughan and suggested that his editor was antiblack. Vaughan knew this was not so and became very angry. Duke and he finally hung up on each other. Work on the book stopped.

Eventually Marian Logan showed up in Vaughan's office. She was wearing a floor-length mink coat, which she took off as she came in and threw across the room. It landed in a heap on the floor, and with great eloquence she asked, "Now, what is this shit between you and Edward?"

Vaughan explained the falling out, and said, "We may have done some things wrong, but it doesn't have anyting to do with color, and I just won't put up with that kind of criticism."

Marian replied, "Now, you know that my husband is Duke's doctor."

Vaughan said, "Of course I do."

She said, "You know that Duke is a hypochondriac."

236

Vaughan agreed. "I know that."

She said, "Well, the difference now is that he's really got it. The big C. Cancer."

That stopped everything in Vaughan's mind. He realized that the whole thing was on a different wave length. He told Logan so, swallowed hard, went to the phone, called Duke and apologized, and they got on with the book.

The final problem was the jacket. It was done in tones of brown, despite the fact that Duke had indicated to Vaughan that he didn't much like brown. Vaughan, not taking Duke's admonition very seriously, let the jacket go through. When the book was finished, Duke was Doubleday's guest at the booksellers' convention in Los Angeles. The band was playing at the Brown Hotel in Dallas. Duke had flown up the night before and would fly back that night, after spending the day promoting the book. Vaughan picked Duke up at his hotel and they drove to the convention site, where Duke knocked everybody off their chairs with his speech at the press conference. Afterward they went down to the exhibit. There was a huge blowup of the jacket of Duke's book, *Music Is My Mistress*, almost covering an entire wall. Done in tones of brown. Duke was aghast. He wasn't having any part of it and was very definite about making his feelings known. He was adamant. Doubleday had no alternative but to hold up the publication date, scrap the brown jacket and remake it in plain blue, with the title in large white letters.

I was sitting in Sam Vaughan's office at Doubleday discussing Duke's book with him. Vaughan smiled in relief as he said, "Thereafter it was a happy story. That's the most of it. It wasn't really bad. There was a down time when I thought the book was going to founder. But Marian Logan was very helpful as an intermediary. I kind of think Duke wanted to get the book out anyhow."

I was curious. "The way the book is written, Sam, everything is moonlight and roses. Everything is great, everything is wonderful. Nobody seems quite human. Why is it written that way? Was it editorial policy?"

Vaughan shook his head. "That book is a mixture of the best and the worst of Ellington. All that love-you-madly stuff goes on and on. We spoke to him about it. We said, 'If you say you love everybody all the time, whether it's true or not, you have no credibility.' I felt if we had had a free hand editorially, we could have made a better book of it."

Vaughan went to the wall of books, saying, "I've got a copy of it here someplace."

I said, "Sam, I remember reading stories in the book where everything is sweetness and light, and everybody loves everybody else, and everything is great, the rulers of the countries are just wonderful; and I said to myself, 'Come on, man, it wasn't like that.' I know, I was there."

Sam thought a moment, then said, "I have a hunch that Duke comes out of a tradition where there is a great respect and a lot of affection for the audience. Especially from the black performers. They give a lot for the money. They make the audience feel good. Duke is part of that. He wants to be loved, and everyone in the audience, one by one, wants to be loved, so what harm is done if he tells them he loves them?"

I replied, "Fine, but how about the other side of the picture? The whole world isn't love. Even Pollyanna must have had her moments."

Vaughan was still looking for the book, saying, "It's one of our better stolen books." Reaching up, he said, "Oh, here it is." He paused, "Don, the value of a memoir is not whether it is accurate. It's a picture of what the man wants you to think. Memoirs are all flawed by self-service, but they still have their value."

My mind wandered back to 1965, when two of the members of the Pulitzer committee resigned in protest because the committee decided to give no Pulitzer Prize that year rather than give it to Duke Ellington, a black man. At the time Duke wrote, "Since I'm not too chronically masochistic, I found no pleasure in all the suffering that was being endured. I realize that it could have been most distressing and distracting as I tried to qualify my first reaction." Then he wrote that much-quoted phrase. "Fate is being very kind to me. Fate doesn't want me to be too famous, too young." He followed this by writing, "Let's say it had happened. I would have been famous, then rich, then fat and stagnant. And then what do you do with your beautiful, young, freckled mind?"

Vaughan finalized: "That's about all there is to it. I was just lucky enough to be the guy who worked on it. This book has its value. The option would have been no attempt on Duke's part to ever write a book."

It was then that it dawned on me that in *Music Is My Mistress*, Duke had spoken about everyone but himself. Once again he had succeeded in remaining concealed behind the charismatic curtain he pulled closed whenever his privacy was threatened.

Dr. Arthur Logan

ONE TUESDAY EVENING MARIAN LOGAN INVITED ME TO HER BROWNSTONE duplex in the West Eighties in New York City, for a TV filming party for the United Negro College Fund, to be shown on a telethon the following Sunday. I arrived early and sat for a while in the small, glass-enclosed terrace off the huge living room, where I had often sat with Duke. There was a stairway in the center of the room from which Martin Luther King, Jr., on more than one occasion had spoken to raise money for his human-rights movement, and where Rose Kennedy had done a bit of motherly electioneering when her son Bobby was running for senator from New York. Birch Bayh, Charles Evers, Robert Wagner, Whitney Young, Nelson Rockefeller and Happy, Shirley MacLaine, Belafonte and Poitier—all had stood on those steps, pitching for money for good and worthy causes. They often raised as much as four or five hundred thousand dollars during an afternoon cocktail party.

Sitting there watching Marian greet the arriving guests, my mind wandered back across the years to the beginnings of Duke and Arthur Logan.

Arthur Logan had just graduated from the Columbia College of Physicians and Surgeons and was interning at Harlem Hospital. Jerry Rhea, Duke's road manager at the time, was a friend and patient of Logan's. One late night Jerry called Logan and asked him to come see Toby Hardwicke, a member of Duke's band, who had asthma. Half-awake, Logan asked what the problem was, and Rhea spelled it out, "A-s-m-a."

Logan went to the Cotton Club and administered to Hardwicke. As he was leaving, Rhea said, "Come on, I want you to meet the boss," and took him into Duke's dressing room.

239

Duke, with his usual charm, said, "Jerry, did you say he was a doctor? He's much too young and much too pretty. He just couldn't be a doctor."

Three days later Logan got a call to see Duke, where he lived on Edgecombe Avenue. From that day on, for thirty-seven years, Arthur Logan was Duke's doctor and one of his closest friends. Duke didn't go to the bathroom without calling Arthur and telling him the color of his urine and asking, "Arthur, how am I feeling today?" It was his favorite line.

Many nights he called, and Logan's wife Marian answered the phone. She'd say, "Edward, Arthur's not here."

"Well, how am I going to know how I feel today? Would you please tell my doctor to call me. I've got to know how I feel."

If Logan was home he'd tell Duke, "You're feeling fine."

"Oh, all right. Are you coming to the club tonight?"

"I don't think so."

"Oh, but you must. I'm sure I need a shot. I'm sure I need something."

Duke, night creature that he was, took to dropping into Logan's brownstone at all hours. He'd ring the bell at three or four o'clock in the morning. Marian, a late-movie bug, would be sitting up watching TV. Logan would be upstairs sleeping, resting up for his early-morning work. Duke came in, gave Marian the usual four kisses (one for each cheek) and said, "Where's my doctor?"

"He's upstairs in bed, Edward."

"Is he scrubbing in the morning?"

"I don't know."

"Well, I'll just go up and give him four kisses."

"Edward, please don't wake him up."

"I wouldn't dare. Don't worry about it."

Duke tiptoed up the stairs to the bedroom where Logan was snoring and gave him the four kisses. Logan in his sleep took Duke's hand, felt his pulse and said, "You're okay, buddy."

Duke, placing his right index finger to his lips, whispered, "Let's go downstairs, Marian. Mustn't disturb the doctor, you know."

Downstairs, he invariably went to the piano and tinkled around for a while.

"What have you got to eat?"

"I've got a steak and I'll fix you a salad."

"Got any grapefruit?"

"Yes, and I've got some lemon rind for your hot water."

Duke opened the window and called out to his driver (he had a big limousine waiting), "Cool it, man, I'll be there in a little while."

After he ate he said, "I wonder what's on the boob tube?"

He loved old Westerns. At that time of night they were the only thing on. He never could see very well, but his vanity wouldn't permit him to wear glasses, so he sat with his hands above his eyes and squinted and watched the movies. "Look at that cat. Isn't this great?"

At the Rainbow Grill Logan came in between shows and before shows. I'd be sitting there in Duke's baby blue dressing room talking to Duke. At the sight of Logan, Duke would say, "Excuse me, Don," and start pulling down his trousers. Logan would spear him in the royal posterior, the same way he did in the living room or the kitchen, when Duke more than occasionally dropped in to visit at the brownstone. It made Duke feel fine. It could have been water. It didn't make any difference to him. His doctor gave him something and he felt better. He was always under the impression he was getting a rainbow shot;* half the time it probably was water. Logan used to tell me, "There's nothing wrong with Edward. It's in his mind. If it makes him happy for me to stick him, I'm going to stick him."

Logan and Sweetpea gave Duke a doctor's bag engraved with the initials E.K.E. in large golden letters. Logan filled it with vitamins and medicines. Duke was so proud of it that he took it everywhere with him. If anyone even sneezed in his presence, he'd give him a fistful of vitamin C and send him to Logan for a checkup.

Late in '63 Duke went on a tour of the Far East for the State Department. His initial comment was, "I got to go to India. What the fuck am I going to do in India? When I get over there I'm going to get sick. Something will happen to me if I go without my doctor."

*Multivitamins.

241

He arranged to have Logan and Strayhorn go with him. They were in Baghdad staying in a hotel opposite the palace when a coup was attempted. The planes were flying over the hotel and dive-bombing the palace. Logan went downstairs and told the manager, "I'm a doctor. I'd like to go to the hospital and help with the injured."

The manager said, "There are no injured in cases like this. Nobody takes prisoners. They're dead or they're alive."

Logan was shocked. He and Strayhorn went up to the roof of the hotel and took pictures of the planes bombing the palace across the street. Duke told them, "You niggers are crazy. Going out there to get shot or something. You might get hurt."

Strayhorn just smiled his nice little smile. When they left the suite, Duke was stretched out under the bed, writing music and hanging onto the six-and-a-half kilos of caviar that the shah of Iran had presented him with when the band played there during an earlier part of the tour.

All the killing was shown on TV in Baghdad. In one scene a man was dragging a decapitated head by its hair through the cobblestoned street. Everyone was happy to get home where nothing like that happened.

The following day President Kennedy was assassinated.

Years later Arthur Logan was working with Percy Sutton, the borough president of Manhattan, to find a site on which the Knickerbocker Hospital could be rebuilt. The entire project was to be called Manhattan Health Park. One Saturday evening Sutton told Logan that the city was contemplating giving them a site at 134th Street and Riverside Drive.

Duke called that evening and said he needed Logan in Europe with him. They made plans for Logan to meet Duke in London the following Monday.

The next morning Arthur was delighted. He said to Marian, "Honey, I'm going to see my patients at the hospital, and then I'm going to look at that site Percy was telling me about. I'll be back to take you to church, and then Buddy Boy (their son Chip) and I are going to the park for a football game."

Forty-five minutes later the police called and asked her to come identify Logan's body.

Percy Sutton took her to the viaduct above 134th Street and

242

Riverside Drive, which overlooked the proposed site of the hospital. There was a low railing, barely hip high, protecting pedestrians from a drop of about one hundred feet, over which Logan had gone.

The media had a holiday. They gave forth various confused conjectures about the cause of Logan's death. Some called it suicide. Others searched for a political motive because of his involvement with Martin Luther King, Jr. Some others said that Logan was going to blow the whistle on some people in Harlem who were putting out drugs for the poor blacks.

Duke was in London when Logan died. They kept the news from him for a few days, but when he found out, he was completely devastated. Strayhorn was gone, and now Logan. Logan's death broke Duke's heart. For the remainder of his life it disturbed him. He always yearned for some explanation of why and how it happened.

Years later Dr. Logan's widow told me what really happened that sunny Sunday morning on the viaduct above Riverside Drive. It is a story that has never been made public and that finally clears up the mystery surrounding what turned out to be the murder of Dr. Logan.

Some months after Logan died, his widow got a phone call that the FBI had become involved in his death. She was still in shock and couldn't deal with the situation, so she turned it over to her attorney.

It seems there were two black dudes in jail in Florida who were reading an old *Jet* magazine that had the story of Logan's death and funeral.

One said, "Hey, that's the cat we tried to roll and pushed off the bridge up North."

The other one said, "I didn't know he was a black cat. I thought he was white." (Logan was light enough to pass in any company.)

Another inmate who overheard the conversation wrote a letter to a reporter, who forwarded it to the FBI, who infiltrated the prison and verified the statements contained in the letter.

Mrs. Logan was asked if she wanted them extradited for trial. She refused because she didn't want another six months of heartbreak or to have her child upset by a trial, because

243

nothing would bring Logan back. She just couldn't deal with it. Besides, the two thugs who had panicked and made such a terribly stupid mistake were already serving sentences of ninety years in the Florida prison for their murderous activities after their unfortunate encounter with Logan.

Laurence Harvey

ONE EVENING IN AUGUST 1973 I WAS SITTING AT THE BAR IN A FRENCH REStaurant called Le Mistral on East Fifty-second Street, which was owned by a gregarious Frenchman named Jean, who was a close friend of Duke's.

Jean and I were drinking wine and chatting when in popped Laurence Harvey, the actor; George Barrie, who owns Faberge; and another chap, a friend of Harvey's.

After some conversation Jean turned to me and said, "Let's all go up to the Rainbow Grill and hear Duke." I said fine and phoned Bigi, the maitre d', to tell Duke we were on the way over. When we arrived, the table right next to the piano was ready for us.

The five of us were talking and drinking for about fifteen or twenty minutes when Harvey's friend whispered something to Jean, who said to me, "Don, please ask Duke to announce Laurence Harvey now, because he has to leave." I leaned over, got Duke's attention and told him the problem. Duke, gracious as always, cut short the number that he was playing, called for a spotlight and announced Harvey, who, as an important and well-liked film star, was very well received.

Jean and George Barrie left with Harvey and his friend, and I remained to spend the rest of the evening at the Grill with Duke.

I didn't find out till later that the reason Harvey had to leave was because he had terminal cancer, and his pain at that moment was almost unbearable. Neither did I know that Duke, sitting at the piano and picking up the microphone to introduce Harvey, also had terminal cancer. One dying man had introduced another dying man, one my brother and the other a new friend. Although at the time I was unaware of their suffering, I did sense a certain mutual vibration and understanding pass between them. Something deep and personal. Something beyond description.

One evening not long afterward, I was watching the news when Chet Huntley announced that Laurence Harvey had died of cancer.

My mind flashed back to that night at the Grill. I remembered how Duke and Harvey had smiled at each other. They couldn't have known about each other's heartache, and yet it seems as though somehow they did. Maybe it was like being in a foreign country and running into a fellow American. You say to yourself, "By Christ, I can communicate with somebody at last." They seemed to know something I didn't know as they waited, unafraid, for the Dark Angel to arrive and lead them to the last Bright Light.

The Rainbow Grill

THE PHONE RANG. I FUMBLED FOR THE LIGHT. IT WAS FOUR A.M. IT HAD TO be Duke. Nobody else ever called at that hour.

"Hello, Duke."

"Oh, you were waiting for my call."

"Sure. I always am. What's happening?"

"I just wanted to remind you to be at the opening tonight at the Grill."

I detected an urgency in his tone. I was wide awake now. "What's so special about tonight? You know I was going to be there."

Duke replied, "I met a writer who has a wonderful project. The three of us are going to work on it together for a movie and a TV series. We're bound to get some great music."

I asked, "What's it about?"

Duke said, "It's a thing called 'Moon Lady.' "

I said, "That's a good title. What's the thought?"

He said, "It's not a man in the moon. It's a lady who comes down to earth and helps people in trouble. There's a very successful book out on it now. We've already written one song for it. I just couldn't turn down the lyric."

"What's the title of the song, Duke?"

He said, " 'What Is It Like Where She Has Gone?' "

I repeated, " 'Where She Has Gone'—does that mean she's departed?"

He said, "Yes."

I almost dropped the phone. Duke would never talk about

death. If you spoke about illness or death in his presence, he'd get up and walk out of the room. (When Louis Armstrong died, instead of Duke saying that he died, he had Money Johnson in the band, who did a great imitation of Louis, come down and sing "Hello, Dolly." Duke turned to the audience and said, "This will be the music of the year two thousand." He was telling the people that in spite of the fact that Louis Armstrong had died, he really would live forever. But he wouldn't use the words *death*, or *passed away* or anything like it.) It was incredible to me until I heard the lyric of the song.

What Is It Like Where She Has Gone?

Like a rainbow glowing in the early dawn
Where the snow is soft and warm
And the rose has no thorn
There are beds of violets in the snow
And silver lilies, shining so.
A hawk's wing shelters the nest of a dove
And everywhere there is love—love—love . . .

It was a beautiful thing. It kind of made you want to leave here so you could enjoy there. I couldn't believe it. Duke actually had written a song with the thought of death in it.

After the first show that night at the Grill, there was a party for the press and close friends in a private area between the Grill and the Rainbow Room. Duke introduced me to the writer.

He said, "Don, come over here and meet a real good writer, Lady Allison Assante. We're going to do a lot of work with her."

I looked at her and I said to myself, "Wow . . . This is some writer. If she can write the way she looks, we're in business." She was blond and she was beautiful. My daughter was with me, and she looked at the lady and looked at me and the way we were staring at each other and said, "I think you two ought to get together."

Lady Allison said to her, "Why would he want me when he has a beautiful young lady like you?"

She smilingly replied, "I'm his daughter."

It was about that time Duke started getting sick. He went to Boston with the band, then to Canada, and returned to the Grill for Christmas. In the meantime Lady Allison was setting up a charity ball for the Children's Cancer Fund at the Waldorf-Astoria, called the Moon Lady Ball. It was in Duke's honor, and he was going to have the band play the music we were creating.

Duke had received every possible award in the world except one: He had never been knighted. Lady Allison was going to sponsor him to be knighted into the Order of the Holy Cross of Jerusalem. She was arranging to have it done in St. Bartholomew's Church, just across the street from the Waldorf. The ceremony was to be performed by the head of the order, the Bishop de Valitch, on the night of the ball. Wanting to surprise Duke, she told him nothing about it. The only people in on the deal were the Bishop de Valitch, Lady Allison and myself. Duke would be the first black American ever to be knighted into this order.

Jackie Onassis accepted the honorary citizenship of the ball, and Serge Obolensky was working with Lady Allison, pulling the society people together. But Lady Allison kept postponing the date for the ball because Duke kept getting sicker and sicker. I kept asking Duke how he felt, and he kept saying, "Don't worry about a thing. I'm going to be there. Besides, it's in my honor." Duke was really confident that he was going to get well. He wasn't going to give up. He was so terribly depressed at the thought of sickness or death, he refused to think about it. He wanted to brush it away, as though it didn't exist. He tried to pretend it wasn't there.

Duke and the band were at the Rainbow Grill. Duke took three days off to get checked at the hospital. He didn't look worried when he returned, but one sensed an underlying feeling of concern. He didn't laugh quite as much. He occasionally became irascible without logical reason. He kept reassuring Lady Allison that he would be at the Moon Lady Ball at the Waldorf-Astoria.

"Duke."

"Yes, Don."

"What did the doctor say?"

247

"He said everything's fine."

"Did you have the same doctor you had a year ago?"

"I didn't have any doctor a year ago."

"Don't you remember? You saw Edmund Anderson's doctor.* He said you had a problem, but it wasn't too bad at the time. He wanted you to go to the hospital back then."

Duke said petulantly, "Well, I didn't go. Do we have to talk about it?"

I said; "Come on, man. Remember what happened to Nat Cole. The last time we saw him at the Copa he did his songs sitting on a stool. He said his back bugged him. When we asked him what the doctor said, he said he hadn't been to any doctor. He was afraid to find out what was wrong, and he waited too long. A few months later he died in that California hospital. The big C." I was worried now. "Don't bullshit me, man, what's going on?"

Duke said placatingly, with an arm around my shoulder, "Take it easy, Don. Everything's fine."

I found out later that he had had a lymph gland removed from his neck in the hospital, but he continued his infernal habit of soaking Kool cigarettes in liquid menthol, drying them out, then smoking them in an attempt to prevent cancer.

Duke and the band flew off to honor a booking in London to perform the Third Sacred Concert.

Westminster Abbey

SEEING WESTMINSTER ABBEY ON THE NIGHT OF DUKE'S THIRD SACRED CONcert was the most extraordinary experience ever. The abbey had never been opened at night and lit up except for coronations and state funerals. The entrance was lined with elaborately uniformed guards standing at ramrod-straight attention, enhancing the pomp that only Britain can maintain. Limousines were pulling up, one Daimler after another, one Rolls after another. All the klieg lights were on, and there was a huge crowd milling about behind a human wall of London bobbies watching the great and the famous arrive.

*Dr. Carl Muschenheim, at New York Hospital.

The inside of the abbey, which was so spectacular even under normal circumstances, was ablaze with the kind of crystal chandeliers that are seen nowhere but in the greatest museums. It looked like a stage set. It was wondrous to see the splendor of the vaults and the ancient stone carvings that were aglow for the first time in anyone's experience. One walked through the Hall of Poets, where all the great English poets, including Chaucer, Browning and Tennyson, are buried; through the Hall of Kings, the final resting place of eighteen monarchs, which had only been seen before in murky darkness, but which now was brilliantly lit; through the entire length of the abbey, and there in the apse came to the prayer part, where during the coronations all the lords sat. This night it was occupied by an array of the most elegantly dressed people, making it seem like a royal occasion.

Suddenly there was a great commotion, and everyone rose as the royal party entered with Princess Margaret and her entourage, including the duke of Bedford, the duchess of Norfolk, Lauren Bacall (who was appearing in London in the musical *Applause*) and many ladies and lords, some of the men in white tie and tails and some in their baronet capes, and what looked like the royal crown jewels on every titled, tiaraed woman.

Duke was seated at the piano, which had been placed on the raised main altar. The band was almost encircling him. There wasn't an empty chair in the choir loft directly behind them. It was a startling thing to see an all-black orchestra on the podium in Westminster Abbey. Some of the dukes and duchesses were looking a bit askance because they weren't royal Africans, they weren't slaves of the Empire—they were the honored guests.

The sacred concert began with music played behind a recitation. It was extremely moving. Duke began with the spoken word, reciting a biblical paraphrase that he had written, which was mostly about the love of the Lord. Toney Watkins continued reciting, and then the music swelled up. At first everybody behaved as though it were a church service. There was silence and tremendous dignity. As the concert proceeded it built up into a very fast, upbeat tempo. There were some magnificent solos, and you could feel the audience begin to melt from their very stiff British attitude.

Faintly first, you could hear feet tapping in time with the music. Toward the end of the concert the band performed a segment called "Joy." The songs (all written by Duke) were of a liturgical nature. Toney Watkins began a dance on the altar level, then came down to the abbey floor, where Anita Moore joined him, followed by the entire choir, and the message of the songs changed to joy and love. Within a few minutes the entire audience, including the stuffiest of the stuffed shirts (you almost had the feeling that they were tearing their collars off), started clapping. As the choir and Toney and Anita continued dancing in the enormous Coronation Aisle of the abbey, the entire audience, headed by Princess Margaret and Prime Minister Heath and including every old lady with her jewels, was bobbing up and down. They were sent.

Duke wasn't feeling well. He had left the piano at one point to go to where Jim Lowe, his valet, was waiting for him behind a screen in front of the choir loft with an empty bottle ready for his use. By that time Duke's cancer, which had started in the prostate, was so bad that he had to go to the john all the time. The audience was unaware of what was happening, as Duke often walked away from the piano when the band was performing parts in which the piano wasn't needed. He just walked off, waving his arms as though he were conducting the choir, and disappeared for a few minutes.

When all the commotion started, Duke stood there clapping his hands, then snapping his fingers and going into his familiar rolling-hip motion, egging them on. Everyone joined the dancers. The scene was incredible. The ovation lasted a good ten minutes, everyone dancing and the choir bursting into song and Toney Watkins doing the wildest dance, and the orchestra coming to full crescendo and then the applause.

Ordinarily, with the kind of people there, Duke would have taken numerous curtain calls and bows; he would have done some kind of love-you-madly bit.

But he never said a thing. He just very stiffly bowed once and disappeared. The audience kept applauding, but he never returned to take a curtain call.

It was so novel for people to be in the abbey at night and to see it lit up that they didn't just leave. A lot of them sort of visited with each other, chatting and walking around, looking at the paintings and the sculptures.

Suddenly there was Duke in his white cashmere polo coat. He went over and whispered something to Prime Minister Heath. Whether he told him at the time that he was unable to come to the reception later that had been prepared for him at 10 Downing Street by Heath and Princess Margaret, nobody knows. A lot of people tried to grab Duke and shake him by the hand, but with Jim Lowe running interference in front of him, he got out of the crowd in a hurry.

It was the first time that Duke had shown any sign of how sick he really was. Despite his illness, Duke continued on the tour that had been booked for the band. He continued on to Africa as scheduled, then returned to London for two concerts without uttering one word of complaint.

While he was there, Robert Farnum, the Governor of Writing, perhaps having a premonition that something was amiss, persuaded him to do an album (the last one he ever did) and a television show to be put on at the Philharmonic. He obviously wanted Duke to smell the roses on what he suspected might be his last go-round. When Duke returned to the States, he took about five weeks off.

St. Clare's Hospital Benefit

IN FEBRUARY, FOR THE FIRST TIME IN THIRTY YEARS, I HEAR DUKE CONFESS that he feels sick. The B$_{12}$ shots and the rainbow shots in his rear end aren't helping him much anymore. They don't give him the bounce he needs.

But Duke doesn't stop with his ladies. If anything his interest seems to increase, not only in the physical area, but in the reminiscences and the conversations of the affairs and the ladies of the past, to the extent of sitting around and often for entire evenings discussing and chuckling and talking about the fun and games and ladies we had shared together.

More and more he talks about his childhood in Washington; about his growing-up days; about people he used to know. He keeps forgetting things. He appears to be growing thinner, smaller.

In March he keeps a promise to play a charity benefit for St. Clare's Hospital at the Starlight Roof of the Waldorf-Astoria Hotel. The room is filled with ladies and gentlemen of the

251

cloth; the sisters who donate their activities to the needy at the hospital; the priests and bishops and an occasional cardinal, all sitting around the flower-festooned, candlelit tables in soft, smiling conversation with one another. There is a concert-grand piano in one corner of the dance floor, and a small electric piano, which I later find out is a backup to be used when it is necessary to pinch-hit for Duke, who has been assigned a suite on the floor below to prepare for the concert and to rest between sets.

When I greet him he seems so much in pain as to be irritable, not even wanting to talk. For the first time since I know him, he almost doesn't acknowledge me. It is obviously taking all his effort to conserve his energy, to say the most necessary things to the most necessary people. He is just feeling like hell. When it is time for him to go up and play the first of his three sets, he can't raise up from the chair by himself but has to be helped to his feet.

He plays clinkers all over the place. It sounds like he doesn't care at all what he's playing. One of the priests comes over with a request. Duke doesn't seem to hear him. The same priest comes over with the same request during Duke's second set, and gets the same response. He walks away puzzled, looking back over his shoulder at Duke.

Duke starts the third set, playing all the old chestnuts that everyone is so familiar with. He turns to me and asks, "What was the name of the song that priest requested?" He ignores my reply and starts playing some beautiful music that I'd never heard before. Obviously it is fresh and new, something he has composed just for the occasion.

Brooks Kerr, the blind, young, white piano player, who is standing watch with me, grasps my arm. "Don, what's he playing? Have you ever heard it before?"

Shaking my head, I answer, "Brooks, he's telling us something. He's telling us that he knows. This is his September music."

Back in the dressing room at the end of the affair, they're helping Duke on with his coat.

This is my buddy, my main man. We've been so close for thirty years, we don't have to talk. We look in each other's eyes, and I hear his silent scream.

252

"Goddamn it, I'm Duke Ellington. Why the fuck did this have to happen to me? I'm the greatest thing that ever came out of a pussy, and *this shit* has to happen to me?"

I watch as they help him into the elevator, and the door closes.

Harkness Pavilion

ON APRIL 29, 1974, DUKE'S SEVENTY-FIFTH BIRTHDAY, HE IS AT THE HARKness Pavilion, a hospital on the Upper West Side of Manhattan, overlooking the Hudson River, which is renowned for the compassionate treatment and care given to its terminal inhabitants.

There is a problem getting in to see Duke. The powers that be have barred everybody but family. It's one thing protecting a man when he's sick—it's all right to keep out the strange apples and weirdos and autograph seekers and nuts and popping cameramen; but to try and keep people like Sonny Greer and Brooks Kerr and myself away is sheer murder. After all, we've bled with Duke.

We knew the family came later in the day and we might not get in with them around, so at 11 A.M. Sonny, Brooks and I took the elevator up to the wing where Duke's room was situated. The solitary nurse on duty outside the door attempted to bar our way.

"You can't go in there. I have strict orders to keep everyone out but the family."

Remembering the ploy that had worked so well so many years ago at the Capitol Theatre, when I first walked into Duke's life, I said, "That's all right. I'm his brother." I smiled and kept walking. She hesitantly permitted us to enter.

I couldn't believe what I saw. Duke, hearing our voices, had gotten out of bed to receive us. He was sitting propped up on a beautiful chaise longue, wearing a robe. I looked at his face and I said, "Now wait a minute." I couldn't believe it was a face, it was so shriveled; and the next thing I noticed was the outline of his hair and I said, "Oh, my God." He had shriveled so much but his hair hadn't; it looked like an oversize wig that had been plopped on.

In spite of everything he was cheerful, just saying, "How are you? How are things? How's Ricki?" (my daughter, who always claimed Duke as her favorite uncle). There was no mention of his own suffering. Though he was weak, he was only concerned about being gracious and cordial. All his manners came to the fore. We were in his room, he was our host and he was going to entertain.

A few mornings later I went back, again at 11 A.M., with Sonny Greer and Brooks Kerr. Fortunately the same nurse was on duty, and she let us in. We had brought a copy of John Wilson's review of the third Sacred Concert, which had taken place on Duke's birthday at the Central Presbyterian Church on Sixty-fourth Street and Park Avenue. It had been conducted by Toney Watkins, and Wilson noted that Brooks Kerr had played excellently in Duke's absence. But Duke didn't seem to comprehend anything we were saying.

Sonny eventually lightened the situation by asking, "Duke, what can I get you? Can I get you anything? Can I get you a little Japanese girl?"

Duke just beamed and said. "The feet. She can walk on my back with the feet." He looked and sounded like a little child. Then he turned and said to Sonny, "Hey, Nasty [his pet name for Sonny], I got a stable of nieces on 125th Street for you to take care of."

The visit ended on an up note.

That was the last time I saw Duke alive. He died on May 24, 1974, at 3:10 A.M.

Funeral Parlor

PAUL GONSALVES AND TYREE GLENN BOTH WERE BURIED ON THE DAY DUKE died. Paul and Tyree had been playing in Duke's band until his final illness. When the Angel struck he took them all within the same week. Now the three of them were together in Cooke's funeral parlor, in the chapel at the same time, tuning up for their journey to the great beyond. For about ten minutes after the arrival of Duke's body, they were alone together for their final farewells, until Paul and Tyree were escorted to their final resting places and Duke reigned in lonely splendor in his seamless copper casket.

Upwards of 65,000 people came to view the body. At times

254

there were lines four abreast that spanned two city blocks. Prominent among the mourners were Count Basie, Ella Fitzgerald, Joe Williams, Dizzy Gillespie, Tony Bennett, Pearl Bailey and Louis Bellson. Frank Sinatra sent flowers. President Nixon sent Stan Scott as his representative. People flew in from every country to affirm their love and respect for Edward. The funeral chapel remained open twenty-four hours a day. (It was rumored that Bing Crosby had paid his respects *après* midnight.)

It was a magnificent outpouring. People coming in to view him were well composed but broke down completely upon entering the funeral parlor. They put all kinds of things in the casket; rabbit's feet, good-luck charms, various types of plant life and objects of various kinds. After a few hours John Joyce, the funeral director, thought that Duke was rising out of the casket with all the things people put in there.

People shook his hands and kissed him. He must have been kissed by more than a thousand people. An old West Coast love was stopped in the attempt to remove one of his shoes. Calls kept coming in from all over the world: Europe, South America, Japan. A call came from Orly Airport in Paris, from a man on his way to Teheran. He had heard the news while changing planes and phoned for verification. Messages poured in from France, England and the Far East. The former king of Thailand, a jazz enthusiast with whom Duke had been very friendly, who played better-than-good clarinet, sent his condolences.

Duke was being remembered with more love, affection and respect than any head of state. He was being treated like the head of state of the entire world. Oddly enough, on his chest he wore only two of his incredible number of awards: the French Legion of Honor and a medal from Ethiopia.

About three o'clock in the morning, Fernanda, who had been one of Duke's more permanent lovers through the years, showed up at Gregory's, a bistro on First Avenue, where Brooks Kerr, Sonny Greer and Russell Procope had a trio featuring Ellington music. She was completely distraught and wanted to lead a parade from Gregory's to the funeral parlor. When she was dissuaded, she insisted that the trio accompany her there. She was beside herself and could hardly be controlled. When they left her, she was on her knees, crying into Duke's face.

Count Basie kept saying, "I loved him, Don. I loved him."

Duke was buried on Memorial Day at Woodlawn Cemetery. Never before or since has there been a burial on Memorial Day, when traditionally all cemeteries are closed insofar as burials are concerned.

Over nine thousand written requests for prayer cards with Duke's name and a religious verse imprinted on them were honored by the funeral parlor.

Tony Bennett told me how he had first learned of Duke's true condition. "Louis Bellson tipped me off that he was in really bad shape. He said to keep calling him, so I kept calling him at the hospital. The very last thing he said to me was, 'Take care of your mother, take care of your sister, and God bless you.' He didn't go through the self-pity trip I might have gone through. The last night I talked to him he was in so much pain, and when he told me to take care of my family he was just sort of clenching his teeth because of the pain. And that was the very last thing he said to me."

Richard Burton, as sensitive as he is talented, completely unburdened his heart and poured out his great affection for Duke: "Don, I actually appeared on stage with the Duke once in the Rainbow Grill. I was sitting in the audience with my daughter when the Duke called me up onto the stage. I said, 'What do you want me to do?' He said, 'You talk and I'll play.' I spoke Shakespeare, I spoke iambic pentameter and iambic hexameter, while the Duke's fabulously infatuated brown fingers stroked the keys. It was a thrilling and extraordinary experience, one of the greatest theatrical experiences that I've ever had.

"I told him I'd do anything to be able to do what he did, and he said he'd give a great deal to be able to do what I did, and he actually gave me a lecture in which he said, 'You know, with your natural voice, your naturally God-gifted voice, you should have been a singer as well as an actor.' He said, 'I shall force you to go and have voice lessons and I want to hear you sing 'Ridi Pagliacci,' I don't know whether he was joking or not, but he was very courteous and very kind.

"The Duke was aptly named. He was one of the world's great aristocrats, a duke in every sense of the word. He talked to everyone. I met him alone, or I met him with forty people around, or a hundred people around, and he had a peculiar genius for talking to everybody as if they were the most important person in the world. He made my daughter feel that way, and he made me feel that way too."

Burton smiled, remembering, "The very last time I saw him, the audience was thronged with young people, people under the age of twenty-five, some of them in their teens, and they reacted to him as if he were also a teenager. He was remarkable . . . he was the concentrated essence of everything that's gifted and courteous. There were times when the Duke could make the short, atavistic hairs rise on the back of your neck when he gave forth with that extraordinary soul of his."

Burton paused, shaking his head sadly. "It's a tremendous shock to me that I shall never see him alive again. I loved him and I know that as long as music is played the Duke will always be with us."

St. John the Divine

THE CATHEDRAL OF ST. JOHN THE DIVINE, LOCATED ON 113TH STREET IN THE lower reaches of New York's Harlem, is one of the most heart clutching structures in the American Northeast. Architecturally superb and emotionally overpowering, it is seldom forgotten by the supplicants who make their personal pilgrimages to its door.

It was there that the services for Duke Ellington were held. The cathedral was packed to overflowing, and outside thousands of other mourners were held back by the police.

After the eulogy by Duke's friend and quondam ghostwriter, Stanley Dance, Joe Williams climbed a vocal mountain to a height that had been unreachable by him before. He was singing for love, not money, and the emotional impact was tremendous.

Father John Gensel, the jazz priest for whom Duke had written and dedicated a composition called "The Shepherd," conducted the services, during which Bill "Count" Basie was literally crying his heart out. The tears kept streaming down his face till it was all I could do not to go over and put my arms around him. Father Jerry Pocock, Duke's friend and spiritual adviser from Montreal, was standing just to the left of Lady Allison Assante and myself, weeping unashamedly, mixing his tears with ours. All Duke's friends, buddies, co-workers and erstwhile sweethearts, including all his nieces from 125th Street, were there, among the thousands upon thousands of souls who had come to mourn him.

After the service the police cleared a way for us to the row of limousines that would follow the funeral cortege on its slow parade through Harlem, before winding up at Woodlawn Cemetery, which was to be Duke's last earthly resting place on the journey to his private Valhalla.

Lady Allison and I found ourselves in a limousine with friends Harry Carney and Sonny Greer for the almost-silent trip.

"What's been happening with you, Sonny?"

"Brooks Kerr, Russell Procope and I have a trio, Don. We're working over on First Avenue." Waving his hand. "But I don't feel like talking about that now." Silence again. "Say, Don, did you know that Duke paid my salary all those years I wasn't working? He didn't have to, but he did."

During the ceremony at the cemetery, Duke's spirit was consecrated to the proper gods as his coffin was gently lowered into the grave. There were blankets of red roses, and during the additional tears of an unexpected drizzle, hundreds of people lined up to purloin a rose from Duke's coffin.

We climbed back into the same big black limousine with Harry and Sonny and headed for the house on Riverside Drive, where a great number of us, as is the custom, were gathering to eat, drink and exchange fond remembrances of Duke.

To lighten the ride (and to ease the pain), I began to tease Sonny and Harry. I told them of the great band Duke was undoubtedly rehearsing up there; Johnny Hodges, Tyree Glenn, Paul Gonsalves, Webster, Joe Benjamin, Tricky Sam

258

Nanton, Sweetpea to help write the arrangements and old friend Nat Cole on vocals.

Sonny Greer shook his head. "Don't look at me, man. I'm sure they've got a drummer."

Harry Carney stared straight ahead. "I'm not going to live much longer," he said.

"Come on, Harry. We all feel badly."

Harry softly repeated. "I'm not going to live much longer."

"Come off it, Harry. You look great. There's nothing wrong with you."

"Duke's dead."

"We know that, Harry."

Harry slowly shook his head. "With Duke dead, I have nothing to live for." (Harry died shortly afterwards. There was nothing physically wrong with him, except perhaps his broken heart.)

We were preceded to 333 Riverside Drive by a large number of friends, acquaintances and well wishers of the family. It seemed more of a party than a wake. Duke had been terminal for some time, and most of the people had become conditioned to the inevitability of the situation. Tony Bennett, who was one of the last persons Duke had spoken to, was there with his sister Mary and her husband. Pearl Bailey and Louis Bellson were having a drink with Ed Dudley, presiding justice of the New York Supreme Court. In one corner Lena Horne was engaged in earnest conversation with her manager Ralph Harris. And overseeing the proceedings, making sure everyone had enough to eat and drink and someone to talk to, was that very gracious lady, Ruth Ellington.

A trumpet, a saxophone and a drum were wailing some blues and people were dancing in a trophy room amidst the hundreds of awards that had gravitated to Duke's genius throughout his incredible career: the Grammy awards, Downbeat awards, the keys to many cities; ribbons and decorations and swords and canes from just about every country in the civilized and not-so-civilized worlds.

There were show people and politicians and celebrities from all walks of life, half-mourning, half-celebrating the occasion.

259

It was exactly the way Duke would have planned it, had he been there. He loved to see people having a good time.

Moon Lady Ball

IT WAS DECIDED TO HOLD THE MOON LADY BALL POSTHUMOUSLY TO HONOR Duke's memory. Jackie Onassis remained as honorary chairwoman, and we wanted Richard Burton to be the guest of honor. He was starring on Broadway at the time in a play called *Equus.* I went to see him at the theater one Saturday, between the matinee and the evening performances. He was extremely cordial and apologized profusely for not having anything to offer me to drink. "Not even wine, I'm afraid." I told him the purpose of my visit and he readily agreed to be guest of honor at the ball. He loved Duke very much, and really missed him.

The date of the ball was set. In addition to Duke's posthumous award, there was an award to be made to Burton as the greatest living male actor.

A few weeks later I read in Earl Wilson's column that Burton's contract in *Equus* would terminate two weeks before the date of the ball. I phoned him at the Hotel Lombardy, where he was staying, and I said, "By the way, I read in the paper that your contract is up two weeks before the date of the ball and that you're leaving the country."

He said, "Don, I've taken care of that. True, my contract was up, but I gave my word to be at the ball, so I called Alexander Cohen, my producer, and extended my contract for two weeks to keep my word to you."

I said to myself, "What a man this is. You dream about people like this, but you never expect to meet them. You hear so many terrible stories about guys like that. They're always controversial, they're temperamental, they're this and they're that." I thought back to when Burton was married to Elizabeth Taylor. They adopted children. The children lived with them. They took care of them and loved them: handicapped children; foreign children; children that nobody else wanted. Burton and Duke had similar qualities. When you sat with Burton, he made you feel the same way Duke did. They looked at you and talked to you and they wrapped you up. You knew that as far

260

as they were concerned, you were the only person in the whole damn world.

The Grand Ballroom of the Waldorf-Astoria was an incredibly beautiful sight on the night of the Moon Lady Ball. The stage was set with moon craters, moon figures and a huge illuminated moon in the background. There were pale blue clouds and soft white doves floating in the air, and silver flowers on every table. The entire room was a shimmering, pale, gossamer, silver and blue moonscape. Breathtaking; ethereal; exquisite.

Entering that room was like entering another world, a world tenanted by beautiful people. People like Lady Allison and Richard Burton, both wearing blue, Duke's favorite color. Lady Allison in a pale blue Moon Lady gown designed by Scaasi, which was covered with silver sequin moons and stars. Burton in his velvet, royal blue tuxedo, looking like every lady's favorite 2 A.M. dream.

The affair was a social smash. Among those present to pay their respects to Duke's memory, were Mrs. Cornelius Vanderbilt Whitney, Mr. and Mrs. David Rockefeller, Mrs. George Vanderbilt, Mrs. Vincent Astor, Princess Giovanna Pignatelli, Countess Pier Braschi, Mr. and Mrs. Nicola Bulgari, Otto Preminger, Earl Wilson, Patrice Munsel and so many other luminaries of the royal, social, theatrical and musical worlds that it boggled the mind. NASA sent Dr. Mark Morton to make a speech about the astronauts and the space program.

There was a forty-piece orchestra and a vocal choir playing background music during dinner, and dance music afterwards, but one thing was inconsolably apparent. Our arms were around only the memory of Duke, which was everywhere. He was leading the band. He was seated in the empty chair at the head of the honor table. He led the choir singing "I'm Beginning to See the Light."

Lady Allison came to the microphone and recited the lyric of the song she and Duke had written,"What Is It Like Where He Has Gone?" At the end of the reading, she raised her hands in devotion, looked upward and said, almost to herself,"Duke, you said you'd be here and you are."

Richard Burton came to the microphone to receive his award and said, "Yes, I feel Duke's presence here, and I know he's proud we didn't give up the ball in his honor."

Duke's sister Ruth came to the podium and with great charm and Ellingtonian dignity accepted Duke's posthumous award.

From the greats of the world who were in that room—from the titled lords and ladies to the waiters and the musicians—everyone, even the seldom silent paparazzi, paid homage to the memory of Duke, which was indelibly engraved in the hearts and souls of all of us he left behind.

After the ball was over, after the music faded, after the last dancer had left, I sat alone at a table in a corner of the darkened ballroom, remembering, remembering. . . .

I think of Duke more often now than I did when he was alive. I often feel him looking over my shoulder. Sometimes I wake in the middle of the night and hear the lonely whisper of a fragile piano playing a melody that seems to be calling for a Don George lyric.

Bye, bye, buddy. See you soon.

About the Author

DON GEORGE WROTE MANY SONGS WITH DUKE ELLINGTON. AMONG THEM are "I'm Beginning to See the Light," "Everything but You," "To Know You Is to Love You," "The Wonder of You."

He has written songs for the films *Giant, Road House, With a Song in My Heart, The Fabulous Dorseys* and many others; and with Duke "Every Hour on the Hour (I Fall in Love with You)" for the film *People Are Funny*.

Don's songs with Duke have been recorded by dozens of major recording artists, including the Dorseys, Woody Herman, Harry James, Nat "King" Cole, Al Hibbler, Joe Williams, Johnny Mathis, Frank Sinatra, Sarah Vaughan and the Pointer Sisters.

Don is the sole writer of the song "The Yellow Rose of Texas."

He is a member of the American Society of Composers, Authors and Publishers. He is on the council and is chairman of the Membership Committee of the American Guild of Authors and Composers and is also on the council of the New York Music Task Force. He is a member of the Dramatists Guild and the Screen Actors Guild.

Among his buddies and friends are Richard Burton, Steve Allen, Dick Clark, Sammy Davis, Jr., Mitch Miller, Pearl Bailey, Peggy Lee, Tony Bennett, José Ferrer, Roosevelt Grier, Otto Preminger, Lady Allison Assante, etc.

Don wrote two songs with Duke for the hit Broadway musical *Sophisticated Ladies*: "Hit Me with a Hot Note and Watch Me Bounce" and "I'm Beginning to See the Light."

He has had a one-man show of his paintings.

Index